FINANCIAL MANAGEMENT FOR NONPROFIT HUMAN SERVICE AGENCIES

FINANCIAL MANAGEMENT FOR NONPROFIT HUMAN SERVICE AGENCIES

Text • Cases • Readings

By

RAYMOND SANCHEZ MAYERS, Ph.D.

Graduate School of Social Work
University of Texas at Arlington

CHARLES C THOMAS • PUBLISHER
Springfield • Illinois • U.S.A.

Published and Distributed Throughout the World by

CHARLES C THOMAS • PUBLISHER
2600 South First Street
Springfield, Illinois 62794-9265

© *1989 by* CHARLES C THOMAS • PUBLISHER

ISBN 0-398-05571-8

Library of Congress Catalog Card Number: 88-36846

Printed in the United States of America
SC-R-3

Library of Congress Cataloging-in-Publication Data

Mayers, Raymond Sanchez.
    Financial management for nonprofit human service agencies : text,
cases, readings / by Raymond Sanchez Mayers.
       p.   cm.
    Bibliography: p.
    Includes index.
    1. Human services—United States—Finance.   2. Corporation,
Nonprofit—United States—Finance.   I. Title.
HV95.M33   1989
361'.0068'1—dc 19   88-36846
                                                      CIP

For Carann, Jordan, and Sara Caitlin

PREFACE

This book is intended for graduate or undergraduate students in the human services. It is not intended to be an entry-level text in accounting for nonprofit organizations. Rather, it is to familiarize the student with the financial terms, concepts, required forms and procedures to be used in the nonprofit human service agency. To this end, I have endeavored to supplement the text with other materials such as cases, short readings, and exercises.

The central organizing theme for this book is the acquisition, distribution, and reporting of agency resources within a systems framework. Human service organizations take in resources that they convert into goods and services. To be accountable, they must record and report on the distribution and use of the resources they receive. This book tries to teach key concepts and skills in each of the major areas of the financial management process. The book is divided into sections relating to parts of the process.

Section I is an overview that covers the systems concept and unique characteristics of nonprofit organizations. Section II covers the planning and acquisition of resources by the agency. This involves planning and budgeting skills as well as fundraising skills. Section III covers distribution of the acquired resources through internal control, budgeting, and investments. Section IV covers the recording and reporting of the agency's financial activities. Included here are basic accounting techniques as well as financial reporting guidelines.

Admittedly, there are some arbitrary distinctions made in the division of the topics. Real life is not so neat and tidy. Certainly those who work in human service agencies know that the activities of budgeting, recording and fundraising go on simultaneously. The division of topics and the order in which they are presented are due to didactic attempts to show a logical flow from inputs (acquiring resources) to outputs (reporting of what happened to the resources), and to show the cyclical nature of the processes involved.

There are several features of this book that distinguish it from other texts for human services students:

Exercises

Each chapter is supplemented with one or more exercises, cases, and readings. The exercises are intended to be a practical application of some aspect of the material in each chapter, and many of them are to be used at the student's field placement or job site. However, it is not necessary for the student to have a field placement or job to do the exercises. In many instances, the exercise may give the student the opportunity to become familiar with one or more human service agencies in the community.

Cases

The cases included at the end of each chapter are also intended to be practical applications. They usually ask the student—given the situation of this agency, what would you do or recommend? All of the cases relate to nonprofit human service agencies. In some cases the agencies are public rather than private agencies, but they have been included because they illustrate an important topic or issue related to the chapter.

Readings

The readings at the end of each chapter are intended to give the student additional information to that contained in the chapter. The readings are excerpted from newspapers, magazines and other sources to help give the student "practical," as opposed to theoretical, information that may be used in their later work. They also usually ask questions of the student, mainly for purposes of discussion.

Acknowledgments

Most of the material included here was reviewed by my classes in Budgeting and Financial Management, their comments have been extremely useful. There are too many to mention by name, but I would like to thank all of the students who gave their thoughtful comments and helped make the topics covered here understandable to other human service students. Most students who take this course will eventually be in managerial or supervisory positions in human service agencies and will, hopefully, benefit from being exposed to these ideas.

There are many others who gave ideas, input, support, and help. My wife, Carann, provided much needed support and encouragement in countless ways; as well as taking the time to read and critique numerous manuscript drafts. Dr. Paul Glasser was an inspiration and also gave much encouragement. Darlene Mendez should be credited for the illustrations used in the book. Connie Chabarria was helpful with the bibliography.

To all those who gave their time and support, I say thank you, knowing that any errors or ommissions are my responsibility.

CONTENTS

I. *OVERVIEW*

  1. **The Financial Management System** 5
     Financial Management. Nonprofit and For-Profit
     Organizations: Similarities Between Profit-oriented and
     Nonprofit Organizations; Characteristics of Nonprofit
     Human Service Agencies. The Agency as a System.
     The Financial Management Process.

II. *RESOURCE ACQUISITION*

  2. **Planning and Budgeting** 25
     Functions of the Budget. Budgetary Processes.
     Budgetary Documents.
     Exercise 2-1: Analyzing an Agency's Budget
     Exercise 2-2: Goals/Budget Analysis
     Case 2-1: The Metro County Mental Health Association
     Reading 2-1: "Budget Systems: Make the Right Choice"
     Jae C. Park

  3. **Program-Planning and Budgeting** 47
     Planning: Designing Planned Budgeting Structure;
     Organizational Analysis; Defining Broad Goals and Mission;
     Developing Tentative Objectives; Gathering and
     Analyzing Data; Setting Objectives. Programming. Budgeting:
     Forecasting Service Volume; Developing Expense Budgets;
     Estimating Public Support and Revenue; Estimating Cash Flow;
     Preparing Budgeted Financial Statements; Modifying and
     Adopting a Balanced Budget.
     Exercise 3-1: The Kimball County Substance
     Abuse Center, Inc.
     Case 3-1: The Family Life Center, Inc.
     Reading 3-1: "Preparing, Presenting and
     Defending the Budget"

xi

4. **Fundraising** 79
Acquiring Funds. Fundraising as Marketing.
Fundraising Programs. The Marketing Process Applied
to the Human Service Agency.
Exercise 4-1: Analysis of Agency Marketing
Exercise 4-2: Fundraising Plan
Case 4-1: "Firm Cited For Violating Permit:
Fund Raising Practices Reported"
John Haakenson
Reading 4-1: "Five Steps to Progressive Fundraising"
Brian Rust

5. **Grantwriting** 103
The Grantwriting Process. Writing the Grant Proposal.
Exercise 5-1: Government RFP.
Exercise 5-2: Foundation Guidelines
Case 5-1: Multipurpose Center of Urban County, Inc.
Reading 5-1: "Proposal Development and Preparation"
Reading 5-2: "Reflections of a Proposal Reviewer"
Dick Schoech

III. *RESOURCE DISTRIBUTION AND CONTROL*
6. **Control** 133
The Agency Control System. Controlling Costs:
The Chart of Accounts; Allocating Costs; Figuring Costs;
Variance Budgets. Controlling Cash: Personnel Controls;
Transaction Controls; Physical Controls.
Exercise 6-1: Cost Analysis
Case 6-1: The Murray Children's Home
Reading 6-1: "The $35.50 Solution"

7. **Investments** 159
Fixed-Income Investments. Variable-Income Investments.
Mutual Funds. Investment Planning for Human Service
Agencies. Selecting an Investment Counselor.
Exercise 7-1: Developing an Investment Strategy
Case 7-1: Senior Citizens Centers of Metro County, Inc.
Reading 7-1: How to Read the Financial Pages
of the Newspaper

Reading 7-2: "Investing for the Ford Foundation"
Ed Doherty

IV. *RESOURCE RECORDING AND REPORTING*

8. **Basic Accounting** 187
Types of Accounting Systems. Basic Accounting
Principles and Concepts. Unique Accounting
Characteristics of Nonprofit Organizations.
The Accounting Equation. Financial Statements.
Exercise 8-1: Transaction Effects on Cash
Exercise 8-2: Transaction Effects on the
Accounting Equation
Case 8-1: Metropolitan Family Counseling Services, Inc.
Reading 8-1: "A Private Group Whose Word is Law"

9. **Nonprofit Accounting** 213
Fund Accounting. The Accounting Equation.
The Accounting Cycle.
The Accounting Cycle:
The Case of the Metropolitan Family Service
Center, Inc.
Exercise 9-1: The Metro County I & R Service
Exercise 9-2: The Family Counseling Center, Inc.
Case 9-1: "Accounting and the Small Nonprofit
Organization"
Reading 9-1: "Evaluating Accounting Firms"
John T. Schiffman

10. **Financial Statements** 245
Purposes of Financial Reports. Users of
Financial Reports. Qualitative Aspects of Financial
Statements. Required Financial Statements. Audits.
Types of Audit Opinions. Analysis of Financial Statements.
Exercise 10-1: Financial Statement Analysis
Case 10-1: "Suite Charity"
Larry Williams and Clifford Teutsch
Reading 10-1: "Checklist for Charitable Nonprofit
Organizations"
Gary N. Scrivner

11. **Computerized Financial Information Systems** 287
Information Systems. Computer Systems.
Advantages and Disadvantages of Computerized Systems.
Computer Acquisition Decisions.
Exercise 11-1: Analyzing and Choosing a System
Case 11-1: "Nonprofit Accounting:
The Search for a Solution"
Arnold B. Simonse
Reading 11-1: "Learning to Compute:
'No Train, No Gain'?"
Emmanuel Rosales

  V. *BIBLIOGRAPHY* 321
 VI. *APPENDICES* 331
A-1: Foundation Center Regional Collections
A-2: Guide to Grant Sources
A-3: Excerpts from Section 501 of the Tax Code
A-4: Fund Accounting Software Vendors

FINANCIAL MANAGEMENT FOR NONPROFIT HUMAN SERVICE AGENCIES

I. OVERVIEW

Chapter One

THE FINANCIAL MANAGEMENT SYSTEM

After reading this chapter you should be able to:

1. Define the functions of financial management;
2. Compare and contrast nonprofit and for-profit organizations;
3. Describe the human service agency in systems terms;
4. Have an understanding of the place of financial management within the human service agency.

INTRODUCTION

"WOMEN'S SHELTER FACES $15,000 FUNDING CUT"
(Fort Worth Star-Telegram, January 24, 1984)

United Way of Tarrant County plans to cut $15,000 from the $80,000 allocation that had been expected for the Arlington Women's Shelter. Board members who oversee the shelter's operation call this a major snag in their efforts to raise a $200,000 operating budget for the shelter and $350,000 needed to buy and improve a larger facility. [The United Way Director]...said, "We have to put things in perspective...there were a lot of equally high priority programs. Unfortunately, we had more needs than we had dollars to spend."

The cry of so many needs and fewer available resource dollars is becoming a frequent one in the human services. This is an age of accountability; an age in which the impulse to charity is viewed in terms of unit costs, reimbursement fees, and financial statements. It is a time when human service professionals are expected to be familiar with the financial aspects of human service management. Unfortunately, due to the traditional nature of career advancement in the human services, very few human service professionals who rise to administrative positions are equipped to deal with financial matters in their agencies.

In the tradition of social work and other human services, an agency administrator usually starts his or her career as a line worker. With increasing experience and demonstration of competence, the worker moves up the hierarchy of the organization to supervisory positions such as unit supervisor or casework supervisor. With each successive rise in administrative duty the worker moves into areas where tasks and functions are unrelated to previous training and experience. The popular notion is that these new tasks, such as supervising, planning, budgeting, and so forth, involve skills that can be learned on the job. But what essentially happens is that the effective caseworker is promoted to his or her level of incompetence. Most have muddled through with varying degrees of success.

The lack of skills in the area of financial management has been particularly detrimental to human service agencies and the human service professions in general. The inconsistent reporting and evaluating that takes place in some agencies has left the human service professions open to criticism as being inefficient and unaccountable. The response in the past has been that the human services deal with the qualitative, and that quantitative analyses and reports do not provide an accurate picture of the work done with a client. While it is true that the human services do have a definite qualitative aspect, there are other areas that can be quantified, indeed, should be quantified. Those who work in the human services are stewards of the public trust, and as such must be accountable to their constituencies—clients, boards and committees, colleagues and peers, funding sources, the community, and public at large.

FINANCIAL MANAGEMENT

One important measurable way that agencies can be accountable is in the recording and reporting of their financial transactions. Financial management is a term that denotes a wide range of activities that take place in an organization. Some of these activities are fund raising, budgeting, grantwriting, accounting, and so forth. Therefore, financial management may be defined as the importation, recording, control, allocation and planning for the use of the financial and material resources of an agency. You can see that financial management involves a number of diverse activities:

Planning: is the use of a rational approach to short- and long-term strategies to be employed by the organization to ensure its fiscal solvency.

Importation: is the gathering in of human, material, and economic resources by the agency, using means such as fundraising, grant writing, contractual arrangements, charging of fees, buying of merchandise, hiring of staff, etc.

Allocation: is the distribution of resources imported into the agency. This distribution may be internal, that is, budgeting a specific amount of money to each department for expenses such as salary and other overhead. It may also be external, for example, contracting for services with an outside agency or consultant and paying for those services.

Control: is the establishment of standardized policies and procedures relating to all transactions and events involving monetary items to ensure that generally accepted accounting principles and procedures are followed by the agency.

Recording/Reporting: is the use of some sort of manual, automated or computerized system to list all transactions of a financial nature in journals and ledgers and to generate periodic financial statements and reports.

Evaluating: is the periodic review of financial activities in order to assess their efficiency and effectiveness in meeting agency and funder requirements for fiscal accountability. Periodic evaluation is done to check that the control system established by the agency is working as it was intended to do. It may also entail a review of agency activities to make sure that they are in the furtherance of stated agency goals and objectives.

While the human service administrator does not need to be an accountant, he or she is responsible for the total management and operations of the agency. Other agency staff, such as program or project directors and supervisors, are often called upon to write a budget for their program or unit, or serve on a budgeting committee. Therefore, it is incumbant upon the administrator, supervisor, or project leader to have some working knowledge of financial management.

In this chapter the financial activities of the agency will be placed in perspective by viewing them within the context of the human service agency and its other activities. First, characteristics of nonprofit human service agencies, as compared to for-profit organizations, will be discussed. Secondly, systems concepts will be presented. Thirdly, a framework for understanding the role and function of the financial management subsystem within the human service agency will be described. Finally, the financial management process as a framework for the presentation of topics and materials in this book will be discussed.

NONPROFIT AND FOR-PROFIT ORGANIZATIONS

Throughout this book the term nonprofit organization will be used synonymously with human service organization. While human service organizations are a type of nonprofit organization, they are not the only type. For example, colleges, universities, hospitals, and churches are all types of nonprofit entities. They have been excluded from the discussion in this text because they have some specific accounting procedures that differ from the kinds of agencies that will be discussed here. For similar reasons, municipal, state, and federal governmental units are excluded. All human service agencies are not necessarily nonprofit, but the only type that will be referred to here is the nonprofit organization. Therefore, nonprofit human service agencies shall be defined here as private voluntary organizations whose primary aim is to provide a social welfare service rather than to make a profit.

Similarities Between Profit-Oriented and Nonprofit Organizations

There are many similarities between profit-oriented business enterprises and nonprofit organizations (FASB, 1981:8–9). Some of these similarities are:

Both Acquire External Resources

Although they vary in size, complexity, and goals, both types of organizations have to compete for, and acquire, valuable and scarce resources from their environments. Some of these resources include skilled, qualified personnel, money, and customers.

Both May Provide Similar Goods or Services

Profit-oriented businesses and nonprofits may sometimes offer essentially the same goods or services. For example, there are profit making marriage and family guidance clinics, for-profit home help services, counseling services, adoption services, and child care facilities. Previously, those clients with money went out into the market place and purchased the goods or services they needed so that there was almost a two-tiered system of social service provision. The poor used public social services and those with means purchased services privately. Now it is much more complex than that because of other funding mechanisms available whereby individuals as well as the government may contract for public or private services that may be paid with third-party or public monies (Kamerman, 1983).

Both Produce and Distribute Goods or Services

Both types of organizations are in business to produce and/or distribute goods and services. They must develop marketing strategies to attract a specific clientele. In the case of the human services, even though many times clientele have few other alternative sources for the good or service there is still the problem of utilization. Underutilization of services is sometimes a problem because all those eligible for a service may not know about it, may associate it with stigma, or may prefer informal networks of family and friends. The human service agency must learn to market and distribute its goods or services to its target population in much the same way that business does. Some agencies are obviously more sophisticated than others at doing this.

Both Incur Financial Obligations

In order to acquire the resources that it needs to accomplish its mission, the human service agency may incur financial obligations in much the same way that any business enterprise does. Both need to obtain labor, material, and facilities, and must pay for them in the present or at a future time. In paying for the goods and materials acquired in the course of operations, both types of organizations may borrow funds through loans or mortgages from creditors who must evaluate their financial viability.

Both Must Stay Financially Viable

In order to continue operations, both types of organizations must stay financially viable by taking in more resources than they use. While governmental entities and public utilities may function on deficit budgets, neither private profits nor nonprofits can stay in business long under those conditions. So the goal of the nonprofit is to use its available resources for providing services and in doing so to: 1) break-even financially, or 2) have a surplus that could be carried over into a new fiscal period to provide a cushion for on-going programs, or even seed money for new programs.

Both Have Limited Pool of Resources and Resource Providers

Obviously, all organizations do not have unlimited access to the resources in their environments. There are other organizations competing for some of the same resources. There are resource providers who may be interested in one type of organization and not another and vice versa. Finally, there are only finite amounts of money, educated personnel, and potential consumers, or clients.

Both May Charge Fees for Services

While the two types of organizations may charge a fee for the services they provide, the purpose of the fee is different for the two types of entities. Most profit-oriented companies try to sell goods or services at a price that exceeds their costs, thus making a profit. Nonprofit organizations typically offer their services at or less than cost, many times even free. Many human service agencies do charge something, usually on a sliding-fee scale, to clients. Often the purpose of the charge is not to make a profit, but rather it is to act as a motivating factor for the client. Nonprofit organizations are generally not expected to cover all or even a large proportion of their costs because they are providing a useful and necessary service that may not be obtainable anywhere in the market economy at a price that the client is willing or able to pay. Rather, human service agencies have to rely on other sources of funding for a significant part of their budgets.

Characteristics of Nonprofit Human Service Organizations

While there are many similarities between the two types of organizations, nonprofit human service agencies differ from business or profit-oriented enterprises in many ways. This is why accounting procedures for the two types of organizations differ. Some of the distinguishing features of nonprofit human service agencies are (Gross and Warshauer, 1979; Anthony and Herzlinger, 1975; Sarri, 1971):

Socially Useful Service

The primary goal of a nonprofit human service agency is to provide a socially useful service, as defined by the community, rather than to make a profit. Because the agencies are not concerned with profit, the financial statements of nonprofits have a different emphasis. There may be an excess of revenue over expenses, but this surplus is to be used for the programs, not to enrich the owners.

Clients are Both Inputs and Outputs

A profit-oriented business such as a manufacturing firm takes in raw materials such as steel, plastic, aluminum, etc., to make a new product such as a car. In contrast, the nonprofit agency takes in clients with problems or needs, and processes and/or changes them so that one of the "products" of the human service agency is a changed and/or processed client.

Little Dependence on Clients for Revenue

Many clients served by human service agencies cannot afford to pay for the services they receive. The purpose of the alternative sources of funds used by the agency is to be able to provide the service without worrying about whether the client has the ability to pay. Even if an agency has a sliding fee schedule, in most cases its major source of income is not the client.

Reliance on Human Relations Technologies and Professionals

Human service agencies rely on technologies based on theories and assumptions about human nature. Some technologies used by agencies may include behavior modification, biofeedback, gestalt therapy, and psychoanalytic therapy. The human service agency also is, in many cases, staffed and run by professionals themselves. For-profit organizations may use the expertise of professional staff, but in many cases human relations professionals are in adjunct positions performing tasks peripheral to the main goals of the organization.

High Proportion of Nonroutine Events

The human services deal with people and their problems. It is therefore almost impossible to routinize the nature of the tasks that need to be performed to alleviate the problems. It is possible to routinize forms and procedures, but agencies must also cope with a myriad of emergencies that arise with people in trouble. And these emergencies have to be dealt with immediately; for example, someone has to be on call at the child welfare office to place children found abandoned in the middle of the night.

Resources are not Loans

Nonprofit organizations receive vast amounts of resources in the form of gifts, bequests, donations, allocations, and grants. The provider(s) of these resources do not usually expect economic gain or repayment for their contributions. Rather, these resources are given to be used for the public good without tangible economic benefit expected in return. There are, of course, some direct and indirect benefits to those who wish to take advantage of them in the form of tax write-offs for charitable expenses, and status in the community.

Accountability and Stewardship

The goal of nonprofits is public service and resources accrue to them on this basis. These agencies have a public responsibility to account for the funds that they have received. Human service agencies are stewards or managers of public funds, thus they should not only account for funds given for specific projects, but they also have a duty to use all the resources of the organization in the most efficient and effective manner possible.

Outside Constraints

While all organizations are somewhat constrained by governmental and legal regulations regarding their activities, there are other constraints placed by funding sources on the goals, policies, plans, and implementation strategies of human service organizations. Many times human service agencies have to provide services as dictated by an outside agency. For example, to get funds for a children's shelter an agency may have to have a certain number of staff with specified qualifications. In some cases, an agency may also be constrained from offering other services that a funding source does not approve of—for example, abortion counseling. The old saying "Money rules—who has the money makes the rules" is no more true than in the human services. No matter whether the funder is a government agency, United Way or other allocation body, these outside constraints are many times more powerful than agency management or the governing board.

No Stockholders

There are no stockholders nor is there owner's equity in the nonprofit organization. This means that there are no ownership interests that can be bought and sold as in a profit-oriented company where stock may be issued or proprietorship passed or transferred to others. In the nonprofit agency, control rests with a board of directors who are supposed to represent the community, and a professional administrative staff.

Blurred Lines of Responsibility

In many nonprofit agencies the line of responsibility is not often very clear. Outside agencies often dictate goals and activities of the nonprofit organization. Also, the governing boards of nonprofits seem to be less influential in decision-making than the boards of profit-oriented companies. Although the governing board is ultimately responsible for the agency, members are rarely paid for their services. They tend to be recruited from the elites in the community to help give the agency an aura of legitimacy, to help in fund raising, and so forth. Many times elites like to sit on boards as a badge of prestige and community service. They are supposed to represent the public interest, but in many cases they are made up of the largest contributors. Although they are legally responsible for the agency, they rarely, except in extreme cases of crisis, get involved in the day-to-day running of the agency.

These then, are the major similarities and differences between the nonprofit and for-profit organization. The differences have a large impact on the type of financial management system used by the nonprofit agency. Before we discuss this in more detail, let us try to view the financial management function within the framework of the agency as a total system.

THE AGENCY AS A SYSTEM

Systems theory has pervaded the physical and social sciences and has provided a framework with which to view many different types of processes. Concepts and techniques of systems theory are important in financial management for a number of reasons. First of all, they are the bases for the development of computerized information systems found frequently in all types of organizations today. An organizational systems analysis is an integral part of the planning and development of a computerized information system. Systems techniques, such as flow charting, are used in programming. Secondly, modern auditing today includes in its evaluations a systems review (Bodnar, 1980:26). Thus, they are very important for accounting and auditing functions. Thirdly, systems con-

cepts help give us a way to look at the human service agency, its subsystems, and processes in some kind of totality.

"A system is composed of interacting parts that operate together to
achieve an objective or purpose. Systems are not random collections of
objects. Systems consist of coherent, patterned, purposeful sets of elements"
(Bodnar: 26). The boundary of the human service organization is made
of its material and human resources, its technologies, as well as its actual
organizational structure. The environment of the human service organization is a complex net of social values and events, economic conditions,
political constraints or facilitating factors, including federal and local
laws and regulations.

If we take a systems view of the human service organization we may be
able to see more graphically the place and function of the financial
management subsystem within the agency. First of all, let us look at the
concept of the open system. Human service agencies are open systems
because they are in interaction with their environments, there is a
twoway exchange of energy and resources between the agency and its
environment. Each can influence and impact the other.

Some Characteristics of Open Systems

Katz and Kahn (1978) describe a number of characteristics of open
systems:

Input

As no organization is self-contained, every organization must take in
energy in the form of resources from its external environment. In the
human service agency these resources are called inputs. Inputs are
material in the form of money, supplies, equipment, and so forth. Inputs
may also be human resources in the form of personnel for the agency,
and the clients the agency is to serve (see Figure 1-1).

Through-Put

Open systems transform or convert the energy they take in. This
means that some process occurs in the organization for the conversion to
take place. In human service agencies material and human resources are
used to process and/or change clients (Hasenfeld, 1974; Vinter, 1974).
The processes or technologies used are varied and include casework,

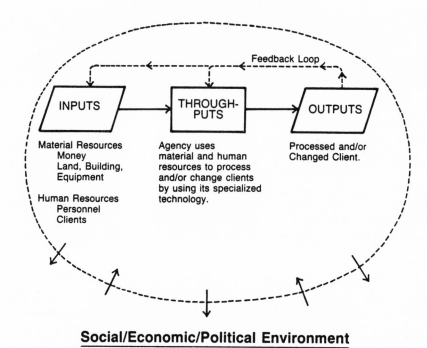

Figure 1-1: A Systems View of the Human Service Agency

groupwork, assessment, diagnosis, behavior modification, and assertive-
ness training, to name just a few.

Output

After through-put, the result of the processing is returned to the
environment. In the case of the nonprofit organization, this output is the
processed and/or changed client. For example, in a home for delinquent
youth, the youth may be seen as an "input" into the home's system; the
treatment he receives in the home is the "through-put," and the changed,
presumably, non-delinquent youth who leaves the home is the "output."

Feedback

Inputs into an open system are not just of a material nature, there are
informational inputs as well. These informative inputs (feedback) may
come from the outputs of the agency and thus are cyclical in nature.
They tell the organization about its environment and its own functioning
in relation to that environment. The information that the agency receives
regarding the results of its processes may be used to alter the process
itself. In the example of the home for delinquent youth, if the youths

discharged from the home are again involved in delinquent acts soon after leaving, the home may receive "feedback" in terms of complaints by parents, teachers, police, courts, and the general community. If the home wanted to continue to treat delinquents, it would use the feedback as a basis for re-evaluating and modifying its program.

Cycles of Events

The exchange of energy (resources flowing through the agency) has a cyclical nature about it. That is, the output from the system may provide the resources for the cycle of activities to continue. If the outputs of the human service agency are seen as successful, this information is relayed to funding sources and the community which in turn means that a continuing supply of clients and funds will be channeled to the agency.

Negative Entropy

Entropy is a process by which all forms of organization move toward deterioration, even death. Open systems must try to retard or reverse this process by acquiring negative entropy. The open system can do this by taking in more resources from its environment than it uses, thus storing up additional energy and keeping it in reserve. How do human service agencies do this? Since they do not make a profit, in many instances they cannot store up reserves of funds. For example, if they have received government grants, all unexpended funds must usually be returned to the funding agency at the end of the fiscal year. But sometimes human service agencies do have a surplus, an excess of revenues over expenses, that can be invested or put into new or ongoing programs. Another thing that most agencies have an abundance of is human resources in the form of clients. Most human service agencies have long waiting lists of clients. By keeping these long waiting lists, the agency can demonstrate the need and demand for their services.

Steady State and Dynamic Homeostasis

The process of importing resources into the human service system, transforming them, and exporting them back into the environment means that the level of energy and relations between parts of the system must remain somewhat constant. This is what is meant by a "steady state" and helps us understand why organizations at times commit acts that appear on the surface to be irrational or confusing. If there are disruptions to the system, either internally or externally, the system moves rapidly to restore itself to its previous state or a new steady state. Through dynamic homeostasis the system may attempt to preserve its character by growth and expansion. Human service agencies try to maintain a steady state and homeostasis in many different ways. They try to keep a steady flow of clients and resources into the agency. They try to maintain a stable source of revenue. Those agencies too dependent on one type of funding source have found in times of cutback and retrenchment that their agencies have been placed in precarious positions leading to uncertainty and instability in the agency.

Differentiation

Open systems move from simple organizational structures to more complex ones with elaborate and specialized roles. A human service agency that may have started with one social worker responsible for all tasks in a small office may grow to a large agency with very specialized professional staff such as intake workers, case workers, art and music therapists, and group workers.

Equifinality

A system can reach the same goal from different initial situations and by a variety of means; this is called equifinality. There are obviously more ways than one of reaching any given objective. For human service agencies this means that, while we tend to think one therapeutic method is superior to others depending on our own theoretical orientations, there are many methods and strategies for helping clients become healthy and lead productive lives. It also means that there are a myriad of strategies that the human service agency may apply in planning for, acquiring, and using the resources available to it.

Subsystems

A system is many times made up of subsystems. "A subsystem is a system whose boundaries are contained within the boundaries of a larger system" (Bodnar, 1980:29). Even a small human service agency may be made up of a number of subsystems. The primary subsystem is one whose activities encompass the main goals and objectives of the agency. This is usually the client subsystem, which exists to help clients (see Figure 1-2). The agency may also have support subsystems which pursue activities to help the primary subsystem achieve its goals. A typical agency will have a personnel subsystem and a financial subsystem, but a larger agency may have even more subsystems. The personnel subsystem is concerned with recruiting, hiring, training, and evaluating employees. The financial subsystem is concerned with the activities that are the focus of this book, the economic activities of the agency.

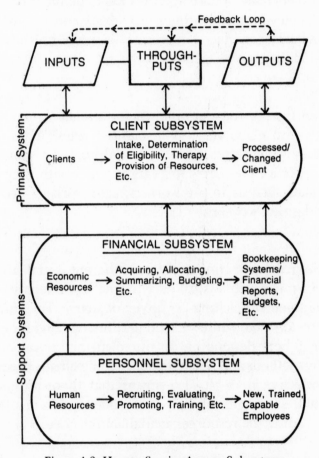

Figure 1-2: Human Service Agency Subsystems

Subsystems are in constant interaction with each other, so the activities in one subsystem have an effect on the other subsystems of the agency. There are a myriad of ways in which the client subsystem and the personnel subsystem all produce voluminous data about activities going on in the agency, and when these activities involve either the accumulation and/or the expenditure of agency monies, then these are recorded and/or distributed through the financial subsystem.

Obviously, agencies are of many different sizes and the larger the agency, the more specialized it tends to become (this is the process of differentiation). For example, a very small agency may only have a part-time bookkeeper, an accountant who periodically comes in on a fee-for-services basis to prepare financial reports, and an auditor who comes in once a year to audit the books. A larger agency may have a full-time bookkeeper and an accountant who comes in more frequently. A very large agency may not only have an accounting department, but the whole financial subsystem may be divided into separate units such as payroll, travel, and so forth. Although the title of the department may vary according to the size of the agency, the principles are the same, the point is the same: a large part of what goes on in the human service agency involves the receipt or expenditure of money, and it is the job of the human service accounting department to record these events, to disburse monies when necessary, and to be able, in a coherent manner, to account for all monies received and disbursed.

For example, in the client subsystem, when a client either receives or pays a bill for services rendered, a copy of the bill or the money itself is sent to the accounting department (financial subsystem) to be entered on the books and deposited in the bank. When an employee goes to work or provides an hour of service (personnel subsystem) this may be entered on a time sheet and sent to the accounting department for payroll purposes. When a caseworker makes a home visit, a travel form is usually filled out and sent to the accounting department so that the worker can be reimbursed. The recruitment of staff also affects different subsystems. It may entail the expense of having an ad printed in the newspaper, or the printing of flyers to post as announcements. The bill for the newspaper ad or the flyers and the paper used for the flyers goes to the accounting or bookkeeping department. Similarly, the forms used in client intake are printed and paid for by sending a bill or purchase voucher to the accounting department. The receptionist who first greets the client, the intake worker who interviews the client, and the worker subsequently assigned to the case are all salaried employees who are listed on the payroll account in the accounting department. They are paid by checks drawn up in that department and signed by the director of the agency.

Each agency has responsibility for the large sums of money allocated to it from various funding sources, public as well as private. Every time monies are received from a different source, the transaction is (or should be) entered into a separate fund account. The agency, through the accounting department, has a checking account to enable it to pay for supplies, bills, payroll, etc. This checking account gets a monthly statement just as a personal account does, and someone in the department has to do the job of reconciling the statement, or "balancing the account." In accepting financial resources from outside funding organizations, the agency has a public, professional, legal, and moral responsibility to be able to account for the disposition of the resources in a way that is understandable to resource providers, as well as other interested third-parties, in a manner consistent with generally accepted accounting principles (GAAP).

The average human service worker does not usually think of, or care about, this interaction between subsystems for he/she may have very little personal contact with the accounting department except for routine chores such as filling out a W-4 form or submitting requests for travel reimbursement. For the human service administrator, however, what goes on in that department has just as much, if not more, relevance as the services provided because the daily transactions recorded by the accounting department form the basis of the annual financial reports that are submitted to funding sources at budget review time. The administrator will have to work closely with his or her chief financial officer not only for budgeting, but to aid in planning and decisionmaking. While the administrator is not expected to do the bookkeeping, he/she should know the basic principles of financial management to be able to converse intelligently about it, and, most importantly, to be able to use the financial management subsystem as a tool for providing more efficient and effective services.

THE FINANCIAL MANAGEMENT PROCESS

This book has been arranged to provide the student with a systems view of the financial management process. In the systems framework, the agency takes in resources as inputs; converts or processes them for its use; and has outputs in the form of clients, goods, or services. The foci of this book are the various stages of the process. Obviously, all the activities to be discussed go on simultaneously in agencies. Also, the process is iterative and looping, each part is dependent on the other, it is a continuous cycle of events that are at once sequential yet simultaneous. However, for learning purposes these activities are broken down into small, discrete units.

In the first stage of the financial management process, the agency is concerned with the acquisition of resources (see Figure 1-3). To acquire resources effectively, the agency must have a clear idea of its mission, goals, and objectives. From its goals the agency can develop a plan of operation that includes projections of amounts of resources needed over a specific period of time. Developing short- and long-term plans are an integral part of budgeting as well as fund raising. The first stage of the financial management process then, is concerned with the future. The agency needs to answer such questions as: How much money and material resources will we need to fulfill our mission? How can we raise this money most successfully? What potential contributors are available? How do we find them? How can we write grants that will be funded? How can we ascertain an appropriate fee schedule?

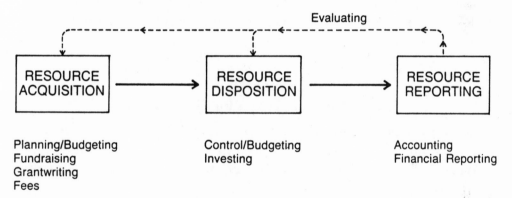

Figure 1-3: The Financial Management Process

The second stage of the process begins at the point that the money or other resources are acquired. This stage is concerned with present time events and with the control and disposition of agency resources. Questions confronting the agency at this stage are: How do we develop good cash management systems? How can we ensure that we fulfill our stewardship responsibility in the most efficient manner possible? What shall we do with the endowment funds given us? How can we make sure that monies allocated for programs are used most efficiently? How do we build in a good control system?

The third stage of the process is an historical perspective; it looks at what the agency has done with its resources. In this stage every financial transaction that takes place in the agency is recorded and then periodically summarized and reported. It forces the agency to evaluate its activities and answer questions such as: What has the agency done with the resources given it over the last year (or other designated time period)? How much has the agency spent for fundraising as opposed to services? What is the ratio of the agency's program costs to its administrative costs?

In this book, methods of nonprofit accounting and reporting, as well as other tools and techniques such as fundraising, grantwriting, and investing will be explained. Tools and techniques needed for efficient management of agency resources will be described. Chapters are arranged around the three main aspects of the financial management process— acquisition, disposition, and reporting of resources. The chapters on resource acquisition include planning and budgeting, fundraising, and grantwriting. Those chapters on disposition of resources include topics such as budgeting and control, and investments. Chapters on reporting of resources are comprised of the areas of accounting, financial statements, and computerized financial information systems.

Chapter One
Questions and Topics for Discussion

1. What is financial management?
2. What kinds of activities are involved in financial management?
3. What are the similarities between nonprofit and for-profit organizations?
4. In what ways do profit and nonprofit organizations differ?
5. What are the characteristics of open systems?
6. What kinds of subsystems might a human service agency have?
7. How would you describe the role of the financial management system in the human service agency?
8. Why is it important for the human service professional to understand something about financial management?
9. What are the stages in the financial management process? How do they overlap?

II. RESOURCE ACQUISITION

Chapter Two

PLANNING AND BUDGETING

After reading this chapter you should be able to:

1. Understand the relationship of planning to the budget process.
2. Describe the purposes of budgets.
3. Explain the different types of budgets.
4. Understand approaches to the budget process.

INTRODUCTION

The key to an agency's financial management system is a well thought out, well documented plan. The agency master plan is the guide for the financial plan that will then be developed to implement the agency's long- and short-term plans. The master plan is the result of overall agency planning, and a reflection of the mission, goals, and objectives of the agency. While a goal is a broad statement of a desired future state, a budget is an expression of a desired future state described in monetary terms.

Budgeting is one of the singular most important activities that takes place in the human service agency. As an activity, budgeting involves planning for the acquisition and allocation of resources for future agency programs. The outcome of the process is one or more budget documents that not only delineate resources assigned to personnel, materials, and programs, but also to a large extent reflect agency goals and priorities. Thus the budget is more than "a plan set forth in financial terms" (Abels and Murphy, 1981:148), it is " . . . a summary of organizational process, policy, and program. It is a statement of goals, priorities, political trade-offs, decisions, authority structures . . . " (Miringoff, 1980:115).

In systems terms, the planning and budgeting process may be viewed as one in which the agency scans its environment, takes in resources in the form of data and information, processes these data, and produces a plan that includes a budget (see Figure 2-1). The information used by the agency may be historical in nature and include such things as past

25

budgets, financial statements, records of client flow, and so forth. Data may also include projections of demographic trends, client flow, and future social problems. Current information that may be used by the agency includes figures on operating expenses, unit costs, break-even costs, as well as information on client needs. The agency takes in this information and has to process it in a meaningful way. The planning/ budgeting process involves a number of crucial decisions on the part of the agency planning team. Key decisions involve the structure of the planning committee, positions of authority and responsibility, the mission, goals, and objectives of the agency, and the necessary tasks to implement them. Decisions are also involved in developing time frames to complete tasks, and formulate desirable, measurable outcomes. Finally, the outputs of the process may be long-term and short-term (up to one year) plans, and the budget documents that accompany them.

FUNCTIONS OF THE BUDGET

The budgeting process and the resulting budget documents can serve a number of useful functions for an agency (Powell, 1980:3–4):

Clarification

The budget can aid in clarification of goals. When a new agency is formed, its board of directors writes up a charter that states its mission and goals. But the human service agency is a dynamic, open system—its mission and goals may change over time. A periodic reevaluation is healthy for the agency. If the budget is used as part of a larger planning process in which the agency periodically reassesses its direction, clarification of underlying assumptions about the mission and goals of the agency can be useful to board, staff, clients, and the community at large.

Coordination

The budget can aid in coordination of activities. In the process of planning, programming, and preparing the budget, overlapping or competing activities of various departments may be highlighted and corrective actions taken. In programming for the delivery of planned services, the process may point to areas where reorganization of units may need to take place, or where clarification of authority and responsibility of different departments is needed. Also, because of the typically tight budgets of most human service agencies, coordination of units and

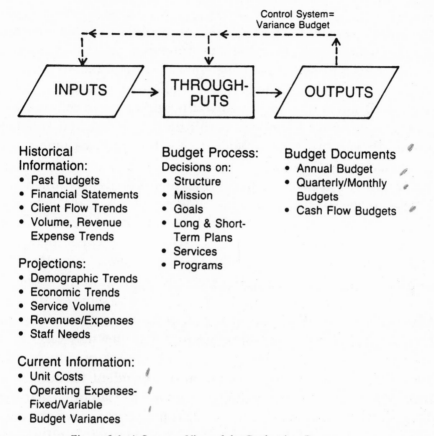

Figure 2-1: A Systems View of the Budgeting Process

departments is needed in order to use agency resources most efficiently. The budgeting process forces the agency to look for ways to increase coordination.

Communication

The budget can aid in communication of agency objectives. The budget is a reflection of agency goals, objectives, and priorities stated in monetary terms and thus communicates to staff and funders alike the direction that the agency plans to take in a specified period of time. The goals of the agency as reflected in the budget can also be communicated to the community at large. This is usually done through media developed for the agency such as annual reports and brochures which may use simple charts to illustrate how the agency has allocated its funds.

Control

The budget can aid in control. Control involves feedback mechanisms to help the agency make sure that it is proceeding with the completion of its stated goals and objectives. The agency can monitor its activities in numerous ways, and budgeting is a very effective, measurable means of doing this. Control may also involve the setting up of monitoring systems to ensure that the agency is fulfilling its fiscal and stewardship responsibilities. This aspect of budgeting will be discussed more fully in another chapter.

There are two aspects of budgeting that will be examined in this chapter—budgetary processes and budgetary documents. The budget processes used by an agency and the documents generated are many times dictated by outside funding sources. As a process, budgeting is very much a political activity, both internally and externally. That is, many human service organizations receive some funding from either federal or state agencies. This means that they are to some extent dependent on political decisions far removed from their agencies as to the nature, level, and extent of future funding that they may receive. Decisions made in Congress and state capitals impact greatly on human service agencies. Many agencies are also dependent for funds on the United Way or other federated agencies such as Catholic Charities, or the Jewish Federation. The decision-making that goes on at the community level of these funding agencies involves community politics and the values, needs, and priorities set by the local funding source. Politics and trade-offs may be involved in the negotiating that goes on between the community or federated funding source and the agency during budget hearings. And finally, there are internal politics that influence budget making because of the differing views, goals, values, and needs of individual board and staff members.

At the agency level, there are a variety of approaches used in the preparation of the budget. Some of the most common approaches to the budgeting process are incremental budgeting, zero-base budgeting, and planning-programming-budgeting.

BUDGETARY PROCESSES

It must be emphasized again that the type of approach to developing a budget used by an agency is many times mandated by the major funding source of that agency. Sometimes the documents to be used are closely tied to the budgetary process as, for example, in zero based budgeting. It becomes quite cumbersome for an agency when it must fill out a myriad of different forms for a variety of funding sources. However, this section will present an overview of the most common types of budgeting process used by the nonprofit agency today.

Incremental Budgeting

The budgeting process is an opportunity for agency administration and staff to re-evaluate and re-order goals and priorities, and to use the budget as a means of planning, control, and accountability. Unfortunately, many times this opportunity is not taken. Instead, previous years' budgets are looked over, an increase to account for inflation is tacked on to the previous figures, and the budget is resubmitted to funding sources as a reflection of "status-quo." This is known as the incremental approach to budgeting.

One of the reasons that the incremental approach is so common is that it is so easy to do. It involves very little calculation beyond the initial decision as to what the incremental amount or percentage should be. Another reason for the persistence of incremental budgeting is that it does not demand analysis of goals or policies (Wildavsky, 1982:11).

Some problems associated with this incremental approach are related to underlying assumptions regarding the ongoing activities of the agency. The incremental approach assumes that the programs and activities in the previous year's budget are essential to the accomplishment of agency goals and should be continued; that they are being performed in an effective, efficient manner, and that they will be cost-effective in the next year (Letzukus, 1982:17). These assumptions may not necessarily be valid, and they need to be examined.

Zero-Base Budgeting

While incremental budgeting starts with an established base of the previous year's operating levels, and seeks to justify changes in the current year, zero-base budgeting (ZBB) attempts to provide some accountability by starting from a base of zero. In ZBB each proposed expenditure must be justified; this encourages the analysis of competing claims on resources, and reduces the possibility of continuing obsolete, inefficient programs. ZBB is not new, it has been implemented at the state and federal levels as well as by some voluntary human service agencies. In principle, the ZBB system can be integrated with other ones such as the Planning, Programming, and the Budgeting System (PPBS) to be discussed below, although it may entail much more paperwork and time than some agencies are willing to spend.

Essentially, the ZBB system is a highly rational approach to planning and budgeting. It forces administrative staff to rationalize the existence and funding level for every program of the agency. It can give decision-makers a choice of options along with the cost of each option. The ZBB process entails five main stages (Kugajevsky, 1981: 179–185):

1. Designating the decision units

A decision unit is a department, program, or some other designated part of an agency that will develop the decision packages. ZBB is output, results oriented, so in choosing the decision units to work on the decision packages, it is most logical to pick those that can be tied to the agency's mission or long-range objectives. In most cases, these units will be the separate programs that make up the agency's primary activities. An important criterion for choosing a decision unit is that each unit have its own budget, and an identifiable manager with authority to establish rules and allocate resources. If these programs have separate budgets it enables the agency to identify the costs of delivering the specific service by that unit.

2. Formulating the decision packages

The decision package is the key to ZBB. It identifies " . . . a discrete activity, function, or operation in a definitive manner for management evaluation and comparison with other activities" (Pyhrr, 1973:6). The decision package is usually a one-page sheet that lists and describes a program activity in terms of its objectives, methods, alternative methods, consequences of not delivering the service or activity, performance measures and outputs, and cost/benefits. The decision packages may be prepared at three different levels of expenditure: high, medium, and low, so that decision makers can compare outputs and costs at various levels of expenditure (see Table 2-1 for a sample decision package form).

3. Ranking the decision packages

After formulating the decision packages, they are then ranked in order of perceived importance by the manager or team working on the budget.

Table 2-1

SAMPLE DECISION PACKAGE

Program: Family Counseling   Rank: 1

Purpose/Objective: To provide professional counseling services to
families of children at risk of being abused.

Method of Performance: Individual, group, and family counseling on
cases referred from Child Welfare and other sources; case management,
follow-up, and evaluation.

Expected Results: Reduction in the number of children neglected and
abused in Metro County.

Consequences of Not Approving: Inadequate provision of services to at-
risk families may lead to increase or, at minimum, continuation of
current trends in child abuse and neglect.

Work Load Measures	FY 86	FY 87	FY 88
1. Number of children seen	251	265	282
2. Number of groups (includes separate childrens, mothers, and fathers groups)	20	26	28
Unit Cost of Service	$20	$22	$23
Positions required	10	12	12
Estimated Expenses for Services			
Personnel	$100,000	$120,000	$126,000
Other Expenses	68,000	81,600	85,680
Total est.	$168,000	201,600	211,680

The ranking process continues as the packages move up the hierarchy of
the organization.

4. Consolidating the decision packages

As the decision packages move through the organization, they are
combined and compared with decision packages from other units.

5. Preparing the budget

After decisions have been made as to the most important and necessary activities for the agency, the ZBB decision packages and budgets are
then converted to the traditional functional budget.

ZBB has been most useful for short-term planning and budgeting. In
addition, it has been combined with other systems such as PPBS. Some
advantages of ZBB are that it identifies and evaluates alternative costs
for a program; it focuses on the high priority goals and objectives of an
agency; it also encourages participatory budgeting in that middle man-

agers are able to formulate the initial decision packages. Some disadvantages of ZBB are that it takes a few years for the system to be fully operational; it creates extra paperwork; the agency staff may be resistant to changing old budgeting habits; and there may be intangible reasons why old programs or activities are carried over that are difficult to rationalize. Staff who have a vested interest in continuing pet programs will be resistant to ZBB.

Planning Programming Budgeting System (PPBS)

The Planning Programming Budgeting System (PPBS) process tries to encourage agencies to think of their programs not as ends in themselves. Instead, the programs are to be seen as means to reaching the desired goals and objectives by competing with alternative and equally deserving programs. This competition among alternatives is crucial to testing the effectiveness and efficiency of proposed as well as current programs. The major components in PPBS are (Schultze, 1981:24–26; Letzkus, 1982:17–25):

1. **Specification and analysis of basic program objectives for each program.** Each agency program must have clearly delineated—measurable objectives that can be periodically analyzed for current congruence with overall agency goals.

2. **Formulation of alternative means to reach the desired objectives.** In systems terms, equifinality means that a goal can be reached in many different ways. Thus, this part of the PPBS process entails a listing of every conceivably possible alternative way of meeting program objectives that have been enumerated.

3. **Analysis of the output of a specific program based on the original objectives.** This means that each alternative program must be examined in terms of how outputs reach agency objectives. Outputs may be such things as number of clients served, number of hot meals delivered, number of counseling sessions during month, number of public education presentations, etc., depending on what the alternative method of service delivery may be.

4. **Measurement of total program costs, not just for the year under analysis, but projecting several years into the future.** For example, even though the initial or current costs of a project or program may be calculated to be

low, that does not mean that future costs may be so. Therefore, projection of costs must include possible expansion of staff and/or space, inflation rates, increased costs, and so forth.

5. **Analysis of alternatives, with a focus on which will be the most effective in achieving the stated objectives for the least cost.** This last step involves cost-benefits analysis as a basis for decision-making on programs that will be incorporated into a final agency budget.

6. **Preparation of a functional budget that ties program costs to specific line item expenses.**

PPBS is a budgeting system that relies heavily on central coordination, this is probably why it was tried in the federal government. But as originally formulated, it was not very workable in the nonprofit sector because it did not take into account the unique nature of nonprofit organizational relationships in which there is a clear delineation between budgeting and allocating. Other criticisms of PPBS are that it concentrates too much on ends rather than means; that it depends too much on economic and "scientific" rationality and has little recognition of the fact that budgeting is a political process that needs organizational consensus; and that it relies too much on the centralization of decisionmaking; in the voluntary sector there is autonomy of the human service agencies from their allocation sources (United Way, 1975:8). Therefore, the allocation source may have little control over individual agency goals.

PPBS was formulated to be a more rational approach to budgeting than the incremental approach. In actuality, it lies somewhere between incremental budgeting and zero-base budgeting. There are two main differences between PPBS and ZBB. First of all, in PPBS there is no annual review of all ongoing programs, usually there is review of all new programs and some selected ongoing ones. Secondly, there is no priority ranking for all programs and activities in PPBS as there is in ZBB. In other ways, they are very similar. That is, they try to tie programs to objectives, and use cost-benefits analysis to decide on alternative means.

This text will use a modified version of PPBS developed by the United Way of America and called the Program-Planning and Budgeting Cycle. This approach to budgeting will be discussed in detail in the next chapter.

While it is difficult to separate the budgeting process from the documents that go with it, this has been done here for ease of discussion. Different types of budget documents are used for a variety of reasons.

BUDGETARY DOCUMENTS

There are a variety of budget documents and formats that an agency may use. Choice of the appropriate documents is dependent on the type of process used by the agency, its own internal needs, and the requirements of funding sources. An agency should try to set up a budgeting system so that its internal budget forms closely conform to those of its major funder, simply for ease in transferring information from one set of forms to another. This may not always be possible, especially if the agency receives large sums from a variety of different sources, all with their own required budget formats. In this case, the agency should devise internal forms that are most convenient for its own internal operations. The most common budget formats are the line-item budget, the program budget, and the functional budget.

Line-Item Budgets

Line item budgets are simply lists by "object category" (for example payroll expense, supplies expense, etc.) of various components of the budget. They do not attempt to tie revenues and expenses in with programs and, in fact, make it almost impossible to figure out the costs of various programs. This type of budget is the oldest and simplest, and may still be found in some small single program agencies. But it is really an obsolete method of budgeting because the simplistic format does not give necessary information needed for decision-making and planning (see Table 2-2 for a sample line-item budget).

Program Budgets

A program budget lists revenues and expenses by program only, so that it is impossible to know specific costs associated with any program. This type of budget may often be seen in agency annual reports, newsletters, and brochures. It is a way of giving some information about the agency without divulging other information that the agency considers confidential (see Table 2-3 for an example of a program budget).

Table 2-2

LINE-ITEM BUDGET 198X

HUMAN SERVICES AGENCY, INC.

Public Support and Revenue

    Contributions $xxxxx.xx

    Allocations   xxxxx.xx

    Grants   xxxxx.xx

    Program Fees   xxxxx.xx

Total Public Support and Revenue $xxxxx.xx

Expenses

    Salaries $xxxxx.xx

    Employee Benefits   xxxxx.xx

    Payroll Taxes   xxxxx.xx

    Supplies   xxxxx.xx

    Occupancy   xxxxx.xx

    Rental of Equipment   xxxxx.xx

Total Expenses $xxxxx.xx

Functional Budgets

Functional budgets are also known as performance budgets and are used in PPBS and PPB. In this approach to budgeting, "objects of expenditure are viewed in relation to the programs they serve" (Swan, 1983:23). Early users of this type of budgeting were some federal departments in the 1930's. One advantage of this system is that it does focus attention on costs per program, which the line-item approach does not. (see Table 2-4 for an example of a functional budget.)

Table 2-3

PROGRAM BUDGET 198X

HUMAN SERVICES AGENCY, INC.

	Revenues	Expenses
	————	————
Support Services		
Administration and general	$xxxxx.xx	$xxxxx.xx
Fundraising	xxxxx.xx	xxxxx.xx
Program Services		
Program A	xxxxx.xx	xxxxx.xx
Program B	xxxxx.xx	xxxxx.xx
Program C	xxxxx.xx	xxxxx.xx
	————	————
Total	$xxxxx.xx	$xxxxx.xx
	════════	════════

The master budget is an expression of an agency's goals expressed in monetary terms. It outlines agency objectives and approaches for achieving them. It aids in planning, in setting measures of performance, and in control of agency activities. It is to the advantage of the agency that staff and board take the time to utilize the budget process to maximize effectiveness and efficiency in the agency.

Chapter Two
Questions and Topics for Discussion

1. What are two important aspects of budgeting?
2. What some functions of budgeting for the human service agency?
3. What are the disadvantages of incremental budgeting?
4. What are the similarities and differences between ZBB and PPBS?
5. What are the advantages and disadvantages of the ZBB and PPBS approaches to budgeting?
6. What is the relationship of defining agency goals and mission to budget making?

Table 2-4

FUNCTIONAL BUDGET 198X

HUMAN SERVICES AGENCY, INC.

	Support Services		Program Services		
	Admin &	Fundraising	A	B	C
Public Support and Revenue					
Contributions	$xxxx.xx	$xxxx.xx	$xxxx.xx	$xxxx.xx	$xxxx.xx
Allocations	xxxx.xx	xxxx.xx	xxxx.xx	xxxx.xx	xxxx.xx
Grants	xxxx.xx	xxxx.xx	xxxx.xx	xxxx.xx	xxxx.xx
Program Fees	xxxx.xx	xxxx.xx	xxxx.xx	xxxx.xx	xxxx.xx
	-------	-------	-------	-------	-------
Tot. Pub.Support and Revenue	$xxxxx.xx	$xxxxx.xx	$xxxxx.xx	$xxxxx.xx	$xxxxx.xx
Expenses					
Salaries	$xxxx.xx	$xxxx.xx	$xxxx.xx	$xxxx.xx	$xxxx.xx
Employee Benefits	xxxx.xx	xxxx.xx	xxxx.xx	xxxx.xx	xxxx.xx
Payroll Taxes	xxxx.xx	xxxx.xx	xxxx.xx	xxxx.xx	xxxx.xx
Supplies	xxxx.xx	xxxx.xx	xxxx.xx	xxxx.xx	xxxx.xx
Occupancy	xxxx.xx	xxxx.xx	xxxx.xx	xxxx.xx	xxxx.xx
Rental of Equipment	xxxx.xx	xxxx.xx	xxxx.xx	xxxx.xx	xxxx.xx
	-------	-------	-------	-------	-------
Total Expenses	$xxxx.xx	$xxxx.xx	$xxxx.xx	$xxxx.xx	$xxxx.xx

7. What are the differences between a line-item budget, a program budget, and a functional budget?

Exercise 2-1: Analyzing an Agency's Budget

Shown below is the budget of a human services agency. In reviewing this budget, please answer the following questions:

1. What type of format is used in this budget (i.e., line-item, programmatic, functional)? Why do you think this format is used here?

2. What is the breakdown (in percentages) of major revenue sources

and expenditures? Do you think funding sources are diverse
enough for this agency? Why or why not?

3. What services are provided by this agency?
4. After carefully examining this budget, write a list of goals that are
   reflective of this agency's budget. (see table 2–5)

Exercise 2-2: Goals/Budget Analysis

Organizational goals are future intended states that the agency wishes
to achieve. But sometimes the agency's goals are not clear to staff or the
community for a variety of reasons, i.e., the goals may be interpreted
differently by different people, there may be philosophical or ideologi-
cal disagreements about them, community needs may have changed, and
so forth. One of the functions of budgeting, as part of the planning
process, is that it aids in clarification of agency goals for staff and the
community at large.

While the budget may not be able to accurately relect all of an agency's
goals, it does reflect allocation of tangible resources. To this extent it
shows areas of agency priority and expenditure of energy, personnel,
and materials.

For this exercise you are to do the following:

1. Using your field placement or job as the unit of analysis, try to
   obtain a list of agency goals. If the agency has no stated goals, try
   to obtain a list of perceived goals by talking to key people in the
   agency. Using this list of goals as a frame of reference, compare the
   agency goals to its budget in a short memo no more than three
   pages long. Please attach a copy of the agency goals and budget to
   your memo.
2. Please include the following categories as subheadings in your
   memo:
   a. Agency description—how does the agency describe itself and
      its mission?
   b. Funding sources—where does the agency receive its funds?
      What agencies or groups? In what amounts (%)?
   c. The budgetary process—what process does the agency go
      through in the formulation and approval of its budget?
   d. Budget format—what format is used for the budget, i.e., line-
      item, program, functional, etc.? Who decides on form?
   e. Budget analysis—What programs/activities have been budgeted?

Table 2-5

ANNUAL BUDGET - 198X

Human Services Agency, Inc.

Public Support and Revenue:

United Way	$ 1,121,843
Program Service Fees	372,762
Allowance for Doubtful Accounts	(38,933)
Membership Dues	5,950
Fees-Grants from Govt. Agencies	2,190,068
Special Events Income	6,329
Investment Income	48,686
Contributions	10,220
Total Public Support and Revenue	$ 3,716,925

Expenses:

Counseling:

Family & Individual	$ 725,455
Drug Abuse	183,540
Crisis Intervention	59,471
Parents Anonymous	36,137

Education:

Family Life & Professional	79,567

Homemaker Home Health Services:

Regular & Expanded Homemaker	392,530
Homemaker Home Health Aide Project	850,675
Hospice	989,920
Management and General	399,630
Total Expenses	$ 3,716,925

What programs/activities reflect an increase/decrease in expenditure? What trends do you see? How efficiently are resources being used, i.e., administrative/program ratio, etc.?

f. Overall analysis—How do the agency's allocations compare with the goals? Is there congruence or a wide discrepancy? If there is a lack of congruence, what do you think accounts for this (i.e., political, economic factors, etc.)? Is it possible for all the agency goals to be reflected in the budget? Why or why not? If not, what kinds of goals are reflected in the budget?

Case 2-1: The Metro County Mental Health Association

The Metro County Mental Health Association (MHA) is a nonprofit human service agency concerned with the issues of mental health and mental illness. It is a voluntary association composed of a local board of directors, a staff of six, and a network of volunteers. The MHA has listed the following goals in its charter:

1. To enhance community acceptance, through public awareness efforts, of persons who are, have been, or are at risk of being mentally ill.
2. To promote mental health through educational and public awareness efforts directed at specific target populations.
3. To develop strategies for individual advocacy of persons who have, or are at risk of having, mental illness.
4. To advocate for a continuum of services for mental health care in Metro county.
5. To advocate for the development of public policy supportive of mental health services.
6. To promote mental health through family life education efforts directed at specific target populations.
7. To demonstrate innovative ways in which volunteers can be instrumental in preventing or alleviating mental illness in a target population.

The MHA of Metro County is a United Way agency and receives part of its funding from the Metro County United Way. In addition, the MHA receives revenue from program service fees, contributions, membership dues, special events, sales, and investments (see below).

The budgetary process begins in the summer for the upcoming fiscal year which starts January 1. The budget is prepared by the executive

Funding Sources of Metro MHA		
United Way		$120,143
Other Support/Revenue		
Fees	$33,160	
Dues	5,500	
Sales	700	
Investments	1,500	
Contributions	24,082	
Special Events	3,500	
Subtotal		68,442
Total Support/Revenue		$188,585

committee of the board, in conjunction with the executive director. The process of formulating the budget, along with the goals and objectives for the coming year, is initiated in discussions during this time. The executive director collects several types of data to help in the development of a preliminary budget. These data may include second-quarter evaluations of budget utilization and units of service provided by program, each presented and justified by the respective program director. The program directors assist in planning for the upcoming year's programs. The data gathering will also include the current United Way priorities study. This study is a major tool used in determining funding of services by the United Way, thus by considering this study in the budgetary process, the executive director has a better idea of how the agency's programs will fare with the United Way's allocation committee.

After the director develops the preliminary budget, it is presented to the MHA budget committee for recommendations and review. The preliminary budget then goes to the executive committee which places it on the agenda for the full membership of the board to review. If the board disagrees with some aspect of the budget, adjustments based on negotiations are made. When the budget is approved, the whole budget package is then submitted to the United Way in September.

The budget is presented to the United Way where it is reviewed by the program-planning and budget committee. At this point the agency must defend and justify its proposed budget and requests. If the committee approves the allocation requests, the complete and balanced budget is reviewed again and given final approval by the MHA board. In most cases, budgets are increased or decreased by the United Way budget committee. This then means that agencies have to modify their proposed budget and restructure their program plans, so the budget will be balanced. This revised budget must be approved by the United Way and the agency board. Final allocations are awarded by the United Way in December.

The MHA's resources are mainly divided among its four program services: family life, services to target population, health education, and volunteer services (See below).

Resource Allocation of MHA

Program Services		
Family Life	$29,013	
Services to target population	37,431	
Health education	51,987	
Volunteer services	40,605	
Total program services		$159,036
Support Services		29,549
Total Program and Support		$188,585

Questions:

1. What percentage of the MHA's funds come from the United Way?
2. Do you think the mix between United Way funding and other sources of revenue/support is a good one for the agency? Why or why not?
3. What other data could the executive director use in preparing the budget for the next fiscal year?
4. What types of budget formats does this agency use? What are advantages and disadvantages of each type?
5. What is the ratio of program costs to support costs?
   a. Is this a good ratio?
   b. Why or why not?
6. Do the allocation of resources in this agency reflect stated agency goals?
   a. Explain your answer using concrete examples.

b. What would some output measures of goal attainment be?
7. How could this budget be re-written in a functional format? Please illustrate by combining figures from Table 1 and Table 2.
8. What else do the figures here tell you about this agency?

Reading 2-1: "Budget Systems: Make the Right Choice" by Jae C. Park*

The literature on budgeting tends to be highly techniques-oriented. It is as if a first-rate budgeting system would somehow emerge and be used effectively, only if such and such techniques are used. But the reality is not that simple; at times the [agency] environment and organizational dynamics may completely overshadow a technically brilliant budget system. It can be said that there is no universally "good" or "perfect" budget . . . system that fits all [organizations]; there are really only alternative approaches to choose from, within a range of reasonably sound alternatives.

. . . A widespread cause of difficulty in establishing an effective budget system is the lack of a commonly accepted definition of budgets . . . In the past, budgeting was commonly perceived as being quite close to pure expense budgeting, very much detailed in the accounting sense. But increasingly, budgets are perceived as being integral with tactical plans. Budgets in the past may have been used to ask how much money would be spent next year for various expense categories, and how much the total would come to. They are now increasingly used to ask why such spendings are necessary, whether such spendings are in accord with the way the [agency] plans to allocate its resources. Budgets, in this context, are detailed, numeric counterparts of tactical plans and extend into manpower, production, productivity, inventory, product marketing, etc.

. . . Consequently, there is a range of choices in how far a company can merge budgets with plans. Much confusion can arise in the budget process, unless the participants agree what a budget is and how far it is to extend into various financial and nonfinancial functions. Clear-cut functional demarcations must be established as clearly as possible among the planning, budgeting, accounting, data processing, and operating areas as to what role each is to play.

Once budgets are viewed in the broader context, it is clear that they must be an integral part of a fully integrated planning system, if they are to be successfully used. Although the need for this integration appears

---

*Excerpted with permission from: Financial Executive, LII(3),26–35, 1984.

easy to understand, it is surprising how often budgets do not conform with plans. This may be due to the fact that the planning function typically falls under a planning department and/or operating department, while a budgeting system may fall under a financial staff. If there are organizational frictions or the coordinating phase is not handled well, serious divergences can emerge.

For an effective implementation of a budget system, the participants in the system must clearly understand the following:

- What budget outputs are required of them, and the formats to be used.
- Who are to receive their outputs.
- What inputs are necessary to produce their budget outputs; who are to supply such inputs.
- What methods are to be used to generate budget outputs.
- Specific timing of each of the information generation and pass-through.

In addition, it is necessary that the participants get an overview of the entire planning/budgeting cycle so that they thoroughly understand how their own particular "piece of the action" fits in within the overall framework.

Senior management must also communicate downward essential plan/budget directives, and this does not always happen effectively. Conversely, there is a need to integrate plans with budgets through a reverse feedback process. In some [organizations], top management may become removed from lower-level managements, and may end up issuing unrealistic, unsound directives. Lower-level managements may not understand what top management wants, become cynical, and engage in game playing in the face of what they consider to be unrealistic or plainly bad senior management directives. Higher-level directives, plans, and budgets must be evaluated and modified, if necessary, through a reiterative feedback process from lower-level inputs.

Smooth coordination and integration of various budget system phases can be achieved through the following measures:

- Institutionalize the coordination process with a formal sign-off procedure;
- integrate the management of planning and budgeting systems under one management responsibility center;

- manage coordination phases of planning and budgeting systems through committees;
- clearly identify and require proper top-to-bottom budget instructions, and bottom-to-top feedback, in order to ensure that necessary modifications do not fall through the cracks.

These steps are not all mutually exclusive, and can be incorporated simultaneously in the planning/budgeting systems.

A well thought-out budget system manual can also help alleviate some of the organizational bottlenecks. A strategic and tactical planning manual may justifiably be largely idea-oriented and descriptive; however, a budget manual should not leave so much leeway; forms-oriented uniformity and more numbers are necessary and inevitable. Typically, data and information that will go through a successive consolidation process need uniformity the most.

. . . Even after all these steps are taken, there can be more insidious problems that can undermine the effective functioning of a budget system. Some examples are incompetence or inexperience, fear of unknowns, refusal to follow instructions, and [organizational] politics. [Organizational] politics may lead at times to deliberate sabotage of the planning/budgeting process. There are no easy solutions to such barriers to effective planning and budgeting, and their solutions probably will take much time and effort. Such dedication to make the budget system work is a prerequisite; the emergence of an effective budget system in any [agency] is an evolutionary and educational process requiring much dedication and patience. Those who are responsible for the management of the budget system must play the role of a catalyst and an educator, without overly appearing to do so. They should also understand that a plan/budget system is probably never a finished product, and should be improved to fit the particular [agency] circumstances year by year.

PROGRAM-PLANNING AND BUDGETING

After reading this chapter you should be able to:

1. Follow the steps to compiling an agency budget;
2. Forecast expenses and revenues;
3. Present a proposed budget to a board or funding source.

INTRODUCTION

This text will use a modified version of PPBS developed by the United Way of America and called the Program-Planning and Budgeting Cycle. Program-Planning and Budgeting (PPB) is a sort of mini-PPBS that follows many of the same steps, yet is geared to the unique characteristics of the human service agency's budgeting process. In this model, adapted from the United Way, the place of budgeting may clearly be seen (see Figure 3-1). That is, it is an integral part of the planning process, in which programs are tied to agency goals and objectives, and revenues and expenses are tied to specific programs. The Program-Planning and Budgeting Cycle has the following components (United Way, 1975:16):

PLANNING

The first part of the PPB process entails the resolution of a number of issues for the agency that revolve around organizational structure and assessment. In this phase, the agency must make sure that it has a structure in place and the necessary data to enable it to carry out its planning and budgeting functions. This involves designing or using a planned budgeting structure, an analysis of organizational capability, and defining mission, goals, and objectives.

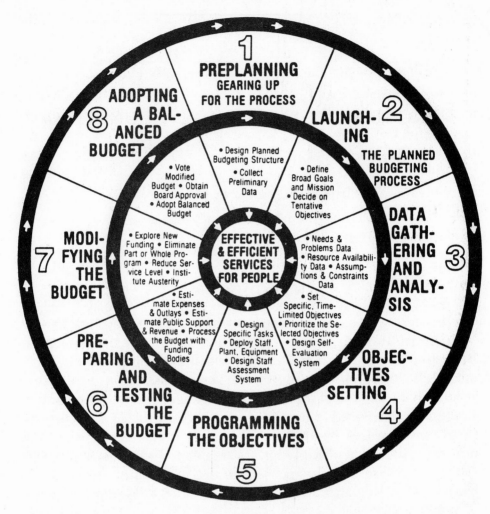

The diagram shows the Program-Planning and Budgeting Cycle:

1. **PREPLANNING** — GEARING UP FOR THE PROCESS
   - Design Planned Budgeting Structure
   - Collect Preliminary Data

2. **LAUNCHING** — THE PLANNED BUDGETING PROCESS
   - Define Broad Goals and Mission
   - Decide on Tentative Objectives

3. **DATA GATHERING AND ANALYSIS**
   - Needs & Problems Data
   - Resource Availability Data
   - Assumptions & Constraints Data

4. **OBJECTIVES SETTING**
   - Set Specific, Time-Limited Objectives
   - Prioritize the Selected Objectives
   - Design Self-Evaluation System

5. **PROGRAMMING THE OBJECTIVES**
   - Design Specific Tasks
   - Deploy Staff, Plant, Equipment
   - Design Staff Assessment System

6. **PREPARING AND TESTING THE BUDGET**
   - Estimate Expenses & Outlays
   - Estimate Public Support & Revenue
   - Process the Budget with Funding Bodies

7. **MODIFYING THE BUDGET**
   - Explore New Funding
   - Eliminate Part or Whole Program
   - Reduce Service Level
   - Institute Austerity

8. **ADOPTING A BALANCED BUDGET**
   - Vote Modified Budget
   - Obtain Board Approval
   - Adopt Balanced Budget

Center: **EFFECTIVE & EFFICIENT SERVICES FOR PEOPLE**

Reprinted with permission from United Way of America, Inc.

Figure 3-1: Program-Planning and Budgeting Cycle

Designing Planned Budgeting Structure

Designing a budgeting structure is really part of designing a total financial management information system. This involves having an organizational structure with clear lines of authority and responsibility, yet that is flexible enough to allow participatory planning, decision-making, and evaluation. At this early stage some crucial decisions have to be made about who will be responsible for budgeting. There are two main approaches to budgeting: the top-down approach and the bottom-up approach.

The Top-Down Approach

In the top-down approach, the development of the budget is done by the administrative staff and the agency board. The budget is then presented to the rest of the human service staff as the plan for next year. In this approach, lower-level staff have no input into the budgeting process. One problem that may arise with this type of approach is that staff who have no input may feel less investment in working toward attaining the goals reflected in the budget.

The Bottom-Up Approach

In the bottom-up approach, there is participation by all levels of staff in the budgeting process. In this approach, the process usually begins with the issuance of general budget guidelines that have been formulated by top management, a budget committee or the funding source. The budget committee may consist of board members, administration, and directors of various programs or units. The guidelines may include agency goals, available resources, projected needs, and similar information. Once the information is received, the individuals who are responsible for achieving the desired goals formulate appropriate budgets for their programs or units. Individual budgets are then grouped together and sent up to top management and the budget committee. Negotiations take place, revisions are made, and the total budget package is eventually completed. As can be seen in the bottom-up approach, ultimate direction is still from the top, but there are some advantages to this more participatory method. For example, in the bottom-up approach, since the budget is constructed by employees who are intimately familiar with the workings in their departments, the budget figures that are derived will probably be more realistic and accurate. Also, if employees have an opportunity to present their views in an atmosphere in which their views are sincerely respected, this can enhance employee morale and job satisfaction.

Organizational Analysis

At this beginning stage of the process, the agency must collect some preliminary data for planning purposes. Types of data the agency board and staff are interested in here do not have to do with clients, but with the agency itself. The agency needs to step back figuratively and ask, Where are we and where do we want to be going? What kind of image do we want our agency to have? What kinds of needs can the agency fill? It also involves gathering of data regarding available agency resources and current beneficiaries of agency programs. It also may involve some analysis as to the situation of the agency vis-a-vis other significant forces in its environment.

Once the structure is in place and preliminary organizational analysis is completed, the agency can now move to the actual planning phase of the process.

Defining Broad Goals and Mission

As stated previously, defining mission and goals is what every new agency must do. After a period of time, many agencies tend to take these goal statements as enduring givens and begin to view them unquestioningly. However, agency administrators should never take for granted that there is an implicit consensus among staff regarding agency goals. Even in the same organization, there may be a wide divergence of opinion regarding the perceived and the preferred goals of an agency by staff and board members. Even if there is consensus to some extent, the actual operationalized goals may be very different than the stated goals. This is the phenomenon known as goal displacement, in which the agency moves into tangential areas in its push for homeostasis and a steady state. Therefore, a periodic (every 3 to 5 years or so) reassessment is necessary (see Table 3-1).

How then does the agency define or re-evaluate its broad goals and mission? A good place to start is in a board/staff brainstorming session in which everyone throws out their ideas for discussion and review. The basic ground rule for a productive brainstormer is that there will be no censoring or negative/positive value attached to any statement made by anyone. Censoring obviously inhibits creative thinking. After all the ideas are looked at and discussed, they need to then be looked at for feasibility and matched with the needs data previously gathered. The agency must ask itself: What is the need? What other group or organization is trying to deal with this problem? Have new problems arisen that our agency has the capability to work on? Are these new goals congruent with our original mission? After a consensus has been reached among

Table 3-1

TIME LINE FOR BUDGETING PROCESS

	Frequency of Activity
Planning	3 - 5 years
Programming	1 - 3 years
Budgeting:	
Budget development	Yearly
Budget control	Monthly/Quarterly

board and staff, it must be voted on by the board for approval. This is the most democratic, participatory approach to goal-setting in that the board has legal responsibility for the agency, but staff must feel that they have input into the goals set for the agency. The top-down method is one in which the board of directors make these decisions and pass them along to the staff for implementation. The bottom-up approach would be one in which the staff drew up a list of tentative goals and presented them to the board for approval. Actually, the board of the agency needs staff input, at least in terms of data, in order to make informed judgements regarding the direction of the agency.

Developing Tentative Objectives

Whereas goals are broad statements of desired future states, objectives are specific, measurable statements that describe means to reach the goals.

Example: "The mission of this agency is to enhance the quality of life for minority youth and their families."

Goal 1.: To encourage minority youth to finish school.

Objectives:

1. To provide 5 remedial counselors and tutors for minority youths having trouble in classes this year.
2. To provide 3 bi-lingual counselors to act as role models and give guidance to high school minority youth.

3. To train 10 peer counselors to help these youth with school and personal problems.

Goal 2.:   To facilitate the entry of minority youth into the world of work.

Objectives:

1. To develop one-day workshops for minority youths on job searching skills.
2. To develop a network of employers who will serve as mentors to minority youth entering the business world.

Tentative objectives are formulated at this time because they need to be tested against the data gathering that the agency will do in the next step of the process, and perhaps revised based on the information obtained.

Gathering and Analyzing Data

At this stage, staff will be involved in the gathering and analysis of data that directly relate to the agency's programs. There are three types of data that the agency will need in order to make decisions regarding the direction that the agency is to take:

1. **Needs and problems data** — These data are important in helping the agency determine if the stated problem is really as severe as perceived by some people in the community. Gathering these data essentially involves a needs assessment as to the extent, level, and severity of a particular problem. Data to be gathered are usually available from a variety of sources, the agency does not necessarily have to go out and do a major survey. The local United Way may have its own community needs assessment study available. Other human service agencies may have completed a recent study. There may be a local college or university that has researchers interested in the problem at hand. There are a myriad of governmental data available through government offices, or college and public libraries.

2. **Resource availability data** — The purpose of gathering these type of data is to give the agency an idea of the resources available to help in its attempt to alleviate the problem. The agency is interested in what groups, organizations, or individuals would be available for material or other types of support. In the preliminary evaluation of possible funding sources, the agency must also consider the positive and negative consequences of accepting resources from a particular organization.

3. **Assumptions and constraints data** — Assumptions are beliefs that are used as the bases for problem formulation and program planning. They are not based on empirical evidence, but are usually the result of experience and informed hunches combined with the empirical data that the agency has collected. In this case, the assumptions are related to social, political, and economic activities or events that may affect the agency and its plans. For example, in targeting high school dropouts as a focus of intervention the agency will have looked at trend data and other information. Based on its findings, the agency may assume that the trend will continue. In another case, with a conservative administration in Washington, an agency may assume that trends in cutting of social programs will continue.

Constraints are external environmental conditions that may inhibit the agency in the accomplishment of its goals. Constraints may also be of a social, political, or economic nature. For example, social values regarding the targeted problem may so greatly interfere with the planned program as to make it almost impossible to carry out. This usually applies to social problems that are highly controversial and where there are wide divergence of views, for example, abortion, or sex education. If the targeted problem becomes highly politicized, there may be a dearth of available resources for the agency. This is not to say that a human service agency should avoid controversial social problems, but rather that it should be quite clear as to the constraints that may impact on its attempts to deal with certain problems.

Setting Objectives

Once the agency has determined its goals, ascertained needs, and available resources, it now should turn to its tentative objectives and reexamine them in the light of the new information obtained. Objectives should be examined for feasibility, that is, can the agency address this problem given the resources available to it? Can it gather enough community support to enable it to pursue its tentative objective(s)? Given that different members of the planning/budgeting team may prefer different approaches to the problem, some consensus may be reached by a prioritizing of the most feasible objectives.

It was stated previously that objectives should be specific and measurable. After the final objectives have been agreed upon, objectives should then also be placed within some time frame. Time frames should be realistic and broken down into units of time such as three to six month segments for purposes of evaluation and feedback. An agency cannot do everything, therefore it must be able to prioritize its objectives so that the most important will be given top priority.

An important ingredient in the setting of objectives is that there be some sort of built-in monitoring or feedback mechanism to enable the agency to evaluate the efficiency and effectiveness of its efforts. There are a variety of evaluation methods, using financial data is one way that will be discussed later in this book.

PROGRAMMING

In the programming phase of the planning/budgeting process, specific tasks, and human and material resources are allocated to programs associated with the objectives. Thus specific tasks need to be defined; specific staff, equipment, and physical plant need to be assigned to the tasks; and an evaluation system needs to be designed.

Designing specific tasks essentially breaks objectives down into units of work. For example, an objective such as "To provide temporary shelter and food to homeless persons" involves a multitude of tasks. Some such pertinent tasks would be selecting a site, checking city zoning laws, obtaining necessary city licenses, finding equipment, etc. After listing all the tasks that need to be undertaken with a specific objective, staff, physical plant, equipment, and measurable outcomes should be listed. For example, the agency could devise a form similar to the one in Table 3-2 for planning purposes:

This form lists the necessary tasks to be performed to meet this objective, the staff required for the completion of the task, equipment needed, any physical plant requirements (e.g., install a kitchen, or building with a kitchen, etc.) and the anticipated cost of the equipment, plant, and staff. The last stage of the programming process involves some sort of evaluation system for staff and their performance of their duties.

Now that the agency has defined its goals and objectives, ascertained community needs, and programmed objectives into meaningful, measurable programs and tasks, it is ready to prepare its budget.

Table 3-2

PROGRAM PLANNING CHART

Objective:(List as a complete sentence)_____

_____

Tasks	Staff Required	$	Cost Equipment	$	Cost Plant	$	Tot. Est. Cost

_____

_____

_____

BUDGETING

There are essentially two types of budgets: the master budget and the capital budget. The master budget covers the agency's planned operations for a one-year period or more. Since the master budget includes plans for operations, it is also known as the operating budget. The master budget is made up of a number of other budgets including:

- a service volume/activity budget
- a public support and revenue budget
- an expense budget
- a salary and wages expense budget
- a cash flow budget
- budgeted financial statements.

The capital budget, on the other hand, is a plan for the future acquisition of major capital assets such as land, buildings, and large equipment. In the sections that follow, the focus will be on the operating or master budget.

Preparing the master budget involves a number of steps that basically entail the preparation of the separate budgets mentioned above. The steps to preparing the budget include (NIMH, 1983:72–78): 1) forecasting service volume; 2) developing expense budgets; 3) estimating public support and revenue; 4) modifying and adopting a balanced budget; 5) estimating cash flow; 6) preparing budgeted financial statements.

Forecasting Service Volume

The first step in preparing the master budget involves a forecast of service volume by each type of service; for example, how many clients are estimated to be seen in the agency's counseling program? In developing the forecast of service units to be provided, a number of factors have to be taken into account such as past levels of service, trends in service levels, demographic trends, public policies that mandate types or content of service, seasonal patterns of service usage, and public attitudes. From this information we can try to extrapolate the coming year's volume, for example, if we can see a trend of 10% increases in service units provided in the last three to five years, we can assume a continuation of this trend. But it should be remembered that forecasts are just that—our best professional estimates of what will happen, for we have no way of knowing for sure. In trying to forecast service volume for a new service that has not been provided as yet, the agency must set a goal of service volume based on what its resources are and the likelihood that the number of service units targeted are feasible for the agency.

Developing Expense Budgets

After service volume has been forecast, the agency must next estimate the cost of providing each service by developing the expense budget and the salary budget.

The Expense Budget

The expense budget shows how money will be allocated in the agency by focusing on operating, administrative, and other costs. In budgeting, the expenses and costs to be incurred must be identified and analyzed as to how the costs will vary according to an anticipated level of service. Basically there are three main categories of expense that need to be looked at in preparing the expense budget:

Variable expenses: Variable expenses are those costs in an agency that vary in direct relation to the volume of services. That is, the more services that are provided or the more clients that are seen the more this expense will rise. For example, the cost of gasoline used in an agency van, or by caseworkers for home visits varies in direct relation to the number of miles driven to provide agency services.

Fixed expenses: Fixed expenses, on the other hand, remain constant no matter how much volume of service you provide. For example, rental on the agency building, typewriter, and other equipment will be the same whether the agency sees 20 clients or 200 clients.

Semivariable or mixed expenses: Semivariable or mixed expenses are those that have both a fixed and variable component. For example, there is a basic (fixed) monthly service charge for utility services such as telephone, gas, and electric. If more than a certain amount is used, additional (variable) charges are assessed to the consumer.

Once these components of expense are identified in relation to a specific item, it becomes relatively simple to allocate amounts to the budget. There are a number of different ways of devising the expense budget based on the individual situation of the agency. Some of these methods are (Moak and Killian, 1963: 128–156; United Way, 1975):

Fixed ceiling budgeting: This means that a stated dollar amount is established prior to the preparation of the budget. The only flexibility the department or program may have is to decide on how most efficiently to use the fixed amount allotted to it. For example, a department may be told that it has $5,000 for supplies and equipment to be spent any way deemed necessary.

Work measurement and unit costing: This method attempts to define units of work and to assign unit costs to these units of work so that the estimated cost can be expressed as: one unit of service = x amount of dollars. This approach focuses on the different types of costs encountered by the agency in the delivery of its services. Unit costing will be more fully discussed in Chapter Six.

Historical analysis: This method uses past expenditures as the basis of estimating future costs. It takes into account such factors as inflation and pricing changes, and estimates a new figure. While historical analysis should be a part of any type of projection, it is probably used most often in incremental budgeting.

Item by item control: This is a review of each expense item with an evaluation as to its necessity in the budget, a sort of ZBB approach. The problem with this approach is that some objective criteria is needed with which to judge necessity and that must be decided by the budget team.

Alternative proposals: In these methods, department heads are required to prepare alternative budgets that are with high, low, and some medium range amounts. For example, the program may estimate expenses based on 110% of last years costs, 90% of last year's costs, and 100% of last year's costs. Another way to approach estimating is based on projected revenue, that is, if revenue is expected to be 115% of last year, then expenses are projected to be based on the same amount. Or if you use service volume, 110% of service volume of last year will equal a 10% increase in expenses.

The Salary Expense Budget

To estimate salary expense, one must be able to determine personnel needs. Therefore, estimating salary expense is based on projected service volume as well as a number of other factors such as: staffing patterns, workload trends, and a review of the use of overtime, prime time, and compensatory time off within a department or unit (Moak and Killian: 132). It is helpful to use a guide such as that in Table 3-2 in planning personnel needs and costs. Prevailing salaries for professional and clerical staff in an area should be surveyed. Benefit packages and inflation rates should be added into the final salary figures. Allocating salary expense when staff have duties in more than one program will be discussed in Chapter 6.

Estimating Public Support and Revenue

Revenue is income earned from the provision of goods and/or services. A revenue budget is "a summary statement of revenue plans for a given period expressed in quantitative terms" (Gaertner, 1982:28). Public support is that income received by the agency in the form of grants and contracts from governmental sources, and contributions from the general public. In for-profit organizations, the revenue budget is usually prepared first. In many nonprofit human service agencies, the revenue budget may be the beginning point on which other budget components may depend. However, as Powell (1980: 22) has stated, there is a critical difference in the budgeting of the two types of organizations. That is, in for-profit enterprises, it is important to develop the revenue budget first in order to be able to allocate revenues. In nonprofit organizations, the level of service should be determined first, then determining the expenditures associated with a given level of service and, finally, policy decisions have to be made as to the financing of these services. Targeting service level and costs associated with the providing of service helps the agency calculate its need for public support through allocations and contributions as well as set revenue levels.

While the revenue for some organizations is almost totally dependent on one major source such as United Way, in this era of scarce resources most agencies have begun to aggressively seek other funding sources. Therefore, it becomes necessary for agencies to try to anticipate this revenue. The revenue budget is usually prepared annually, though it may be broken down into quarterly or monthly periods for comparison.

In budgeting for revenues, timing of revenue inflows is an important factor to consider. There may be three types of revenue inflow patterns in any one agency: regular, seasonal, and random (Gaertner, 1982:30). The regular pattern of obtaining revenue is usually from the on-going activities of an agency such as counseling, crisis intervention, and so forth. By examining trends of fees-for-services the agency may feel comfortable in projecting future trends. Seasonal patterns of revenue usually come from seasonal activities such as an annual campaign or other annual fundraising events. Random revenue may come occasionally without any pattern—for example, unsolicited donations, special bequests, and grants.

The basis of the revenue budget is usually past revenues earned. The human service agency administrator and appropriate staff may review past trends and take into account current environmental conditions (changes in demography of client population, changes in public policies, funding policies, economic conditions, and so forth) to formulate a revenue projection.

Some information that the agency needs to gather in order to estimate revenues includes the following:

- the number of clients currently being served, average number of visits per client, and average user fees paid;
- statistics for the past 3–5 years on revenues from client services;
- plans for change in the number of clients served;
- any planned increase in user fees and the date on which the change will take place;
- an estimate of potential users of service not now being served;
- past revenues from any auxillary services, for example, gift shop, etc.;
- plans for changes in any auxillary services.

Information needed for estimating public support includes such items as:

- statistics of income from public support broken down by source and showing changes and trends by percentages;
- current budget requests to all sources;
- an estimate of priority of agency services by funding sources;
- statistics regarding trends in contributions broken down by year and shown as a percentage of fundraising costs;
- any grant proposals or fundraising projects currently in the works with projected dollar outcomes.

There are other, more sophisticated techniques available for human service agencies today that use already developed computer programs and spreadsheets for projecting trends. The acquisition of such programs will be discussed more fully in Chapter 11.

Estimating Cash Flow

The agency must estimate its cash flow using a cash budget. The cash budget "summarizes planned cash receipts and disbursements" based on budgeted support, revenues, and expenses (Anthony and Herzlinger, 1980:326). The cash budget is influenced to a large extent on the seasonality of operations, that is month-to-month variations in service levels or inflows of revenue. The cash flow equation is simply:

$$CB_b + CR - CD = CB_e$$

Beginning cash balance + cash receipts − cash disbursements = ending cash balance.

Basically, a cash budget has the following components:

1. The beginning cash balance, which would have been carried over from the previous fiscal period;
2. Cash received during the month, which is added to this initial balance;
3. Cash payments made by the agency during the month, which are subtracted from total cash on hand;

These calculations result in an ending cash balance for the month (a simplified cash flow budget can be seen in Table 3-3).

Table 3-3

CASH FLOW BUDGET

For Three Months Ended June 30, 19X1

	April	May	June
Cash balance, beginning	$10,000	$10,700	$11,700
Cash receipts:			
Client Fees	3,000	2,800	2,500
Donations	5,000	5,500	5,300
Total Cash Receipts	8,000	8,300	7,800
	-----	-----	-----
Cash disbursements:			
Operating Expenses (less salaries)	3,200	3,200	3,200
Salaries	4,100	4,100	4,100
Total disbursements	7,300	7,300	7,300
	------	------	-------
Cash balance, ending	$10,700	$11,700	$12,000

Preparing Budgeted Financial Statements

Preparing the budgeted or pro forma financial statements of the agency is usually the last step in the budgeting process. The preparation of financial statements will be discussed in Chapter Ten. These then, are the basic steps in budget preparation. It must be emphasized that budgeting is not just a process in which numbers are fit into a document to be submitted to a board or funding source. Budgeting is a process that involves long-term as well as short-term planning, fitting programs to agency goals and objectives, and choosing the best alternatives so that quality services can be delivered most efficiently and effectively.

Modifying and Adopting a Balanced Budget

The approach that the agency takes to the balancing of its budget depends on the agency's overall planning approach and long-term goals. For example, if an agency administrator and board believe that the agency should take a proactive approach to planning and budgeting, they will aggressively seek alternative funding for programs that they think are important in meeting community needs. On the other hand, if an agency takes a reactive approach, the budget committee will cut expenses to match revenues and feel fortunate in having balanced the budget. A moderate approach would take a proactive stance with new, developing programs and a reactive one with declining ones (Ramanthan, 1982:485).

In any case, any shortfalls in support and revenue entail the revision of the original proposed budget. After the budget is modified by the budget committee, it may be submitted to the board for approval and adopted as the balanced agency budget. But, the budget may need to be revised or modified again after it is submitted to the agency's major funding source at allocation time.

Chapter Three
Questions and Topics for Discussion

1. What components make up the master budget?
2. What are the basic steps in budget preparation?
3. Give some examples of variable costs, fixed costs, and mixed costs.
4. What are some approaches to estimating cost?
5. What are some approaches to estimating revenue?
6. What is a cash flow budget and how is it prepared?

Exercise 3-1: The Kimball County Substance Abuse Center, Inc.

This exercise has been developed to illustrate the basic steps in the preparation of the master budget. It is assumed that the agency has already gone through the necessary prior steps in the budgeting process, i.e., planning, and programming, and is at the point where it is ready to translate its goals and objectives into a budget.

Although the process of developing the master budget may seem technical and mechanical, it does reflect key decisions on types and levels of services, billing rates, staffing assignments, and planned expense levels. Most of the decisions relating to programmatic questions and issues should have been addressed and resolved in the programming phase of the budgeting process.

As you know, the development of the master budget involves the preparation of a number of other budgets including:

—a service volume/activity budget
  a public support/revenue budget
—an expense budget
—a salary and wages expense budget
—a cash flow budget
—budgeted financial statements

In the following exercise, the amount of service volume has been estimated and given. Many of your calculations will be based on this initial estimate. Please complete each step of the budget process as indicated. For this exercise you will not have to complete budgeted financial statements, but you will complete all the other budgets mentioned above.

Step 1. Shown below in Table 3-4 is a quarterly forecast of service volume for this agency. You will note that projections for months outside the quarterly period have also been provided in order to properly project such things as cash flows or purchase requirements. October projections are needed, for example, to determine September purchases.

Table 3-4

SERVICE VOLUME/ACTIVITY BUDGET

1st Quarter

Month:		June	July	Aug	Sept	Quarter Total	Oct
Units:							
Service A	Visits	240	230	220	240	690	242
B	Days	300	290	270	280	840	301

Step 2. Forecast of revenues and support: In most cases, human service agencies should try to project their expenses before their revenues. However, this is not always possible. In this case, the agency is a substance abuse center whose main sources of funding are client fees and county support. It is not allowed to do outside fundraising, and therefore it uses service volume as the basis for its calculations for revenue and support as well as inventory. Please complete the budget in Table 3-5.

Table 3-5

PUBLIC SUPPORT AND REVENUE BUDGET

1st Quarter

	Rate per Unit	June	July	Aug	Sept	Quarter Total	Oct
Services							
On account							
Service A (90%)	$30						
Service B (80%)	40						
Cash							
Service A (10%)	30						
Service B (20%)	40						
Subtotal							
(Service revenue)							
Staffing Grant*		0	4,000	0	0	4,000	0
County Support*		0	0	1,000	6,000	7,000	0
TOTAL							

*Received quarterly

Step 3. Forecast of cash collections: Translate all sources of revenue into monthly cash collections by combining the sources of revenue from the revenue budget. Collections often lag behind the rendering of services, particularly third-party payments. The extent of the lag can be determined by looking at past experience. For this agency, collections run 80 percent of the past month's billings. The remaining 20 percent represents discounts for clients unable to pay and bad debt expense. Please complete the cash collection budget in Table 3-6.

Table 3-6

FORECAST OF CASH COLLECTIONS

1st Quarter

	July	August	September	Quarter Total
Services				
Cash				
Collections*				
Staffing Grant				
County Support				
	-------	-------	-------	-------
TOTAL				
	═══════	═══════	═══════	═══════

----

*80% of prior month's services on account; remaining 20% client discounts and bad debt expense.

Step 4. Prepare expense budget (less salaries). Expenses for the agency will be estimated based on analysis of past records combined with projected patterns of service delivery. These should provide information on expected usage and desired inventory levels. Please complete Table 3-7 below.

Step 5. Estimate salary expense:

Salaries are currently $8750 per month for full and part-time staff. Part-time consultants will be paid $250 in August and $100 in September. Transfer this information to the appropriate place in the cash flow budget (Table 3-8).

Step 6. Prepare cash flow budget:

The budgeted statement of cash receipts and disbursements (cash flow budget) shows the amount of cash available at the beginning of the

Table 3-7

EXPENSE BUDGET

1st Quarter

	July	August	September	Total
Services				
Day care				
contract(1)				
Supplies				
Medication(2)				
Other(3)				
Occupancy(4)				
Telephone(5)				
	-------	-------	---------	---------
Total Expenses				
	=======	=======	=========	=========

----

(1)Contract for purchase of day care @ $30 per day for up to 300 patient-days per month.

(2)Medication currently costs $3.20 per patient day

(3)Supplies inventory is 7.5% of current month's service revenue.

(4)Occupancy includes rent and related items such as utilities, it currently runs $1000 per month.

(5)Telephone expense costs a base rate of $100 for a business phone and extension lines plus 5% of service volume (includes visits and days) per month.

quarter, how the cash position would be affected by the budgeted operations during the quarter, and the cash balance to be available at the end of the period. Please complete Table 3-8 and indicate the source of your information.

Table 3-8

CASH FLOW BUDGET

Budgeted statement of cash receipts and disbursements

for quarter ending September 19xx

Source	July	August	September
Cash balance:beginning*	$15,000		
Cash receipts:			
Total per schedule			
	------	------	------
(W) Total			
Cash disbursements:			
Services and supplies			
Salaries and consultation			
Occupancy			
Telephone			
	------	------	------
(X) Total disbursements			
(Y) Cash balance:ending			
(Y= W - X)			

*Given

Case 3-1: The Family Life Center, Inc.*

The Family Life Center, Inc., is a small voluntary nonprofit human service agency for abusive parents and their children. It has been in operation for nine months and its new fiscal year starts July 1st. It was originally funded the first year with a $45,000 grant from the Federal Government. The program currently has one full-time social worker, one part-time case aide, and one part-time secretary. It has two programs:

1. A counseling program in which it provides counseling services to individuals and families.

---

*Based on a case developed with Carann S. Feazell

2. A family life education program in which volunteer speakers (there is a list of 12) go out to schools, churches, civic groups, and talk on issues related to the family, mental health, parenting, child development, child abuse, and family violence.

In the first nine months of operation, the agency saw:

Counseling Program: 210 clients (family members are counted individually).

Family Life Education Program: 910 individuals in various settings.

The agency is currently housed in a 2-room office in a city building which houses other social agencies. Referrals come from the courts, Department of Social Services, ministers, teachers, doctors, police, and self-referrals. It would like to add another program, a support/follow-up program for children who have been sexually abused. It anticipates the majority of these referrals to come from the State Department of Social Services and the courts, although other sources of referral may be rape crisis centers and shelters for abused women. It would also like to expand its funding base, so it has decided to apply for a United Way allocation as well as to seek alternative funding sources.

This agency is located in a large middle-class suburb which had, until quite recently, been little more than a bedroom community. Consequently, it lacks many social services of its own. Those services which are available are branch offices of county services or small satellite offices of voluntary nonprofit agencies. Even though the city has the highest median family income in the county, there are pockets of real poverty among single-parent families, a small number of minorities, and elderly. In addition, there are soaring rates of crime and child abuse. But since the city has so many upper-middle income professionals, the agency sees real potential for developing a broad funding base.

In searching for alternative funding, the agency has made certain assumptions such as the following:

1. **Political:** Federally funded social programs will continue to be cut, and the Administration in Washington will continue to push the private sector to take over more of the funding and provision of social services. Therefore, the agency expects to receive continuation of its grant, but at a reduced rate of approximately $35,000.

2. **Economic:** Inflation will fluctuate around the 4–5% level in the coming year; interest rates on consumer loans will be in the 12–30% range; interest on treasury notes will fluctuate at the 7–8% level; chari-

table contributions will continue to be a tax-deductible item in any new tax legislation; unemployment will show a slight rise, but not enough to affect fundraising efforts. Therefore, the agency has set a goal of raising $15,000 from its first year's fundraising activities.

3. **Social:** This agency is located in the sunbelt. As the population continues its shift from the Midwest and Northeast to this area in search of jobs, warmer climates, and different life styles there will be increased need for services. Therefore, the agency projects a 15% increase in revenues from client fees.

Attached is the 12-month budget of the Family Life Center, Inc.:

REVENUES		EXPENSES	
Grant	$45,000	Salaries	$32,500
Program fees	8,640	Employee health	3,900
		Payroll taxes	2,200
Total revenue	$53,640	Supplies	600
		Telephone	2,000
		Postage	840
		Occupancy	1,200
		Printing	800
		Transportation	300
		Equipment	7,500
		Utilities	1,800
		Total expenses	$53,640

Programs are allocated: 75% Counseling, 5% Family Life, 20%

Support; Salaries are allocated as follows:

Social worker	$18,500
P/t case aide	7,000
P/t secretary	7,000

Fringes are 12% of salary expense.

You are to do the following:

1. Divide into small groups. Each group is to complete each part.
   A. List your goals, objectives and assumptions regarding the agency and its programs.
   B. Compile a budget for next year using the United Way format (a functional budget format).

Remember to include the new program in your budget.

C. Make sure that you are able to justify any new requests.

D. Prepare to present your request before the Allocation Committee:
1. Anticipate questions you will be asked;
2. Prepare your responses;
3. Decide on your strategy;
4. Pick a spokesperson to present your budget.

2. Identify and select an alternative funding source, e.g., foundation, city government, etc.

A. List your assumptions about this funding source.

B. List your goals, objectives and assumptions regarding the agency and its programs.

C. Prepare a new budget based on your assumptions.

D. Develop a strategy for presenting your budget before the funding source.

E. Pick a spokesperson to present the budget.

As each group presents their budget, the other group will act as the Allocation Committee. A feedback session will take place after each presentation.

Reading 3-1: Preparing, Presenting and Defending the Budget*

THE LOCAL BUDGET PROCESS IN PERSPECTIVE

Perhaps the most important point about the budget process is that it is a long-term management responsibility, not an isolated task to be completed once a year. Successful preparation of a local budget, resulting in approval of adequate funds to accomplish annual program goals, is a complex undertaking. Several observations are in order:

- Committing program goals to paper and tying them to specific amounts of money during the budget preparation phase are exercises in **economic skill.**
- Physical presentation of the budget before the budget authority is an exercise in **salesmanship.**

*Excerpted from: Basic Skills in Creative Financing, Student Manual. EMI Professional Development Series. Federal Emergency Management Agency, National Emergency Training Center, Emergency Management Institute, Emmitsburg, Maryland, 1983, pp. 211–220.

- Daily administration of your program and the budget that makes it possible is an exercise in **management skill.**

These observations illustrate that "presentation" of a budget is not an action that takes place once a year when you appear before the budget authority. Rather, the presentation is reflected in every action you take in managing the program and in every relationship you establish in the community. There is no magic formula for the successful preparation, presentation, or administration of a budget. Your personal credibility and the credibility of your program—coupled with sound working relationships with others in the community—are the keys to the budget process. And these must be established over time.

The Importance of Credibility

A budget hearing is an exercise in salesmanship. You appear before a group of individuals to "sell" a product—maintenance of a sound [program] the budget authority . . . must determine how to allocate specific sums of money in the face of complex and often contradictory claims.

A beautifully prepared "dog and pony show" with charts, graphs, and visuals may overwhelm the average budget authority and result in an adopted budget. But if you appear before the group the next year and have nothing except another "dog and pony show," chances are you will not only face rejection but also lose credibility, seriously hampering all future activities. Even if the budget authority is not perceptive enough to detect the illusion, other program managers competing for local dollars may be happy to point it out. They may also exercise time-honored methods developed by the bureaucracy to hamper every future move you make.

You must be certain your program is sound and shows annual progress. It must be accepted by others competing for the local budget dollar. . . . Once [your agency's] capabilities have been established, the techniques of budget presentation can be applied productively and effectively. But you should not assume that techniques are the reasons the budget is adopted. Techniques receive the most attention because the act of presentation is both visible and dramatic and results in specific actions others can see and evaluate. A smooth, effective, informative budget presentation tends to overshadow the fact that it is the result of days, weeks, months, even years of steady, competent activity within [your program].

. . . . During various steps in the process, you identified real local problems and needs. You mobilized every community resource in support of [this problem]. You sought and applied to outside sources to meet needs not covered by local resources. In conducting these activities, you also talked to many people in the community and told them about your program goals and objectives.

If you have worked through some of these steps before your budget presentation, you may find that your credibility—and that of your program—is already on the rise. [Effective budgeting] is grounded in sound management techniques and approaches. Actions in the process are visible and effective. Results, and their impact on the local situation, can hardly go unnoticed. So, while creative financing is not the only effort you need to build credibility, it is a management tool you can use to improve your program. As your program improves, so will its credibility—and so will yours. As an effective leader and catalyst with a solid record of success, you are in a better position to deal with your local budget authority.

The Importance of Relationships

As you prepare to present the budget, you must also address your relationships with other agencies competing for local dollars. Through awareness of their budget requests, you should point out elements of your proposal that make their objectives more attainable or that enable reductions in overall expenditures through cooperative use of resources.

Results of efforts to do everything possible with local resources can be used to show how services interrelate. You can also describe and document how reductions in overlaps and gaps in services (due to creative strategies) will reduce expenditures in many areas. If you have obtained funds from outside sources, you can demonstrate how this will cut local costs.

. . . As various community programs and services begin to coordinate, cooperation is encouraged. Cooperation, rather than competition, also becomes feasible as roles and functions are clearly defined and overlap and waste reduced.

With this perspective on the local budget process, you can see the significant role overall management activities and successes play in gaining the community dollars you request. . . .

PREPARING THE BUDGET

Budget authorities usually deal simultaneously with requests from many programs. Although it may seem perfectly obvious to you that funds you are requesting are necessary and will be well spent in [your program], you must convince budget officials (who have limited funds) that your program is more deserving than others.

Regardless of the form your budget takes or the philosophy it reflects, it must be the result of thorough research and planning. If you are not thorough in your preparation, it will be evident during your presentation and defense.

One way you can demonstrate the thoroughness with which you have prepared your budget is to include a set of clear, concise statements relating to each specific budget line item. This information might include:

- Resources available to offset the cost of the activity (expense minus outside resources equals requested appropriation);
- The relationship of this expenditure to accomplishment of long-range goals of the program;
- The relative priority of this activity in terms of the overall budget;
- Procedures developed to ensure accurate monitoring of the activity, which demonstrates that the most efficient, economical means of accomplishing the program objectives have been selected;
- Support for overall goals of the community (for example, requested communications equipment can be used by other agencies; economies realized through resource management make funds available for other departments); and
- The impact on program objectives if line item allocations are modified (either increased or decreased).

In researching and documenting your funding needs, the following information can be helpful. Some documents may serve as supporting appendices to your budget.

- Estimates for specific expenditures from reputable sources;
- Resources available by type, origin, and relationship to the program. (resources gained at no cost form a valuable body of information. Their acquisition is testimony to your ability to reduce budget expenditures through maximum use of resources);
- Past budget history of your agency;

- Documents establishing that your program will be receiving support from outside sources;
- Any data prepared by outside sources that show the supportive nature of your operations in relation to other local . . . [public or private agencies].

Next, you will have to select a presentation strategy suitable for your situation and abilities. Completing the following suggested "homework" can help you develop an effective presentation strategy.

- Review all available data on the general budget and on budgets of agencies and programs with which you are interdependent. Identify components of those budgets that will be enhanced by adoption of your budget. Also identify components that make it possible for you to reduce your budget requests, should theirs be adopted.
- Become fully familiar with required local budget forms.
  − Do you have enough of them?
  − Do they clearly show various program elements and activities?
  − Are you certain you are filling them out in accordance with the expectations of the budget authority? (Work closely with the fiscal officer responsible for preparing and reviewing the forms.)
- Determine time frames you must meet in the budget preparation process. Even the best budget faces problems if it comes in late or out of sequence.
- Determine the date, time, and place of your budget hearing. Plan to be there! Be sensitive to such factors as time of day. If you must face the budget authority at the end of a long session, members may be restless and abrupt. Insistence on adhering to a long, detailed presentation may result in an unreasonable (but very human) termination of your presentation and an arbitrary setting of the amount they will approve.
- Review the political and economic climate on the national, state, and local levels. Identify factors that support your program and budget request. Pinpoint factors that may cause criticism of any budget elements and address them, preferably in advance of the budget hearing.
- Identify individuals who advise the budget authority on fiscal matters, especially those dealing with [your type of program].
- Know your audience, both allies and enemies. Review your relation-

ship with members of the budget authority, fiscal office, and other departments and agencies. If you have maintained steady, positive contact with them throughout the year, they should be familiar with your program and conditioned toward acceptance.

- Consider the interests and needs of the budget authorities and how your budget takes those interests and needs into consideration.
- Develop a portfolio of photographs, charts, graphs, and other visuals to illustrate major points.

Finally, in choosing a strategy (or set of strategies), consider the following points:

- What are the advantages and disadvantages inherent in particular strategies?
- What characteristics do individuals on the budget authority possess that would make particular strategies effective or ineffective?
- How would use of particular strategies be viewed by the news media, other officials, and the taxpaying public?

In considering various strategies, bear in mind that they are techniques rather than components of a sound, well-developed, and properly administered program. Techniques have enough validity to be effective under certain circumstances, so be prepared to use any that may improve your presentation. However, their use should be in support of, rather than as a replacement for, day-to-day application of sound management techniques.

Adequate preparation before your presentation is critical to the success of your presentation strategy. If your homework has been thorough, you should be prepared to deal with any issue. Ask yourself the following questions to ensure that you have been as thorough as possible:

- Do I know the history of past budgets—how much was requested and how much granted?
- Am I aware of the total budget picture? What underlying principles will dictate the budget authority's attitudes?
- Do I know the fiscal officer? Have I used the procedures he or she requires for budget document preparation?
- Have I identified all conditions applying to my budget and unique to my program (i.e., federal matching requirements, grants management regulations, personnel pay scales)?

- Have I prepared a brief written statement of support for each line item in my budget?
- Have I included documentation from outside sources attesting to the accuracy of my program assumptions . . . ?
- Am I personally familiar with every item in my budget, and can I personally support each proposed expenditure clearly and effectively?
- Do I have documentation on past budget projections and on program attainments to support those projections?
- Have I identified and included all sources of revenue beyond local dollars?
- Have I clearly identified outside sources of revenue and established their impact on reducing my request to the local budget authority?
- Can I clearly identify and explain portions of my budget over which I have limited control (i.e., mandated services, ongoing commitments, recurring expenses)?
- Can I relate possible cutbacks to specific effects on individual program elements?
- Am I aware of conditions facing the budget authority in relation to my budget (i.e., taxpayer attitudes toward my program, degree of acceptance by other [agencies], misconceptions on the part of individuals serving on the budget authority)?
- Am I familiar with all other program budgets and at least aware of their relationship to the total budget being considered by the budget authority?
- Have I demonstrated internal controls established to assure the budget authority that I am personally concerned with maintaining accountability?

A final suggestion for presentations is to organize your material so that the main message—the point with the most impact—is given as the opening statement. Isolate the most positive point you want to stress, the most startling statistic, the best result your program has achieved, and turn it into the "lead" sentence of your presentation. When you begin, you can be fairly sure of having the full attention of the budget authority. Use these valuable moments to make the most important announcements of your presentation so you can be sure it will get across. You may also be able to hold the authority's attention longer if you have a good, strong opening.

PRESENTING AND DEFENDING THE BUDGET

As you have seen, points that will allow you to defend your budget are built into the document as it is prepared. When you go before the budget authority, you should be so well prepared that you have nothing to think about but last-minute details and communicating effectively. The following points can aid you in giving your presentation smoothly and professionally.

- Be flexible. Remain alert to on-the-scene conditions that may alter the manner in which you should deliver your budget presentation. Everyone attempts to be professional about such activities, but human factors cannot be discounted. If you happen to follow a department that hasbeenengagedinaheatedargumentwiththebudgetauthority,members may carry over their feelings. Be aware of this and adapt to it.

- Key your brief, explanatory remarks to applicable line items, so the budget authority can clearly see the relationship between money requested and goals you expect to accomplish.

- Have present any individuals who can lend professional support to your budget proposal, but resist the temptation to parade a string of "character witnesses" before the budget authority. The budget authority is busy and probably eager to complete the process. If others can contribute concrete testimony, bring them. If not, put their words on paper and offer an appendix.

- Be alert to questions and comments of budget authority members. If they show interest in an area you did not intend to cover fully, switch directions and address their interests. Unresolved issues are normally decided in favor of the action that costs the least. If the members "feel" there are areas not fully addressed, they may reduce the appropriation just to "play it safe."

- Emphasize program successes. Show how previous expenditures have enabled your program to respond effectively to local [problems].

- Point out how your services complement those of other agencies.

- Demonstrate how various aspects of your budget are interrelated, and how lack of funding in one area might jeopardize services in another area.

- Illustrations, examples, charts, graphs, and other visuals should be used only when you are certain they support specific points. Every moment spent displaying visuals not of direct interest is one more moment the viewers can devote to thinking about other matters.

Chapter Four

FUNDRAISING

After reading this chapter you should be able to:

1. Understand concepts of marketing as applied to nonprofit agencies;
2. Discuss the advantages and disadvantages of various fundraising techniques;
3. Plan and design fundraising strategies.

INTRODUCTION

Raising funds to ensure survival of the organization, maintenance of its on-going programs, and the development of new ones is a crucial agency activity. In systems terms, funds are resource inputs that are used in the process stage of the social service system, they are used so that services may be provided. In the systems view, there are other resources used in the fundraising process such as staff, volunteers, donors, and potential solicitors. These resources are used in the planning and solicitation processes in an attempt to secure more resources for the organization (see Figure 4-1).

Fundraising is the importation of assets, either in the form of money or in-kind goods or services, into the agency by means of solicitation. The acquiring of funds in this way is the result of asking individuals, groups, or organizations for resources without always giving a tangible service in return. However, if an agency is receiving funds from an allocation body such as a United Way or even a government agency, the fundraising approach to be used by the agency may be restricted by the allocation source.

Since human service agencies are dependent to a large extent on outside organizations for funding, the level of funding for a specific program is usually a decision made by external bodies. This means that unanticipated additional income in the form of grants or contributions often reduces the level of support from a funder rather than being

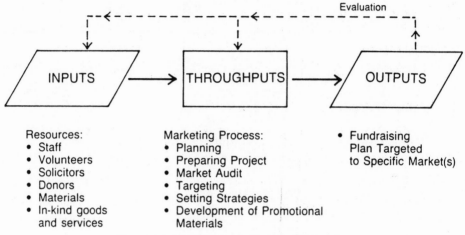

Success of fundraising efforts may be measured by: reaching goals; increased visibility of the agency; positive reactions from constituency and potential donors.

Evaluation

INPUTS → THROUGHPUTS → OUTPUTS

Resources:
• Staff
• Volunteers
• Solicitors
• Donors
• Materials
• In-kind goods
  and services

Marketing Process:
• Planning
• Preparing Project
• Market Audit
• Targeting
• Setting Strategies
• Development of Promotional
  Materials

• Fundraising
  Plan Targeted
  to Specific Market(s)

Figure 4-1: Fundraising in Systems Perspective

available to be used at the board's discretion. In addition, many allocation sources do not want an agency's fundraising to interfere with their own, so an agency may be restricted to fundraising on its own during certain periods of the year. An allocation agency may also have guidelines that specify that certain methods of obtaining operating funds may not be used, since this would mean that certain groups of contributors would be approached twice. These factors must be kept in mind in planning a fundraiser for an agency.

In the past, fundraising (in terms of grantwriting) was thought to be a staff function, while fundraising (in terms of solicitation of contributions) was thought to be an administrative (director and board of directors) and volunteer function. Human service workers in large agencies may not be very involved with fundraising in the organization, but they should be familiar with aspects of it because they will be expected to take on fundraising tasks as they assume increasing administrative responsibility. On the other hand, everyone who works in a small human service agency will be involved in fundraising in some way as part of the job.

In this chapter the concept of marketing as applied to human service agencies will be discussed, as will various types of fundraising, especially campaigns and special events. Also covered are strategies and approaches to these fundraising activities. Grantwriting as an approach to fundraising will be discussed only briefly here, as the next chapter is devoted exclusively to this topic.

ACQUIRING FUNDS

The acquiring of funds by an agency is done in a variety of ways. The most common sources of funds for an agency are the following: 1) fees; 2) contracts; 3) allocations; 4) grants; 5) contributions.

Fees

Fees are earned revenues for the agency. That is, the agency receives money in return for providing a good or service. Fees may be paid directly to the agency by the client receiving the service, but many times the client is unable to pay. In these cases, third-parties such as a Department of Human Services, Department of Rehabilitation Services, Medicaid or Medicare, Blue Cross/Blue Shield or other health plans may pay for the services.

Contracts

Contracts between public and private agencies are frequently negotiated to provide mandated services such as foster care or adoption. This is often done because it is easier and more cost-effective for a public agency to use the services of a private nonprofit which has the demonstrated expertise in the service area. In these cases, the public agency refers the clients to the private agency and the contractee is paid for delivering the service. Recently, agencies have begun to provide contractual services, such as employee assistance programs, to corporate clients, or counseling services to school systems that have no social workers.

Allocations

Allocations are the funds supplied by the federated fundraising and allocation agencies such as the United Way, Jewish Federation, Catholic Charities, and so forth. In this case, the agency must submit a request for funds along with a budget and a justification for the request. Then the request is reviewed by the funding agency's lay allocation and budgeting board which makes the final decision as to amount of allocation.

Grants

Grants are sums of money given for the agency to perform a specific task or to develop a specific program. Grants can be given by public agencies, private foundations, or corporations. In order to receive a grant, in most cases an agency must write a grant proposal, spelling out in detail what it intends to do with the grant money. Writing grant proposals will be discussed more fully in the next chapter.

Contributions

Contributions are sums of money donated by individuals or groups to support the work of the agency. Usually, the money is obtained without the agency having to exchange something tangible in return. That is, the agency does not provide a service to obtain them. Contributions may be in the form of money, or in-kind goods or services. The contributions may be solicited as part of a regular, organized campaign, or by special events that are planned as a one-time occasion for a specific purpose or goal.

While all of these sources of funds are important to the human service agency, in this chapter fundraising as an adjunct means of raising additional funds for the agency will be explored. To be specifically delineated is the art of fundraising from contributions using well-known principles of marketing. It is not intended to infer that other types of fundraising are not important, but allocations were discussed in the last chapter within the budgeting context. Contracts, especially from public agencies, are quite standard in terms of requirements and boundaries. Usually the agency uses forms provided by the funding source, must disclose required information, and must have the ability to provide the needed service or no contract will be made.

A major reason that fundraising is highlighted here is that many agencies are too dependent on limited sources, and thus are at the mercies of the vagaries of the economy, trendy social issues, and shifting political coalitions. Human service agencies need to look to marketing principles as a means of increasing their funding opportunities as well as a way of increasing their client populations, and the effectiveness of service delivery to those populations.

FUNDRAISING AS MARKETING

Marketing may be defined as "the analysis, planning, implementation, and control of carefully formulated programs designed to bring about voluntary exchanges of values with target markets for the purpose of achieving organizational objectives" (Kotler, 1982:5). What does this mean? Actually, marketing involves activities common to all human service organizations. For example, all agencies need to analyze the needs of their client populations, they need to plan services, and be able to implement them. Also, marketing involves carefully formulated programs, again a characteristic of well-run, effective human service organizations. Marketing "utilizes market segmentation, consumer research, concept development, communications, facilitation, incentives and the exchange theory to maximize target group response . . . [it] can be used to bring products, services, organizations, persons, places, or social causes to the attention of a market" (Kotler, 1982:495).

Most central to marketing is the concept of exchange, that is, the reciprocal transfer of something of value. The importance of the principle of exchange must be underscored. The basic idea of exchange is that there is some type of benefit that accrues to both parties in the process. Before an exchange can take place, the agency must try to learn as much as possible about the individuals or groups with whom they want to exchange. These individuals or groups are called "targets" or "publics," and the more a target is understood, the easier will be the process of exchange. Of course, the same applies to the clients that we serve, the more we know about them the easier is the process of helping.

Through the process of exchange, the agency obtains the resources it needs by giving something in return. Just as with the services that it offers, what the agency offers in return for contributions has tangible and intangible components. Tangible aspects include tax deductions, or a seat on an important committee or board; intangible aspects include a feeling of being socially useful, of fulfilling religious commandments to help the needy, of contributing to causes that one believes in, and so forth. This exchange process is obviously very different in the nonprofit area than it is in the for-profit market, where the process has much more tangible aspects. Even in the for-profit sector, though, subconscious motivation plays a part and marketing researchers have spent enormous sums of money trying to understand why people purchase the products that they do. Marketing also involves selecting target markets and concentrating on those market segments that potentially will have the highest possible response to the organization's campaign.

Lastly, achieving the organization's goals and objectives is the purpose of marketing. In business, the goal is profit. In the human services, the goal is community service. But, the important thing for human service agencies to remember is that effective planning and marketing requires that the agency develop specific goals and objectives that can be measured or quantified. In conjunction with planning, it must also be remembered that marketing is user-oriented. That is, it takes into account the needs, wants, desires, and special characteristics of the client, rather than designing services or campaigns that are inappropriate to the client or target population.

Components of Marketing

Marketing uses what is called the "marketing mix" to design an appropriate marketing strategy. The marketing mix is made up of four components, often called the "four P's: product, price, promotion, and place (Genkins, 1985:40; DiGuilio, 1984:232). An agency that wants to develop an effective fundraising campaign must find the right "mix" of these elements for its agency.

Product: refers to the main products or services offered by an organization. Obviously, the services offered by the agency are, or should be, styled and packaged in a way that reflects quality. One of the intangible aspects of an agency's product is the reputation it builds in its community. This reputation is of extreme importance in fundraising because mention of an agency's name should generate a positive response by the public. Product may also refer what is offered to potential donors in return for their contribution. For example, a marketing product developed for a campaign may be an expensive dinner to which tickets must be purchased, art items sold at a fundraising auction, used items sold at a garage sale, craft items sold at a bazaar, etc.

Price: refers to the fees for services charged by the agency. This setting of fees in nonprofits differs from for-profits because the price is not always based on an amount that can cover costs, rather user fees typically only pay a fraction of an agency's overhead. The support garnered from funding sources and service fees is matched against operating costs. The agency must then determine the break-even point or the gap between revenue and expenses. This gap, the excess of expenses over revenue, is usually the amount the agency must target to be raised through its fundraising activities. Price may also refer to the amounts charged for fundraising products. That is, a dinner may be donated by a restaurant, but contributors are charged $50 each for it. They pay this because they know that the money will go to the nonprofit organization, not because they think the dinner is worth $50.

Promotion: involves communication by the agency to its many constituencies to stimulate increased utilization of services or increased contributions. Many times it involves public education to increase public awareness about a particular social problem, or to encourage public utilization of new programs as, for example, child abuse hot-lines, and so forth. Communication is critical in developing or shaping an agency's image and reputation. Some tools of promotion include advertising, personal selling, and publicity. All of these promotional tools need to be utilized in the marketing campaign.

Place: refers to the channels through which an organization distributes its products or services. Distribution or place also refers to transportation, referral arrangements, the organization's physical plant, and so forth. Since most human service agencies are in direct contact with their clients, distribution may not be an important issue in delivery of services. From a marketing point of view, distribution is critical in the link from the agency to its larger public from which it is soliciting funds. That is, what is the best way for a agency to reach the largest number of its target market in order to deliver its fundraising appeal?

All of these components make up the marketing mix of an agency. They can be controlled to some extent internally by agency staff and board, but there are external factors such as government regulation, competition, and social focus which may be constraints on the agency's mix at any point in time (Vanderleest, 1985:20).

Fundraising Programs

There is not just one type of fundraising program that can be used by the human service agency, rather there are a variety of fundraising programs that fulfill different functions. The most common solicitation programs used by agencies may be classified as follows (Freyd, 1983:4-19 to 4-28):

Annual Giving Programs or Campaigns: seek funds from donors who will give repeatedly over time. An annual giving program should be the cornerstone of an agency's fundraising plan. This type of program tries to build up a pool of contributors who will give regularly to support agency activities. The funds received from this type of program will be used for new or on-going programs of the agency. A comparison of some of the costs and benefits of this and other programs may be seen in Table 4-1.

Table 4-1

COMPARISON OF FUND-RAISING PROGRAMS*

Program	Staff time/ Effort	Cost	Productivity
Annual giving program	High	Variable	High
Capital program	High	Low (5-10%)	High
Deferred giving program	Low (but complex)	Minimal	High
Events	High	Variable (50%+/-)	Variable

*Extrapolated from Freyd,"Methods for Successful Fund Raising", pp. 4-19 to 4-28 in Connors (Ed.). The Nonprofit Organization Handbook, 1980.

Capital Programs: usually seek larger gifts, in installments over several years for capital projects such as renovating, buying existing premises, or building new ones. The purpose of this type of program is to have contributors committed to the long-range capital improvement of the agency's facilities.

Deferred Giving Programs: seek monies in the form of endowments that are bequeathed to the agency from an estate or trust. In this form of giving, a contributor may leave money in a will or trust fund for the agency. This type of program takes the expertise of a financial planner, attorney, and accountant to help design a suitable program.

Fund-Raising Events: also called "special events," use a variety of means to seek contributions from those that would not normally give to one's agency. The distinguishing characteristic of an event is that it is usually a one-time occurrence for the agency.

In this chapter, the focus will be mainly on annual campaigns and special events, although the marketing principles discussed apply to all types of fundraising programs. Annual campaigns and events are the most common types of fundraisers for human service agencies. They are also less complicated to plan and implement.

THE MARKETING PROCESS APPLIED TO THE HUMAN SERVICE AGENCY

No matter what type of fundraising program adopted by the agency, marketing principles can be applied. An organized approach may involve a total marketing process. The marketing process usually consists of the following components (Rubright and MacDonald, 1983:9–11): the initial planning stage, selecting the fundraising project, the market audit, setting of objectives, targeting, setting strategies, developing promotional materials, and evaluating.

Initial Planning

The initial planning stage involves setting up a fundraising committee of board members, some staff, and interested volunteers. This committee will be responsible for the design and implementation of the fundraising project. An essential component for membership on a fundraising committee is the enthusiastic commitment of the participants, this enthusiasm and commitment will help keep them going through endless meetings, a thousand tedious details, and occasional setbacks and fatigue.

One of the first tasks of the committee will be to set up a schedule of tasks to be completed with tentative dates for completion. One example of such a schedule or checklist can be seen in Table 4-2.

Table 4-2

AGENCY FUNDRAISING CHECKLIST

Task	Date Completed	Comments
1. Fundraising committee established		
2. Agency goals clarified		
3. Agency need determined		
4. Feasibility study completed		
5. Costs estimated		
6. Budget developed		
7. Market audit completed		
8. Marketing objectives developed		
9. Target markets selected		
10. Marketing strategies chosen		
11. Fundraising approaches selected		
12. Promotional materials developed		
13. Evaluation mechanisms established		

Selecting and Preparing the Marketing Project

The preparation of the marketing project usually involves an analysis of the goals and objectives of the agency as well as determining agency need, estimating costs, developing a budget, and evaluating the congruency of the marketing project with the current and future direction and image of the agency.

The cost of the fundraiser will depend on a number of factors such as type of fundraising strategies chosen, expertise of staff, support of volunteers, image and name-recognition of agency, public attitudes toward the services offered by the agency, size of the agency, and so forth. Initial costs of starting an annual campaign may be very high, depending on approach, but over time the costs should go down. An agency should always try to keep its fundraising costs as low as possible, however, since this is one area in which human services agencies may be publicly criticized if costs are too high in proportion to services.

Some of the components of a fundraising budget may include (Pendleton, 1981:40–42) the following, although all the items may not be applicable to all programs:

- preliminary feasibility study
- salaries, including secretarial (this must be apportioned between fundraising expenses and program expenses)
- office expenses, including rent (this must also be apportioned)
- postage, printing, photography or other art work
- cost of mailing list
- travel and lodging
- meals
- professional fees
- cost of materials or items for resale
- any other miscellaneous costs

All of these and any other related costs must be subtracted from the projected amount of monies obtained through fundraising efforts, something agency planners sometimes forget to do. Without considering the total costs of fundraising, the agency may be very disappointed when the final results of their efforts gain so little.

The Market Audit

A market audit evaluates the agency's markets, services, marketing programs, and overall marketing effectiveness. The audit usually consists of three parts:

- an evaluation of the marketing environment of the agency—its markets, customers, competitors, and macroenvironment.
- an evaluation of the marketing system of the agency—its objectives, programs and implementation.
- an evaluation of the major areas of marketing activity in the agency—its products, pricing, place, and promotion. The audit thus can be the basis for more effective planning by the agency.

Setting Marketing Objectives

It is crucial for an agency to set marketing goals in writing after going through brainstorming and planning sessions with staff and board members. But there is a difference between agency goals and marketing goals. For example, an agency goal might be:

- to provide foster care services to children under 10 years of age.

Some marketing objectives might be to:

- to increase the number of referrals from child welfare agencies, and
- to raise $1.3 million dollars to renovate a group foster home.

Targeting

Targeting involves "the identification of individuals, groups, or people with special characteristics and with whom the organization wants to initiate and manage exchanges" (Rubright and MacDonald, 1983, p. 10). Individuals and groups that are usually targeted for fund-raising include families of clients, ex-clients, other organizations, corporations, and certain groups of contributors. Targeting is a selective process and, most important, high priority groups who are possible givers are targeted first. Once a group is targeted, the next stage involves what is called "market segmentation," breaking up the target market into more homogeneous groups who have a common interest in a particular cause, or who have similar demographic characteristics. For example, if your agency serves children with learning disabilities, then one target market segment might be parents or other relatives of such children. By segmenting the target market, the agency is better able to develop an appeal that will be appropriate for the audience chosen. Thus every segment is viewed as a separate audience. Then potential donors are ranked according to the likelihood that they will be responsive to your campaign.

Setting Strategies

Deciding on marketing strategies involves the delineation of tasks needed to be completed in order to reach your target markets and thus fulfill your marketing objectives. Four general marketing strategies which may be applied to fundraising are:

    a. market penetration: increasing fundraising efforts in the area and to the population currently targeted:

    b. market development: targeting fundraising programs to new markets;

    c. product development: improving present fundraising strategies;

    d. diversification: developing an entirely new campaign.

Once your agency has decided on one or more of general marketing strategies, it must then examine some of the traditional approaches to fundraising, whether for a campaign or special event:

Collections: seek small sums from large numbers of people and most commonly are done in the form of setting canisters out, passing the basket, or going door-to-door with the help of volunteers. This approach may be used as a special event, although it is an annual fundraising approach for some small organizations. This method is very unsophisticated, can be very time-consuming, and may not generate much money for the agency. It is unsophisticated because it uses a "blanket" approach and does not target a market from which it could gain the maximum return for the amount of time invested (see Table 4-3 for a comparison of fundraising approaches.) While not included in the discussion, grant solicitation is shown in the table so as to compare it with other approaches.

Table 4-3

COMPARISON OF FUND-RAISING APPROACHES*

Approaches	Staff time/ Effort	Cost	Productivity
Grant solicitation	High	High	Variable
Collections	Low-staff High-Volunteers	Low	Low
Direct mail	High	High	Variable
Merchandise sales	Medium	Variable	Very low
Advertising	Medium (but complex)	High	Low

*Extrapolated from Freyd,"Methods for Successful Fund Raising", pp. 4-19 to 4-28 in Connors (Ed.) The Nonprofit Organization Handbook, 1980.

Direct mail: seeks gifts through the mail from large groups of donors who could not effectively be reached by other means. This approach is usually used for annual, capital, or endowment campaigns, rarely as a special event. Part of the secret of a successful mail campaign is to have a good mailing list. The development of such a list can be made by using present and former clients and contributors, targeting certain residential sections of the city, or even buying one or more lists from companies that specialize in direct mailing. A list of prospective contributors most useful to a specific agency may take a while to develop. Costs are very high in direct mailings, even with a bulk-rate permit or nonprofit permit, a large part of the cost may be for postage and printing. But if a good list can be developed, there is potential for a good return.

Merchandise Sales: seek sums through the selling of a product. Bazaars, flea markets, and bake sales are some examples of this approach. The investment in staff and volunteer time may be somewhat high, although cost may be negligible. If the agency can use donated items to sell, or goods made by volunteers, then the cost of such an effort will be low. But if the agency has to buy goods to sell, the cost may be too high for the amount of return involved. This approach is also relatively unsophisticated because it does not usually target a market segment, rather it seeks sales from any passerby. This approach is usually part of a special event, although some organizations regularly schedule them as an annual fund-raiser.

Advertising: seeks to reach a great many people quickly with a message. It is most effectively used in crisis situations, for example, if an agency were soliciting funds to be used for the victims of a disaster—fire, flood, etc. This approach may be used either for an annual campaign or special event. A good advertising campaign takes the expertise of a professional who knows how to write good copy. The cost of advertising can be high, therefore, this approach may be out of reach for most small human service agencies. However, all agencies should make use of the free public service announcements that are available through local media to keep their programs in the public eye and increase positive image and name recognition.

The type of fundraising strategy that should be used by a particular agency depends on a number of factors, such as available funds for start-up, expertise of staff and board, commitment of staff, board, and volunteers, time availability of staff, and results of feasibility study. Actually, an agency should use a variety of approaches aimed at different target markets, and marketing should be an on-going activity in every agency. Agencies should also be aware that running a successful fundraiser may take a few initial lean years, each year brings more expertise, more name-recognition in the community, and hopefully, a bigger response to agency efforts.

In addition to choosing one or more of these strategies, the fundraising committee must draw up a schedule of tasks to be completed which includes a time-line and persons responsible for each phase of the project. A GANTT chart is a useful way to do this planning (see Table 4-4). Record keeping is important for tax agencies, credit-rating bureaus, and the general public, so a list of records needed must be drawn up and the agency bookkeeper or accountant or committee treasurer must make sure that record keeping guidelines are adhered to.

Table 4-4

SAMPLE GANTT CHART

Tasks to be Completed for Flea Market Fundraiser

Tasks	Person(s) Responsible	12	11	10	9	8	7	6	5	4	3	2	1
Obtain space	Joe	X											
Obtain permit	Joan	X											
Solicit donated items	Joe,Sylvia,Pete	X	X	X	X	X	X						
Tag and mark items	Sylvia,Ida, Tom					X	X	X					
Contact media	Sue						X	X	X		X		
Schedule volunteers	Fred								X				
etc.													

Weeks Before Event is the heading spanning the numbered columns 12 through 1.

Development of Promotional Materials

Since most small human service agencies cannot afford to pay professionals to develop these materials, they many times have to do it themselves. Other agencies usually have volunteers or board contacts who can provide this service at minimal or no cost. Another place where art help may be obtained at somewhat of a lower cost is at the art departments of colleges and universities. Art students may be hired to help, or faculty members may volunteer their services. Whatever the means, the important thing to remember is that the marketing materials that are developed should be the product of planning to reach appropriate targets.

Evaluation, Feedback, Modification

Lastly, the marketing process should involve evaluation, feedback, and internal adjustment in order to modify or revise any part of the marketing plan that does not seem to be working the way it should. Fundraising is not an end in itself, it is a means to an end—the provision of services to those in need.

Chapter Four
Questions and Topics for Discussion

1. What are the major sources of funds for an agency?
2. Why are marketing concepts useful to the nonprofit agency?
3. How may the process of exchange take place in fundraising?
4. What are the major components of marketing strategy?
5. What factors should be taken into account by an agency in determining its marketing strategy?

Exercise 4-1: Analysis of Agency Marketing.

Using your field placement or job site as the unit of analysis, please examine its marketing approach using the following guidelines. If you have no job or field placement, contact a human service agency in your community.

1. What are the sources of funding for the agency?
2. What is the present mix (in percentages) of public/private funding, fees, grants, contributions, etc.?
3. What are some advantages and disadvantages of the present marketing mix and what mix would be more beneficial to the agency?
4. What types of fundraising strategies are used by the agency at the present time? What market(s) are these strategies aimed at? In your view, how successful are these strategies in reaching their stated goals?
5. What suggestions to improve marketing would you make to this agency?

Exercise 4-2: Fundraising Plan.

You are to write a fundraising plan in memo form in 2–5 pages. Write the plan as though you were presenting it to the agency director or board of directors. Be prepared to present this to the class. In your plan please include the following:

1. The objectives of the fundraising effort, i.e., purpose and amount desired?
2. Target market, i.e., individuals or organizations you want money from?
3. Your assumptions about this market.
4. Your specific plan.
5. Resources needed: personnel, materials, money, volunteers, etc., (please attach a budget).
6. Timetable for completion of specific fundraising tasks: please use a GANTT chart to illustrate it.
7. Attach a cover sheet to your memo that briefly describes the agency, its goals, and how they relate to this fundraising plan.

Case 4-1: "Firm Cited for Violating Permit: Fund-Raising Practices Reported" by John Haakenson*

An Arlington firm that promotes fund-raising activities has been cited by the Dallas Consumer Affairs department for violating permit requirements.

J.C. Clark & Associates was issued two citations for failing to disclose to potential donors that their contributions are not tax deductible, and that 45 percent of gross receipts go to fund-raising expenses, and 55 percent to the stated cause.

Kathy Toler, fund solicitation administrator with the city of Dallas, said Monday that J.C. Clark & Associates was the first business to be cited under a city ordinance that went into effect Nov. 16.

Clark is scheduled to go to court with the citations Jan. 19, Toler said.

Officials from the city and the Better Business Bureau of Metropolitan Dallas, Inc. received complaints from citizens about Clark's fund-raising procedures, according to Toler and Better Business spokesperson Jeannette Kopko.

---

*Reprinted by permission from the Arlington Citizen-Journal. December 21–22, 1983, p. 17A.

Kopko said Clark & Associates was raising funds for Randolph-Sheppard Vendors of Texas Inc., an organization of blind persons that operates snack bars and cafeterias in federal buildings.

Kopko said an investigation revealed that Clark "at least in some cases was not complying with the requirements of the permit." She said Clark's alleged failure to mention tax and gross receipts information are violations.

Clark was unavailable for comment Monday and Tuesday.

"He (Clark) should be aware (of the disclosures requirement), and he should make sure that everyone is following that procedure," Kopko said.

"The unfair part of this is for Randolph-Sheppard—it's on their record too. We don't have any question about Randolph-Sheppard, but we do with J.C. Clark," Kopko said.

Last summer, the Better Business Bureau received inquiries from Dallas residents who had been solicited by Clark for donations to Randolph-Sheppard to support programs for blind vendors.

At the time, Randolph-Sheppard did not have the required permit from the Dallas Fund Solicitation Board, according to Kopko. Randolph-Sheppard later applied for a permit, and told board members it planned to seek donations for a Christmas party for blind children Dec. 17 in Fort Worth.

A permit was issued to Randolph-Sheppard in November with the stipulations about tax and gross receipts information.

In November and December, officials received complaints that the permit requirements were not being met.

Toler said Clark was issued two citations last Thursday.

"We had four complainants who were willing to testify—full disclosures were not made," Toler said.

Kopko said the Better Business Bureau rarely receives complaints about fund-raising permit violations.

"Most people who call here call for information, to help them make up their minds. They don't mind giving, but they want to be sure it's going where they think it's going."

1. What happened in this case?
2. What should Randolph-Sheppard have done to protect the reputation of it's organization?

3. What are the responsibilities of an agency when it contracts with an outside fundraising consultant or organization?
4. What should the organization do now?

Case 4-2: The Women's Shelter of Kimball County, Inc.

The Women's Shelter of Kimball County, Inc. was established in 1975 and became a United Way Agency in 1980. It is open 24 hours a day to battered women and their children. The goal of the shelter is to provide women with a refuge from abusive mates. To achieve this end, the shelter offers a number of services to women. Some of these services are a crisis hot-line, service plan coordination, day care, health and developmental screening for children, health care for the women, and a nutrition program to supply daily food needs.

The agency is staffed by one program manager, one full and one part-time counselor, a part-time nurse practitioner, and a part-time person in charge of building maintenance. A volunteer program supplements staff time in all the above areas, as well as provides public relations for the agency through its Speaker's Bureau.

A total of 30–32 women and children are housed at the Shelter at any one time. Women are allowed to stay up to four weeks, but the average length of stay is a week. The women staying at the Shelter perform most clean-up chores and cook their own meals.

The Shelter is facing a number of problems at the moment, some of which have to do with its external environment. Even though it has been existence for ten years, it must still operate in an ambivalent environment. That is, there are both positive and negative attitudes about the very idea of a women's shelter. Some people in the community still refuse to admit the need for such a home, others see it as undermining the unity of the family, others see it as governmental intrusion into private family matters. There are also a great many attitudes about the women themselves that interfere with the work of the Shelter. For example, some people think battered women are "sick" because they are in abusive relationships, others think they have done something to "deserve" the treatment they have received at the hands of their mates. Yet despite these negative attitudes, the Shelter has an extensive waiting list, sometimes up to three months long.

Another problem the agency faces is the dire need for more space. It is currently housed in a former private residence and has five bedrooms and four bathrooms. The families share a common living area, kitchen, and the bathrooms.

The agency currently receives the majority of its funds from the United Way, although it also receives monies from the City of Kimball, the County of Kimball, the State Department of Social Services, private foundations, church organizations, and individuals. It has just received word that its latest budget request to the United Way has been cut by $25,000. Therefore, it needs to make up the $25,000 for operating expenses from other sources. Also, the agency would like to have a long-range plan to acquire or build another shelter. You are to do the following:

1. Devise a fundraising plan for the Women's Shelter with a target of at least $25,000.
   a. Explain your assumptions about your target market;
   b. Explain how you will reach your target market;
   c. Include a timetable and task list in your plan;
   d. Discuss how the agency will acquire and use needed personnel for its fundraising drive;
   e. Include a budget with your plan.
2. Devise a long-term capital fundraising plan to enable the agency to acquire a building. Include in your plan the components discussed above.

Reading 4-1: "Five Steps to Progressive Fundraising" by Brian Rust*

One need all fundraisers share is to organize and plan efficiently for the campaign. At one time or another, . . . [they] will forego a progressive (step-by-step) process to carry them to their goal. The all-encompassing fundraiser may take the attitude, "Let's use what we have, rather than what we don't have, and cut corners in the plan. Likewise, the large fundraising department, in an effort to "get on with the fundraising campaign," may not always use department resources to their fullest. Expediency sometimes wins out over deliberate planning.

Whether alone or part of a department, one needs to carefully plan and carry out fundraising activities that make the most of the resources at hand. Such deliberate fundraising can be divided into five progressive steps.

---

*Reprinted with permission from *The Nonprofit World Report,* January–February 1985.

1. Prepare the Case Statement.

This is the core of any fundraising effort—the "who, what, when, where, how and why" of your organization or campaign. Preparing the case statement is the exercise of bringing all the elements of your message together into a concise, audience-centered presentation. It is a clear description of your need and a specific request, put into the potential donor's language. It can be as detailed as the situation or donor calls for.

The case statement can be applied to many situations as well. You can develop a case for a specific campaign, a team of people, a conference, or for an entire organization.

Begin by answering seven basic questions about your cause:

1. What need exists for your cause? Whether you're seeking funds for a community center or support for an annual fund drive, describe your service. Explain briefly where and why it exists.

2. Why should a potential donor support your group? Are you or your organization the only one providing this service? Explain what set you apart from your competition and why a gift to your cause is a wise investment.

3. What do you hope to achieve in your work? State specifically your goals for the coming year (should the campaign be successful). For example, how will your project have changed the community a year from now?

4. What is the total cost of your project? Present the budget in terms understood by the layperson. The amount of detail will vary according to the potential donor's wishes. Be prepared.

5. What are you asking of the potential donor? Break the total need into several suggested gift amounts. Tailor the size of the suggested gift to a maximum level at which the donor may be able to contribute. The larger the gift, the fewer gifts one will have to raise.

6. How soon do you need the funds? When is the project scheduled to begin? It is best to set a date even sooner than the actual date so that even late gifts will arrive on time.

7. What will the consequences be if the needed funds aren't raised? This may be conversely stated from question 3. Will something be held up, changed, or lessened if the project is not funded? What might the end result be for the people you serve?

Write your answers to these questions and then boil them down into a concise essay. Practice your presentation before a group of coworkers.

Also try adapting your message into a letter, a phone call, and a brochure format. Different audiences will require different vehicles for your message.

2. List Potential Donors.

Who will you ask for funds? Everyone you can think of? Well, that may be a good first step, but you will need to move beyond mass appeal in order to make the most of your contacts.

Think of the project for which the funds will be raised. Are there current donors to your organization who may be interested in giving toward this new project? . . . . Depending on the project, one may try developing a new network of potential donors. . . .

Next, segment the master list of potential donors into several homogeneous groups. These groups may be segmented by interest (disaster relief), by location (metropolitan Dallas), or by their relation to the project or organization (present donor). When you're done, consider how to communicate the need and donor involvement more personally with each segment. For example, one can refer to a current donor as someone "already concerned about the work" as he or she is asked for a special gift. Or, for a community project appeal, address people by their location: "As a resident of the Brady Park neighborhood . . . "

3. Choose Methods for Contact.

Just about everyone sends mailings to ask for funds. But is that really the most attractive way for one to obtain gifts for a project? Perhaps not. Consider the various means at your disposal—personal visits, phone calls, letters, and brochures. Don't look first at what you are best equipped (or can best afford) to do. Try to determine what method will produce the greatest response. Then see how the organization could adopt that method.

Evidence and wisdom both point to personal contact as the best means to request a gift. But like all things of quality, it costs more. There may not be enough staff available to make personal contacts. Or the people to be contacted may be spread out over too wide an area. But if neither of these is a problem, make an appointment to present your case and ask for a gift in person.

If personal visits are out of the question, consider phoning. Nonprofits that lack the resources to conduct a phone campaign might ask a local company to donate time on its WATS line. Local donors or volunteers from a community group may be tapped to do the calling (if properly trained).

A third option—especially if there are too many people to contact in too short a time—is to send a letter and brochure to begin the fundraising campaign. Although financial response to fundraising letters is not as high as it is via phone or visits, letters can garner a quicker response. Adapt any one or a combination of these methods of fundraising contact to present your case to each segment.

4. Strategize and Plan.

Each segment of a potential donor list requires a tailored approach. Take, for example, donors from Dallas. Depending on where most of them live in that large urban area, one could try to get them together for a fundraising event. A banquet is one such forum. Or, if you can't host such a gathering, try using a combination of approaches. Send a letter introducing your campaign. In your letter, answer the first three question you addressed in your case statement—the need, reasons for supporting the project, and what will be achieved through the project. Then follow up the letter with a phone call to ask for a gift.

After a four or five step strategy has been written for each segment, combine the strategies into a master plan. Time and money can be saved by having separate letters printed at the same time or by visiting prospective donors from a particular area in a block of several days.

5. Maintain Contact.

The possibility of obtaining a second gift isn't the only reason for keeping in touch with donors. Regular contact beyond the first gift has tremendous public relations value. Expressing appreciation and keeping the donor informed of progress toward the goal help reinforce the donor's good feelings about participation. And positive feedback about how you treat donors has a way of influencing others to give.

Evidence shows that the sooner a donor is thanked, the sooner and more likely he or she is to give again. Thank all of your donors as often as they give to the project and as soon as possible.

Regular contact (beyond gift appeals) is important as well. Larger organizations send regular donors publications or newsletters designed to keep donors abreast of project development. Representatives from smaller organizations may write personal letters, call, or meet with donors, especially if their donor list is small. Any such efforts to keep in touch with donors help foster a relationship that could lead to other gifts. Let donors know that giving to your cause is something to remember.

Also give people opportunities to "take" from your organization. Are there any instructive materials you could provide for them? Can you ask their advice on some plan or activity your group has in the works? By lending their opinion, donors frequently get more deeply involved. This leads to more faithful giving, and more donors. Some of the best referrals of new donors are made by current contributors who love your work.

Try this five-step approach to plan your next funding campaign. While the steps themselves are far from new, their progression may help you organize the next funding campaign more efficiently. And the more efficiently and thoroughly we organize, the more effective we can be at raising funds.

Chapter Five

GRANTWRITING

After reading this chapter you should be able to:

1. Understand the grantwriting process;
2. Know where to look for potential funding sources of grants;
3. Write a grant;
4. Know where to go for additional information.

INTRODUCTION

A grant is an allocation of funds from a governmental agency, a private foundation, or sometimes a federated funding source, to a human service agency for a specific program or project. Grants differ tremendously in terms of amounts, eligibility requirements, purposes, and regulations. Some are open to any nonprofit organization; some are restricted to specific purposes or types of organizations. For example, some foundations only fund certain types of activities such as health, welfare, education, alcohol, drug rehabilitation, and so forth. Other foundations only fund organizations in particular geographic areas, such as their home state, or their own county. Each federal department with grant monies available obviously only funds in its area of interest, but within that area of interest the appropriate grantees may be narrowly defined.

The availability of grants also varies with the economic and political climate, so that in the "social reform" era of the 1960's and early 70's there was ample grant money available from the federal government, but in the 1980's this source of funds has become more constricted. As a result, there is increased competition for fewer funds. More and more agencies have begun to look to private and corporate foundations for grants and, as a result, these foundations have been flooded with applications.

To obtain a grant, the agency needs to submit a proposal to the funding source outlining exactly what it intends to do with the money, for what period of time, and agreeing to abide by the evaluation and reporting guidelines of the grantor. While an agency may receive funds

103

from its local United Way and/or other federated funding source for continuous on-going support, most grants are not given for this purpose. Grants are usually given for a limited period of time; so one of the factors an agency must consider when it looks to granting agencies for funds as seed money for new projects or programs is how it will continue the program or services after the grant money is no longer available.

In grantwriting, there are two main concerns of the grantwriter: (1) Where do I find information on funding sources? (2) How do I write the grant proposal? The purpose of this chapter is to acquaint you with the nature of the grantwriting process, which involves a number of different activities culminating in the submission of a grant proposal. The main focus will be the planning necessary in developing a project and the searching for, and screening of, funding sources. A more indepth discussion of the actual mechanics of writing a grant proposal may be found in Reading 5-1. In the following discussion, "the agency" refers to those designated individuals in the agency responsible for the grantwriting effort, as well as administrators and board members who are ultimately responsible for the grant project.

THE GRANTWRITING PROCESS

Grantwriting is a process that involves much more than sitting down and writing a proposal, it is a planning process with colleagues within the agency as well as outside of it. It is also a political activity in the sense that the grantwriter must be able to garner community support, as well as use the available help from the funding source to write a better proposal. There are two main ways that an agency may become involved in writing a grant proposal for funding: one way is in response to an RFP (request for proposal) circulated by a governmental agency or private funding source; the other is in response to a specific community need or problem, in which case the agency initiates the grant proposal and contact with a funding source. In the former case, the agency has a specific funding source in mind and is thus spared the tedious search for an appropriate donor. In the latter case, the agency must expend time and energy to find a suitable funder for its project. In the grantwriting process to be described below, the assumption is that the agency looking for funds is not responding to an RFP and thus has to search for a funding source.

While the grantwriting process may be viewed in different ways, there are some basic steps in the process that may include the following (From Lauffer, 1977:64–86; Lindholm, et al, 1982:15–41; EMI Professional Development Series, 1983): 1) Assign grantwriting responsibility; 2) plan program/project; 3) search for appropriate funding source(s); 4) evaluate and select funding source(s); 5) initiate contact with funding source(s); 6) write and submit grant (see Figure 5-1).

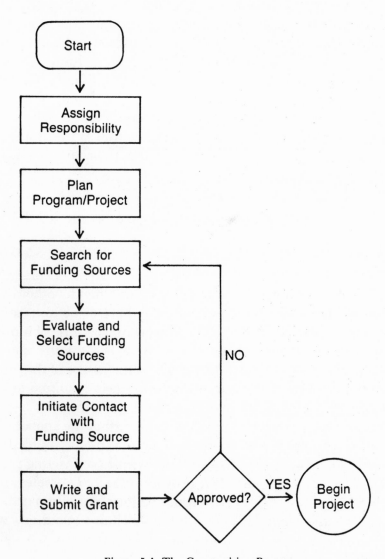

Figure 5-1: The Grantwriting Process

Assign Responsibility

Someone has to be responsible for the grantwriting effort, the coordination of information and resources, the contacting of potential funders, and the sheparding of the actual grant. Often one individual is the actual grantwriter and calls on others within the organization as well as outside of it for help as needed. In other cases, a grantwriting committee is established and the various tasks divided up among the committee members. In either case, someone has to have the responsibility as well as the authority to make decisions regarding the grant, the funding source, and the proposed project. Often this person is the one who will eventually implement the proposal if the grant is funded, since the writer is the most knowledgeable about the project. If only one individual is responsible for writing the grant, he or she should receive assurances that additional help will be forthcoming, as needed, and that agency resources will be available to complete the grant proposal in a timely manner. Once these matters are settled, the actual planning can begin.

Plan Program/Project

Define Your Problems or Needs

The agency may be aware, from a variety of sources, of certain needs or problems in the community that are not being met by other community agencies. These needs or problems may have come to its attention because of the types of clients it is already serving, because of input from other agencies or groups in the community or because the agency has done a systematic assessment of needs. Due to the nature of the problems and the mission of the agency, it may feel uniquely qualified to deliver services to meet these needs or problems. The services that need to be delivered may be necessary adjuncts to services that the agency already provides. For example, if the agency is one that treats troubled youth, then a logical offshoot program would be a family counseling program, or a teen pregnancy program. If it provides meals to homeless people, then other logical adjunct services could be job counseling, or housing placement. Or the agency may desire to branch out into a new area of service because it knows the needs are there and it has the staff with expertise to provide the service.

In defining the need or problem area for a grant proposal, the agency must be able to tell how it knows the needs or problems exist in the community. In other words, it must be able to document the needs or problems. There are a number of different ways to do this. The agency may want to do a needs assessment in the community, or if it does not have the time, money, or expertise to carry on such a study it could try to collect data from secondary sources such as a United Way, a University, a city planning department, or a community group. Other sources of information include libraries which have census data, key informants in the community, and staffs of elected officials.

The documentation should be able to illustrate who is affected by the problem; that is, what segments of the population, what age groups, ethnic groups, etc., and how many in the community are affected. The documentation should also describe the ways in which the target population is affected by the problem or need, and what will happen if intervention does not take place. Sometimes it is very difficult to state definitively all the ways that people are affected by a problem, especially since some problems are not manifest for years. In these cases, the proposal writer could extrapolate from what is known now about the affects of some problems and project how these would impact on the population in the community or the community itself in the future.

Develop Goals, Objectives, and Strategies to Meet Needs and/or Solve Problems

After an examination of the existing human service needs in the community, the agency can then move on to developing goals, objectives, and strategies to meet these needs or problems. The writing of goals and objectives was discussed previously in another chapter. Remember that goals are broad statements of desired future states, while objectives are specific, measurable, time-limited means to reach goals. Strategies are specific actions to reach objectives. In the case of most human service agencies, objectives involve choosing the most appropriate level or method of intervention to reach the target population with the stated problem.

Once objectives are formulated they should be prioritized, first by how congruent they are with the current short- and long-range goals of the organization; second, on the basis of a number of different variables, including costs, the existing resources of the organization, its capabilities, staff available or needed to be hired, and what is known about the most effective ways of ameliorating certain human conditions. Other factors include the priorities of the potential funding source(s), if known at this time, and the projected effect on current clients and programs.

After objectives have been prioritized, agency staff can start developing strategies to meet each objective. A program plan can be developed that includes tasks involved, a timetable, a budget, staff and material resources needed, duties and responsibilities of staff, and some measures to evaluate the effectiveness of the program. Use of a program planning chart or Gantt chart is useful in clarifying the implementation steps of the proposed project and reflects in-depth thought on the part of the staff.

Describe the Strengths and Capabilities of the Organization.

After defining needs, goals, and objectives, the agency must look to its capabilities in meeting the stated needs for which grant money is desired. Information that can be used in describing the capabilities and achievements of the organization are annual reports, brochures, and other materials that have, in all, probability already been prepared for other purposes. In addition, some summary of the qualifications of existing program staff to manage the proposed project or activity should be prepared. Up-to-date resumes of staff should always be kept on hand, or be readily available for this purpose.

In addition to staff qualifications, other information needed to describe the strengths of the organizations relates to current programs and clients served, and how the proposed project fits or deviates from current organizational goals and activities. Physical plant and other resources of the agency should be described, as well as agency location and accessibility to the target population and other community resources.

Based on the data available, the agency has started building its case for grant funds, but the agency should be honest with itself and the funding source in answering these questions: Do these problems or needs lend themselves to funding as a solution, or is the real purpose of this grant proposal just a scheme to keep the agency afloat? Are there really no alternative means to dealing with the stated need or problem besides the installation of a new service or program? If the agency is not willing to ask these questions, be assured that the funding source will.

Now that you know what it is your agency wants to do, it is now time to find an appropriate funder for your project if you have not already done so by replying to an RFP.

Search for Appropriate Funding Source

One of the most important aspects of obtaining grants is knowing where to look for sources that award grants. It is not enough just to have a good idea, or to know the techniques of writing. If you cannot communicate your idea to the people who are interested in funding the type of problem your agency is trying to address, then you are wasting your time. This is why it is necessary to spend some time on the crucial step of matching your agency priorities with those of an appropriate funding source. It is not wise to use the "shot-gun" approach by submitting proposals to every foundation and government agency whose address is available. Rather, you should take some time to research whether this funding source is most appropriate for your agency.

Where then, does one look to find out where the money is? There are three main sources of funds: governments (federal, state, and local), foundations, and corporations. The first place to go for information on most of these sources is your local public or university library. Many libraries have a section devoted to information on grants, in fact there are federal regional depositories as well as regional depositories of the Foundation Center all over the country (see Appendix for list). If your library does not have such a center, ask the librarian for some of the publications discussed below as well as those in the list of grant resources in the Appendix of this book.

Governmental Funding Sources

For information on federal government grants, the two best sources are the Catalog of Domestic Assistance and the Federal Register. These are published by the Federal Government and are available from the Superintendent of Documents or a local library.

The Catalog of Domestic Assistance: The Catalog of Federal Domestic Assistance identifies over one thousand assistance programs administered by 51 Federal government agencies. It is the basic reference source for information about Federal government programs, since it is a compilation of programs administered by various Federal departments and agencies all in one place. It is a useful tool in identifying programs which may be of interest to the grant writer. A flow-chart depicting how one may apply for federal grant monies using the Catalog may be seen in Figure 5-2. The Catalog is published annually, usually in June, and an update with the latest information on monies available after the passage of the Federal budget is usually published in December.

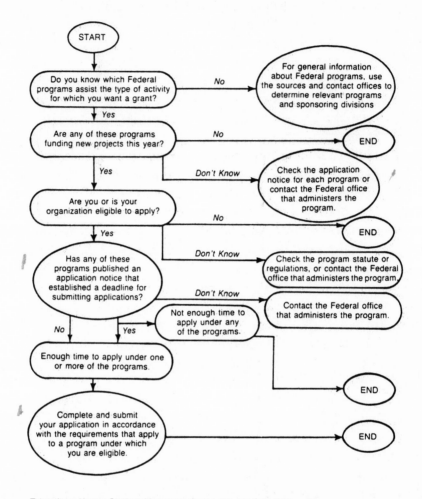

Taken from: Human Services Monograph Series, No. 19, April 1981, p. 36.

Figure 5-2: Applying for Federal Assistance Using the Catalog of Domestic Federal Assistance

The Federal Register: The Federal Register is published daily, Monday through Friday, throughout the year. It publishes legal notices issued by Federal Agencies, thus, it is the place to look for Requests for Proposals (RFP's). An abbreviated example of guidelines for a grant preapplication from the Federal Register may be found in Exercise 5-1. The Requests for Proposals published in the Federal Register contain the general guidelines and other information pertinent to the proposal.

The RFP's also contain contact persons names and numbers for more information in each state. Since the Register is published every day, it has more up-to-date information than the Catalog, but the Catalog is a good place to start to get a general overview. Certain times of the year seem to be best for using the Register. For example, after the annual federal budget is passed, there are likely to be RFP's issued by the Department of Health and Human Services, and other agencies. When major legislation relating to human services is passed throughout the year, there will be a good possibility that RFP's will be issued when monies are available.

State and Local Funding Sources: There may not be information on state and local governmental funding readily available in some states. The grantwriter must call relevant agencies, for example, Departments of Human Services, Social Services, Youth Services, Drug and Alcohol Abuse, and so forth, and ask to be put on a mailing list to receive announcements of RFP's when they are issued by that department. At the county and city level, again, calling is useful, but so is being up-to-date on the politics in the local area. Being in contact with city planning and council staff may be useful. In some areas, a proposal has to be presented before the city council or county commissioners. The grantwriter has to explore the specifics of the local area.

Foundation Funding Sources

For information on foundations, there are national and state foundation directories available, even county foundation directories available in some cases. Some of the best sources for national and state information are the Foundation Directory and the Annual Register of Grant Support.

The Foundation Directory: The Foundation Directory is one of the best sources for getting information on foundations interested in your subject area. It provides information on the nation's largest foundations which make grants, those which have assets of over $1 million and which give at least $100,000 in grants annually. The Directory is arranged by state and alphabetically by foundation name within each state. It lists much useful information about each foundation, including types of grants, interest areas, and so forth. A Directory is published by the Foundation Center, which also publishes other resource materials for grantwriters.

Annual Register of Grant Support: The Annual Register of Grant Support includes information on grant programs of governmental agencies, public and private foundations, as well as other types of special interest organizations. The Annual Register lists over 2,600 entries in its latest edition.

There are a number of other resources available to the grantwriter, but the ones mentioned here are the best places to start looking. For those willing and able to pay for a computer search of the same information, The Foundation Center has available COMSEARCH printouts which are computer listings of foundation grants in 70 major donor categories. Also, if you are interested in more detailed information about a particular foundation, about 500 foundations publish annual reports which the prospective grantee can obtain on request.

Information on Corporate Funding Sources

Corporations should be the last resort for the grantwriter, as they give much less money to social programs than either government or foundations. The new tax laws make it less attractive than it used to be for corporations to do this, although they have never been a major funder in the social service area. However, they should not be totally ruled out, as some of the large corporations in a community may be willing to donate monies or in-kind goods and services if your organization can present a good case and the project is one that interests the funder.

There are two main ways that a corporation may donate money to an agency or human service project: indirectly, through a corporate foundation set up for this purpose; or directly, through a corporate committee set up to screen such requests.

Approaching the corporate foundation is done the same as approaching any other foundation, as will be discussed below. Approaching the corporation directly involves finding and contacting the person in charge of community relations activities in the organization. Once this person is identified, the contact involves doing some of the same kind of screening as for any other funding source, that is, what types of activities does the company give grant monies for? What is the average amount of grant? What are the application procedures? How long does the review process take?

Two resources for finding out about corporations are the Taft Corporate Giving Directory and the Corporate Fund Raising Directory.

Taft Corporate Giving Directory: This book profiles more than 500 corporate giving programs, the type of support they provide, whom to contact, and how much money is available.

The Corporate Fund Raising Directory: This book provides information on over 600 corporations, contact persons, headquarters, geographic preferences for giving, and corporations that issue guidelines.

Once likely candidates for funding are located, they must be evaluated for appropriateness.

Evaluate and Select Appropriate Funding Source

As the grantwriter searches through directories of assistance for possible funding sources, some criteria should be kept in mind for evaluating and selecting possible sources for further inquiry. This will help eliminate those resources that are not appropriate for the agency. A screening list such as that shown in Table 5-3 may be helpful.

Table 5-1: Screening Funding Sources

	Yes	No	Unknown—Need more Information
1. Does this source fund in my agency's geographical area?	___	___	___
2. Does this source fund programs similar to my agency's?	___	___	___
3. Does this source have enough resources to fund the project?	___	___	___
4. Is the potential dollar amount adequate?	___	___	___
5. Does my agency meet the minimal eligibility requirements?	___	___	___
6. Is the grant duration sufficient?	___	___	___

Does This Source Fund in Your Agency's Geographical Area?

What are the geographical boundaries of the funding, e.g., local, regional, national? This is one of the first things to be ascertained in screening a funding source, if the organization is not interested in funding in your geographical area, you are wasting your time and it should be automatically eliminated from further consideration.

Does This Source Want to Fund the Types of Programs/Activities That are Similar to What Your Agency Wants to Do?

What kinds of programs/activities have recently received funding from this source? Look to see what types of projects or programs the organization has targeted for its funding. Most funding organizations will list their funding priorities. Are these activities in any way related to the types of activities your agency has in mind? If so, continue to scan for more information.

Does the Source Have Enough Resources to Fund This Project?

In looking at the resources of the funder, one of the most important questions is whether or not it has enough to fund your project. Usually most foundations have their assets listed, so one needs to look for information such as: how much money has it given recently? You might also try to ascertain the dollar amount that the organization has reserved for grants for the coming year.

Is the Potential Dollar Amount of the Grant What the Agency is Seeking?

What is the average size grant? Determining the average size grant awarded in the past gives a clue as to the amount of grant that is likely to be funded in the coming year. Finding this information helps give clues as to the appropriateness of the funder for your agency's proposal. That is, if the average size grant is much smaller than your agency was looking for, chances are slim that you will get the amount you want from this source.

Does my Agency Meet the Minimal Eligibility Requirements?

Given that this funding source funds in your geographical area, is interested in your stated problem or need, and has grant monies available in the amounts you are requesting, try to gauge whether your organization meets the eligibility requirements of the funder. Even though your agency may be nonprofit, established for charitable purposes, it may still not meet the requirements of the funder who may specify a certain type of organization that it is seeking to fund; for example, one that serves a specific population or group—the handicapped, women, minorities, children, and so forth.

Is the Duration of the Grant of Sufficient Length?

Look to see what the duration of the grant is and whether it is long enough to complete the agency's new program, or at least demonstrate its effectiveness or feasibility. Try to ascertain whether renewals of the grant will be considered. If not, then additional funding for ongoing operations must be explored.

After these basic criteria have been used to screen potential funding sources, some may be selected at this point for further information. Usually a contact person is listed in the directory and whether or not he/she will accept queries by phone.

Initiate Contact with Funding Sources

After the potential funding sources have been narrowed down to those which appear most likely to fit the agency in terms of goals, amounts provided, interests, and so forth, someone from the agency needs to call or write the contact person at the funding organization who is listed on the RFP or grant directory. The most likely person to do this is the executive director of the agency, who will, in all likelihood, be involved in the grantwriting effort.

The director or staff person should try to get as much information as possible regarding what is involved in the application process, including forms, procedures for submission of the proposal, guidelines for the proposal, criteria for review of proposal, how often the review committee meets, funding dates, and so forth. Try to find out from the contact person whether your proposal falls within the interests of the funding organization, and whether funder staff are willing to provide any technical assistance or feedback regarding your grant proposal. If you have ascertained that your project falls within the purview of the funder, ask for application instructions and materials from the sources selected.

If the agency or grantwriter has followed all the steps list here, he or she will now be ready to write the grant proposal.

WRITING THE GRANT PROPOSAL

The second concern, writing the grant proposal, will be addressed in a general way in Reading 5-1, since most funders have specific guidelines for the proposals that they will accept for review. The writer(s) must follow the guidelines of the funding source in writing and submitting a grant proposal or risk rejection before the proposal itself is even read. Therefore, the comments in Reading 5-1 are offered as a general overview of the most common elements in a proposal. In discussing the mechanics of putting together a proposal, there are certain aspects of the writing that are assumed here: namely, that the writer is able to write clearly, concisely, using correct English grammar and style, that the plan has been well conceived and can be explained simply in a logical fashion. Given these factors and the adherence to the specific requirements of the funding source, the grantwriter will be on the right track to getting in the competition for the scarce resources needed by the human service agency to fulfill its social mission.

Chapter Five
Questions and Topics for Discussion

1. What are some types of grants?
2. What are some of the tasks involved in planning a program or project that will be the basis of a grant proposal?
3. Where are some places to go to look for grant information?
4. Does your local public library or university library have a grants center? Find out from the librarian what grant information is available there.
5. What kinds of information should you look for as you review catalogues and directories of grant sources?

Exercise 5-1: Government RFP

Sometimes, in order to reduce the number of grant proposals to be read, a governmental agency will request preapplications to be submitted for grants. Successful agencies with well-thought out preapplications are then invited to submit final applications for consideration. The benefit to the grantwriters is that the pool of applicants will have been narrowed by the time the final application is written. Following are excerpts from an actual government RFP (Request for Proposal). Using the guidelines given here, write a preapplication for a grant.

Instructions for Project Narrative*

Describe the project you propose in response to this announcement. Your narrative (10 pages typed double-spaced, or five pages typed single-spaced, maximum, on 8½" × 11" plain white bond with 1" margins on both sides) should provide information on how the preapplication meets the review criteria. We strongly suggest that you follow these format and page limitations:

a. **State of Need for the Proposed Project** (2 pages maximum.) This portion of the preapplication should state the objectives of the project, including clear specification of the concrete outcome(s) expected of the project and HDS populations targeted. In addition, this portion should document the need for and importance of the issues to be addressed beyond the local area of the project. It should also describe how the proposed project builds upon previous work and how it advances the state of knowledge from a national perspective.

b. **Results and Benefits Expected** (1 page maximum.) this portion of the program narrative should briefly summarize the anticipated results and delineate the benefits which are expected. Emphasis should be placed on outcomes as opposed to process measures. Projects should result, for example, in the employment of a specific number of people rather than just the training of people to increase employability.

c. **Approach. Project Design** (5 pages maximum.) This portion of the program narrative should describe specific plans for conducting the project. It should include relevant information about: (a) hypotheses to be tested (if appropriate); (b) data to be collected (including specification of data sources); (c) plan for data analysis; (d) what the project will do; (e) who will do it.

d. **Utilization and Dissemination** (1 page maximum). This portion of the narrative should address the project's responsibility to serve as a source of information to other agencies and/or researchers. This section should describe ways in which the project will share its experiences and findings with the field of human services in general and, specifically, with agencies or organizations capable of developing improved service delivery and management.

---

* Taken from: Federal Register. Part V, Department of Health and Human Services, Office of Human Development Services, FY 1984, Coordinated Discretionary Funds Program, October 18, 1983, pp. 48392–48397.

e. Level of Effort (1 page maximum.) This part of the narrative should describe what staff, money, facilities and time would be required to complete the project as envisioned. Describe the resources needed to carry out the project. State the total Federal funds required to complete the project as proposed.

Organizational Capability Statement:

A brief (maximum 2 pages double-spaced or one page single-spaced) background description of how the applicant agency is organized and the types and quantity of services it provides or research capabilities it possesses. Include descriptions of any current or previous relevant experience. Describe the competence of the project team and its demonstrated ability to produce a final product that is readily comprehensible and usable. The qualifications of key staff should be described in a few paragraphs rather than in formal vitae. (A copy of (Standard Form [SF] 424 is shown in Appendix.)

Exercise 5-2: Foundation Guidelines

Following are guidelines for grant proposals issued by a foundation. Using these guidelines, write a grant proposal on a topic of your choice. Alternatively, use your field placement, job site, or a human service agency in your community that you are familiar with, and write a grant proposal for your chosen agency.

OUTLINE FOR GRANT APPLICATION
XYZ FOUNDATION

Grant applications should not be lengthy. It is helpful in evaluating grant requests if the prepared material follows the format suggested in the outline below:

I. A concise, one-page statement, summarizing the elements of the grant request.

II. Background information on organization seeking funds:

    A. Name and purpose of organization
    B. Summary of organization's activities
    C. Names of Board of Directors and their business affiliations
    D. Names of professional staff, positions held, and qualifications

E. Financial statements
   1. Balance sheet
   2. Current operating budget
   3. Analysis of sources of funding
F. A copy of I.R.S. letter of notification indicating the type of exempt classification the organization has qualified for and all subsequent communications from I.R.S. concerning exempt status.
G. Signed statement from administrator that no funds granted to the organization will be used for activities prohibited by the 1969 Tax Reform Act.
H. Letter of approval from Chief Administrator if request is signed by Division or Department Head of a large institution or organization.

III. Summary of Proposed Activity for Which Funds Are Being Sought:

A. Nature of the problem
B. Goals and objectives of the project
C. Justification for need
D. Plans for administration and operation of proposed activity
E. Dates for implementation and conclusion
F. Plans for evaluating the impact or success of the project
G. Statement of all budgeted expenditures itemized by account
H. Funds on hand or pledged (if any) and other potential sources of funds
I. Nature and source of long-term funding commitments
J. Specified amount requested from the XYZ Foundation
K. Pictures, diagrams, or other descriptive information (if appropriate and available)

IV. Copies of Other Supportive Material (if available)

A. Letters of support from local authorities
B. Letters of support from affiliated national organizations
C. Research studies or reports justifying need
D. Names of key persons backing projects

Case 5-1: Multipurpose Center of Urban County, Inc.

The Multipurpose Center of Urban County, Inc. is a voluntary, non-profit human service agency whose goal is to strengthen families and individuals by helping with life problems through counseling, crisis intervention, home health services, and family life education. The counseling services include services to individuals and families in the areas of child abuse, drug abuse, and the sponsorship of a parents anonymous group. The agency employs a staff of about 50, of which 10 are administrative/support, 20 are employed in counseling (both full and part-time), 2 are in crisis intervention, 3 are in family life education, and 15 are involved in home health services, mainly as home help aids.

The agency receives funds from five main sources at the present time: government fees and grants, United Way allocations, client fees, contributions, and investment income. The breakdown is as follows:

Govt. fees and grants	55%
United Way	25%
Client fees	10%
Investment income	5%
Contributions	5%
	100%

The government fees and grants are monies from contracts with the State Department of Social Services, Division of Child Welfare, to provide counseling services to abusive parents and their children. The United Way allocation helps subsidize the other programs offered by the agency, as most clients are unable to pay very much. The agency uses a sliding scale fee, whose minimum was recently raised from $0 to $2.50. Even with this increase, client fees make up only a small percentage of the revenue for this agency.

The agency would like to start a new program of counseling youth between the ages of 12 and 17, as it has done a needs assessment survey and found that Urban County youth have serious problems: the county has one of the highest school dropout rates and one of the highest teen pregnancy rates in the nation. Teen runaways, suicides, and substance abuse are also problems.

The agency has a well-deserved highly respected reputation in the community for delivering quality services. It would need additional staff and space to be able to provide the proposed new service. You have been hired by this agency as a consultant to help obtain a grant for the agency's proposed new youth counseling/outreach program. The agency is particularly interested in foundation funding, which it has no experience in. What steps would you take to find a suitable funding source for this agency?

Reading 5-1: Proposal Development and Preparation*

One of the most common mistakes made in proposal efforts is immediately assigning people to begin writing. The writing phase of a proposal effort is important, but this is the second step of the process. The FIRST STEP is to plan an effective approach to the project or activity you want supported and to collect documentation that will make a strong case for support. No amount of writing ability can disguise thin content or mediocre strategies. So be aware that proposal efforts have two distinct phases:

• The development (or strategy) phase focuses on the CONTENT of the proposal. In other words, you plan WHAT to say.

• The preparation (or writing and packaging) phase focuses on the ORGANIZATION, STYLE, and PRESENTATION of the proposal. In other words, you decide HOW to communicate key content points effectively.

Before the content discussion begins, it will be helpful for the proposal-development group to be aware of the items review committees typically look for in proposals. These include the following:

• The proposed project/activity matches the objectives and priorities of the source of support.
• The proposed project/activity matches the overall goals of the applicant organization.
• The proposed project/activity will solve a real problem or meet a real need.
• The applicant organization is qualified to manage and conduct the proposed project/activity.
• The applicant organization demonstrates a state-of-the-art knowledge in the field of the proposed project/activity, including:
  • What has been accomplished in this area in the past.
  • What others have done about similar problems or needs.
• The applicant organization has community support for the proposed project/activity, if appropriate.

The group will want to be sure to cover all these topics thoroughly as it develops the content of the proposal. In addition, they should be aware that proposals are rejected for four basic reasons:

―――――――――
*Reprinted from: BASIC SKILLS IN CREATIVE FINANCING, Student Manual. EMI Professional Development Series, Federal Emergency Management Agency, National Emergency Training Center, Emergency Management Institute, Summer 1983, pp. 185–196.

- The applicant organization fails to demonstrate its credibility.
- The proposed project/activity is not feasible or lacks a sound strategy for implementation.
- The applicant organization fails to follow application instructions or procedures.
- The proposal content, style, and/or packaging are sloppy.

During the content planning session, the group should focus on developing approaches and information to be included in all nine elements of the proposal. These elements are described in detail in the next part of this section. The group should take time to become familiar with the general content to be included in each of these standard elements before beginning the discussion.

In addition, as you learn about the standard proposal elements, you will see that documentation you collected during previous steps of the . . . [proposal] process will come in handy now. You should have data on problems and needs as well as on local resources. Don't hesitate to offer this documentation if it is pertinent to the proposal. Your facts and figures may be just the right concrete information to convince an outside source that your community has a real problem. Your information can also be used to show that your community is doing everything possible with existing local resources. With these facts established, it is relatively easy to show why you are seeking support.

PREPARING THE FINAL PROPOSAL

In preparing most proposals to either public or private sources, writers will want to follow a format that includes the nine standard proposal elements described below.

Basic Elements of a Proposal

The following nine standard elements are described in the order in which they should appear in the final proposal.

The ABSTRACT should summarize key content points made throughout the proposal. This is the last section to be written but the first to be read. The abstract should briefly describe the capabilities of the applicant organization. It should also discuss the need for the proposed project and the expected results (or benefits) to local . . . [agency] efforts. The abstract should present the nature and scope of the proposed project, the project objectives, an overview of implementation methods to be used, and an overall cost figure. It should not be longer than one page.

The INTRODUCTION should describe the qualifications, credibility, and experience of the applicant organization. It should include a statement of how and why the applicant organization was founded and an overview of recent successes and accomplishments. It should discuss how the organization is managed and structured and what staff has achieved. The introduction may also mention community support or other endorsements. In general, the introduction should convince the source that the applicant organization can manage projects and funds competently. In preparing the introduction, "canned" materials containing irrelevant information should be avoided in favor of facts pertinent to the proposal at hand. The introduction should be specific about organizational accomplishments similar to the proposed project.

The PROBLEM STATEMENT is the keystone of the proposal. It should document the problem to be solved through the proposed project and describe how support from the outside source will be used. In developing the problem statement, it is best to avoid negative terms such as "lack of" or "failure to."

In preparing problem statements, it may be helpful to ask the following questions:

- What is the specific problem?
- Who is affected?
- Where are those affected located?
- What is the extent of the problem?

The PROJECT OBJECTIVES section of the proposal defines what will be accomplished or changed in relation to the problem. If the problem has been defined clearly, it should not be difficult to describe expected results in measurable terms. However, objectives should not be confused with methods. Objectives are measurable results; methods are the means of achieving objectives.

In developing objectives, it may be helpful to ask:

- What will be achieved?
- When will it be achieved?
- Who will benefit?
- Where will change take place?

The STRATEGY AND METHODS section should describe how project objectives will be achieved and how the applicant organization will use its resources to change the situation or problem. It should include some statements on the proposed overall strategy and specific descriptions of proposed activities during the period of funding. This section should also clarify reasons why this particular strategy was selected: how it was chosen, if similar programs elsewhere are working, and why this is the best approach to achieve results. In describing strategy and methods, the following points should be addressed:

- Development of the proposed project;
- Benefits of the proposed approach;
- How this approach will meet the need defined in the problem statement;
- The proposed project organization:
  - Staff and functions,
  - Performance milestones,
  - Operating procedures, and
  - Resources available to support the proposed project; and
- How the proposed project (including funds) will be managed.

The EVALUATION DESIGN should describe how progress toward achievement of the stated project objectives will be measured. The evaluation design should be an integral part of the proposal and project. Evaluation is an ongoing process that strengthens accountability to the community, the outside source, and public officials. It is also more than a collection of monthly reports, noting such things as the number of people served or problems solved. The project evaluation should generate evidence that change did or did not take place. It should answer questions such as:

- What did the project achieve?
- Where was it achieved?
- Who benefited from the change?
- How was achievement implemented? Was this the most effective way to accomplish objectives?
- Were project costs justified?

The evaluation design in the proposal should describe clearly:

- Specifically, what will be evaluated and what criteria will be used to measure progress;

- How the evaluation will be carried out:
  - Who will conduct it (staff or consultants);
  - How will it be conducted;
- What the time frame will be for evaluation results;
- Who will carry out the evaluation and what their credentials are;
- How the evaluation results will be used:
  - To modify the project;
  - To improve the project; and
  - To demonstrate that the project could be replicated in other communities.

The section of the proposal on FUTURE/OTHER FUNDING should describe a specific and concrete plan for project continuation. The plan could be based on getting guarantees from other funding sources or generating funds through the project. The outside sources will want to know what steps the applicant organization has taken to secure future funds and what commitments have already been made. Some . . . [creative strategies are]:

- Fees for services,
- Fund-raising efforts,
- Profit-making activities,
- Donated equipment from private corporations, and
- Use of volunteer services.

This section of the proposal is particularly important if the outside source requires local agencies to "match" their dollars with cash or noncash contributions.

The proposal BUDGET should clearly delineate estimated costs to be met by the outside source as well as costs to be provided by the applicant or other parties. It should also list specific cost items, justify these cost items, and correlate with the project strategy and methods. The format of the budget should follow what is required by the outside source and should provide the necessary detail. Personnel (or direct) costs would include such items as:

- Salaries and wages;
- Fringe benefits; and
- Consultant and contract services.

Nonpersonnel costs would include items such as:

- Facilities;

- Rental, lease, or purchase or equipment;
- Consumable supplies;
- Travel;
- Telephone;
- Printing; and
- Auditing.

APPENDICES containing additional information pertinent to the proposal may be attached. Appendices should contain all major documentation required by the outside source and any information necessary to substantiate the proposed project. Separate appendices may include:

- Letters of support or endorsement from key people in the community;
- Statistical charts, graphs, or tables to clarify points made in the proposal;
- Maps and brochures;
- Newspaper articles;
- Photographs;
- Organizational charts;
- Job descriptions;
- Government-required compliance or assurance forms; and
- A statement of approval of the proposed project prepared by local elected or appointed officials.

Appendices should not be overloaded with irrelevant information, and all items included should be referenced in the body of the proposal.

By including these nine elements in your proposal, you will be able to meet the requirements of most outside sources of support.

Stylizing the Proposal for Different Sources of Support

In approaching either federal or state sources of support, you will find they usually require that an application form with specific instructions be completed. Most federal sources use the Standard Form (SF) 424 application package. . . . requirements for the narrative portion of SF 424 correspond to the nine standard proposal elements discussed above. In completing SF 424 or any other special application package from a public source, be sure to follow instructions exactly. Remember that failure to follow application instructions is one of the major reasons why review committees reject proposals.

Foundations and other private sources usually do not provide a specific application form or package. They may provide general instructions about application requirements and procedures and expect you to take it from there. The best proposal to a private source will be a letter no more than five or six pages in length. The nine standard elements described above can be used to structure the narrative portion of the letter. Your proposed budget should be a separate, highly detailed attachment. Private sources are generally more interested in content than in form. But following the structure of the nine standard elements can ensure that your material is organized, thorough, and clear.

. . . . Especially with corporations, a written proposal alone will not automatically obtain support. Personal contact, organizational credibility, and the ability to "sell" your idea to executive management will be equally important. Have a top official in your community deal directly with a top executive in the corporation you wish to approach. Send your "brass" to deal with their "brass." A solid base of personal contact and interaction will probably have to be established before you reach the stage of putting anything in writing. In some cases, your top officials may be able to obtain a corporate contribution through negotiation alone.

Additional Tips on Writing and Packaging

Outside sources will view the proposal as a reflection of your organizational skills and abilities. Since you will be presenting your organization as credible, well-managed, and capable, you will want your proposal to be the best it can be. When writing and packaging your proposal, remember the following suggestions:

- Present all key content points in a logical and organized fashion.
- Use clear, direct, simple language. Avoid jargon. If you must use technical terms, acronyms, or terms known only to those in your local area, provide definitions.
- Document statements. Avoid unsupported assumptions such as "Everyone knows that . . . "
- Adopt a tone that is persuasive but not pleading, authoritative, but not authoritarian.
- Avoid negative language. Do not make accusations.
- Make sure the proposal is neatly and correctly typed.
- If your proposal is lengthy, you may want to bind it in an inexpensive folder (available at office supply stores). Add marked tabs between sections, if these will make the proposal easier to review.

- Have someone unfamiliar with your proposed project read the draft to see if it makes sense.

Distance yourself from the proposal, and try to view it as the review committee will.

Reading 5-2: Reflections of a Proposal Reviewer by Dick Schoech*

The following reflects my experience with reviewing proposals as a regional planner and as a reviewer for the Department of Health and Human Services.

Grant writing involves two related processes. The first is obtaining all necessary information from the granting agency while making a favorable impression. Agency staff are usually quite busy and do not have time for detailed conversations with all applicants. Be well organized before contacting them to ensure the receipt of relevant information.

The second process is technical writing. When writing the proposal, keep the reviewer in mind. Imagine yourself the reviewer sitting in a meeting or hotel room with 10 to 25 proposals to read and score in a day or two. After 8 to 10 hours of reading your eyes hurt, you are tired of sitting, you would like to socialize with other reviewers, and the many sights of Washington are just outside. Consider that the reviewers usually cannot devote over one-half hour to read and write up their comments on each concept paper or over one and one-half hours for each full proposal. If reviewers cannot understand your proposal from a quick reading, they will probably not rank it high. Prevent information overload. Key information should stand out. A well-organized format helps the reviewer skim for the crucial information. Do not be afraid to state the obvious because what may be obvious to you may not be obvious to the reviewer.

Know and use the review criteria. Reviewers usually do exactly as they are told. Request a copy of the review criteria and the reviewer's work sheets. If unavailable, request a copy of the previous year's and ask how the criteria has changed. Ask one or two of your colleagues who are totally unfamiliar with your proposal to critique it based on the review criteria. Try to simulate the actual review as closely as possible.

Determine what to include and exclude. A concept paper may only

---

*Reprinted with permission of author from Research Review, 11(9): 2–3, May 1984, Office of Sponsored Projects, University of Texas at Arlington.

need to present a good idea in an attractive manner. It might make the reviewer say, "this is an excellent concept and the applicant is well-qualified to implement it." Working details, such as budgetary specifics, may be better left to the full proposal where space is available to provide the necessary explanations. Review the criteria to see where the emphasis lies.

Cost is usually a key factor. Try to obtain a sense of the average grant award by reviewing previous awards. In reviewing at the local (city-county) level, I found the lower the overall cost the more favorably the agency viewed it. Many small grants result in more satisfied applicants and more community recognition. Grant monitoring is not problematic since the applicant and reviewers reside in the same community.

At the national level the process seems to be reversed. Grants are harder to monitor since staff is minimal and projects are distant. Monitoring many small grants can be a nightmare. Thus, large grants may be preferable to small projects. You may wish to make your proposal modular so that the budget can be cut without destroying the total project.

Allow enough time and use it wisely. In essence, the proposal preparation process should be divided into the three steps of (1) writing, (2) review, and (3) rewriting. Time may be a major factor. Make a time chart. Work backwards from the application due date and set deadlines for yourself. Allow extra time for unexpected problems. Use a word processor so that changes may be facilitated. Standard cover sheets should be substantially completed immediately since these forms often take longer than anticipated. Key information—budget, title, etc.—can be added at the last minute.

Don't take rejection personally. Proposals are not funded for many reasons other than quality. For example, a[n] . . . applicant may have received a grant last year and the agency wishes to share funding with other [agencies]. Submitting essentially the same proposal the following year may result in an award.

Proposal writing is like playing Bingo. You have to buy a card (write a proposal) to get in the game. You can increase your odds by paying attention to details and staying alert. However, the game is still one of chance and the odds of winning are never in your favor.

III. RESOURCE DISTRIBUTION AND CONTROL

Chapter Six

CONTROL

After reading this chapter you should be able to:

1. Understand the role of control techniques in financial management;
2. Set up a system for controlling costs;
3. Find unit costs for agency services;
4. Develop variance budgets;
5. Set up a system for control of cash in an agency.

INTRODUCTION

Management control involves the "measurement and correction of performance in order to make sure that enterprise objectives and the plans devised to attain them are being accomplished" (Koontz, O'Donnell, and Weirich, 1982:463). No matter what aspect of the agency is under scrutiny, there are certain aspects of control that apply in every case. That is, control as a process involves three steps: "(1) establishing standards, (2) measuring performance against these standards, and (3) correcting variations from standards and plans (Koontz, O'Donnell, and Weirich:464).

In systems terms, control is a sort of sensing procedure that continually scans and checks internal agency processes as well as the environmental climate and brings feedback to the organization so that it may make whatever adjustments are necessary to achieve its goals and maintain homeostasis. The usual analogy given in discussing control is that of a thermostat and the way it regulates temperature to stay at a constant level. There are many types of information that the agency uses in order to regulate its many service related and maintenance related activities. Service related activities involve direct service delivery, and thus service related information may include numbers of clients seen and number of units of service delivered—for example, hours of counseling, number of meals served, number of families referred for shelter, etc. Maintenance related activities are those tasks the agency needs to do in order to

133

survive or maintain itself. Maintenance related information may include such things as how much money was raised from fundraising efforts, how much income was derived from investments, how much in-kind goods and services were donated to the agency, and so forth.

Once the agency has gathered and received this feedback, it must measure its findings with the goals, plans, policies, procedures, and budgets that it has formulated. It must then take the necessary steps to discover and correct the causes of the variations that it has discovered (see Figure 6-1 for a systems view of the control process). In the discussion that follows, the focus will be on control mechanisms that involve the financial management subsystem of the agency.

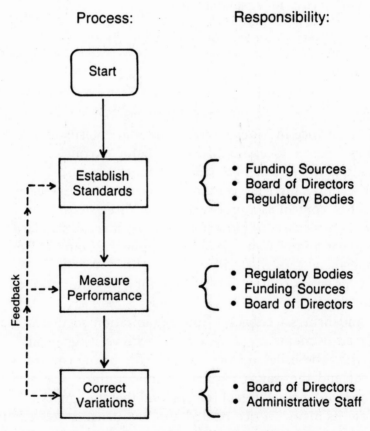

Figure 6-1: A Systems View of the Control Process

THE AGENCY CONTROL SYSTEM

The control system developed by the agency must be based on the plans that it has set for itself. It should be part of the evaluation system built into the agency's financial information system. There are a number of important factors to consider in the structuring of such a system. An effective control system should:

Fit the Organizational Climate: That is, the control system must be designed to be congruent with the particular demands and constraints of a given agency setting. Human service agencies are so unique and diverse that a control system set up to monitor one organization would be inappropriate in another.

Be Tailored to Plans and Positions: Any control system that is set up by the agency must reflect the long-range goals and plans of the agency, for, in effect, these are what the control system is set up to monitor. In addition, the system should be developed in such a way that it can quickly and accurately convey information to those in different positions in the organization. The control system should be able to meet the varying needs of different persons in different positions in the organization. For example, information needed by the clinical director may not be the same as that needed by the director of budgeting and planning, or the administrator of the agency.

Point Up Exceptions at Critical Points: An effective and efficient financial management system runs according to the rules of management by exception. That is, smoothly running activities are not routinely reported; rather those activities and events that deviate from the norm are reported so that analysis and corrective action may be taken.

Be Objective: While elements of subjectivity creep into any human system, an effective control system should be constructed in such a way that measurable standards of performance can be used in periodic review to judge the progress of agency and individual activities.

Be Flexible: No system should be so rigid that revisions cannot easily be made. Some provision should be made for periodic review, and revising, or modifying existing guidelines, policies and procedures.

Be Economical: A control system must efficiently do the job at a price that the agency can afford. This is a crucial factor in human service agencies, which usually have to operate with "bare-bones" budgets. How much a system will cost in terms of time, personnel, and materials must be evaluated in deciding on any control system.

Have a Reporting Provision: This applies in several ways. First of all, standards and criteria must be communicated to all employees. Second of all, instances of deviations from the norm should be communicated through appropriate channels. In some cases, this communication may just be in the form of discussion between a worker and a supervisor. In more serious cases, written documentation may be needed. Thirdly, forms which concisely and graphically display pertinent report information should be developed and used.

Be Meaningful: There must be some logic and rationale for the system developed, and this must be communicated to employees. Any system developed will be counter-productive if employees feel as though they are engaged in "busywork" by having to fill out forms for which they see no use.

Be Enforceable: Some method must be built into the system to ensure that policies, procedures, and rules will be enforced. That is, there must be sanctions for those who do not follow agency procedures, and there must be positive reinforcement or motivators for those that do (Koontz et al, 1982:473–481; Lohman, 1980:200–202).

In the following discussion, the focus will be on two main types of control in the human service agency: controlling costs and controlling cash and other assets. Controlling costs involves an understanding of how to figure and allocate costs. Control of cash and other assets involves the setting up of a system of checks and balances to minimize the potential of loss to the agency. Developing the kinds of control mechanisms described here will help the agency more effectively use the limited resources that it has.

CONTROLLING COSTS

Every human service agency operates in an environment in which it must compete with other valued entities and activities for scarce resources. For example, $150,000 that goes to one agency means that $150,000 will not be able to be used for a competing, but equally worthwhile, program because resources are finite. Thus the social programs that human service agencies use to promote the general welfare of a community and its citizens not only produce a social good, but have a cost as well.

Remember that when the agency prepares its operating budget, it estimates various costs related to its programs. But these are just estimates and plans of how funds will be allocated, rather than an actual list of expenditures that have taken place. In addition, the costs of certain agency activities are often hidden in the master budget because they are either part of a larger activity, or may be spread across programs. Thus, while budgets may serve as monetary reflections of agency goals and desired levels of programmatic activity expressed in dollars, they do not tell us the "true" costs of providing programs and serving clients. To be able to control costs, the agency must first be able to isolate and identify costs. It must also be able to allocate costs by program or service unit. Finally, it must be able to report variances from budgets on a regular basis. One of the first steps in devising a system for controlling costs is the setting up of a chart of accounts.

The Chart of Accounts

A chart of accounts may be defined as "a system for identifying and classifying various account titles and accounting transactions by:
"(1) The type of account or nature of transaction (what is it?), and
(2) The function of the accounting transaction (for what purpose did the transaction take place?); and,
may incorporate a coding scheme composed of numerals and/or letters of the alphabet" (United Way, 1974:34).

A chart of accounts is an integral part; indeed, it is at the core of an accounting system in an agency. The purpose of the chart of accounts is to enable users to use, identify, and classify agency activities easily, quickly, and in a uniform manner. Some of the other purposes of a chart of accounts are:

1. To facilitate the recording of financial transactions in a methodical, organized way;
2. to facilitate the posting of data with a minimum of effort; and
3. to facilitate the gathering and reporting of financial information to interested outsiders.

While a chart of accounts does not necessarily require a coding system, it does facilitate accounting operations, especially if the agency wants to computerize its operations. Table 6-1 illustrates the chart of accounts system developed by the United Way of America.

Table 6-1

UWAACS, UNITED WAY OF AMERICA ACCOUNTING CODING SYSTEM

In the UWAAC System, the core accounting codes are designated as follows:

Core Accounting Codes

0-0000

Fund Codes	Balance Sheet Accounts
1: Current Unrestricted	1000-1999: Assets
2: Current Restricted	2000-2999: Liabilites
3: Land, Bldg and Equipment	3000-3999: Fund Balances & Chgs
4: Endowment	4000-4999: Public Support
5: Custodian	5000-5999: Fees&Grants from Govt
6: Add if Necessary (AIN)	6000-6999: Other Revenue
7: AIN	7000-7999: Employee Compensation
8: Loan	8000-8999: Other Expenses
9: Annuity	9000-9999: Other Expenses

The first column on the left is reserved for fund codes, numerals one through nine. For example, 1 is reserved for the current unrestricted fund, 2 for the current restricted fund, and so forth.

The middle set of numbers are reserved for balance sheet accounts, with codes numbering 1000-9999. So in this case, 1000-1999 are for asset accounts, 2000-2999 are for liability accounts, and so forth.

If an agency had a account coded as follows: 1-1999 this would mean that monies received were to go to the current unrestricted fund, in an asset account.

Allocating Costs

Once an agency has set up a chart of accounts to help it properly code and classify its transactions, it must set up some type of system to allocate its costs. This is not a problem in the small, one program agency, because the agency knows that all the expenses it incurs are related to that one program. It becomes much more of a problem to allocate costs when there are a number of different programs in an agency.

While it is almost impossible to accurately allocate all of the costs in a multi-program agency, here are some steps that an agency can take to achieve this end (Standards, 1974:101–108):

Record Expenses by Function

At the point of original entry into the journal, expense transactions should be coded not just as to object category, but to program category whenever possible. When an expense benefits more than one program, the expense can be determined in different ways. For example, expenses such as rent, electricity, and heating can be determined according to the space used by various programs. Space used can be ascertained by measuring floor area, or by counting rooms. To illustrate, suppose an agency had a counseling program and a public education program in an office with eight rooms. One room would be a waiting room/secretarial area, another would be used by the executive director, one would be used by the public education program, one would be a conference room, and four rooms would be used for counseling. Since the counseling program uses fifty percent of the rooms, fifty percent of the overhead costs may be charged to that program.

Some expenses such as travel expenses, and salaries can be broken down according to time spent on a particular function. Determining time spent on various functions necessitates some method of analyzing and reporting employee duties periodically. This may entail the use of time reporting, as explained below.

Use Time Reporting

Personnel costs usually make up the largest proportion of costs in a human service agency. In large agencies, as an example of the principle of differentiation, job categories tend to be much more rigid and workers tend to fill one job or program function only. In small agencies, on the other hand, work loads tend to be much more flexible and workers must fill in wherever help is needed. In these cases, it is even more important for time/function sheets to be used. However, the method of reporting chosen by the agency should not be burdensome to the workers and create what they will perceive as additional, unnecessary paperwork. A daily time record form could be used at periodic intervals to survey amount of work performed in various functions. This type of random sampling should give the agency a fair idea of the amount of time spent by employees whose jobs span more than one programmatic area.

Some Key Points in Setting Up a Time Report System:

- Randomly select representative employees. That is, not all employees should have to fill out the forms every time. Choose different employees who are representative of key positions. For example, rather than all child welfare workers having to time report, only a few from different offices or units would be sufficient.
- Train these employees, not just in filling out the form, but in the importance of the form. If they do not understand the reasons for the form, they will view it as busywork.
- Require that reports be completed on a periodic basis, for example, one week a month per quarter.
- Make sure the reports are reviewed and signed by the appropriate supervisor. The supervisor should check and verify with the employee that the time reported for tasks listed is an accurate reflection of what the employee actually did that week.
- In designing the report form, ease and simplicity should be the key. Remember to include items such as task performed, hours spent on task, and program related to task (see Table 6-2).
- Finally, develop a summary report that can be used in preparing the Statement of Functional Expenses.

Set up Responsibility/Cost Centers

A responsibility/cost center is a program, department, or unit of an agency that is responsible for its own budget and expenses. This type of center thus has to keep track of its expenses. A system such as this, common in the business world, makes managers much more cognizant and careful of the expenses they incur. Each responsibility/cost center will have to tie its goals to the budget it develops, be able to justify its expenses, and use variance budgeting to monitor its progress. Variance budgeting will be discussed later in this chapter.

Figuring Costs

Once the agency has developed its chart of accounts and some method for allocating costs, it can then proceed to an analysis of its costs. There are a number of different techniques that have been developed to calculate the costs of human services programs. These costing methods differ in three main ways: 1) in addressing the question of who incurs the cost;

Table 6-2

SAMPLE TIME REPORT FORM

Name_____ Date_____

Department/Unit/Program_____

Time Start	Time End	Task Performed	Program
----------	--------	-----------------------	-------------
----------	--------	-----------------------	-------------
----------	--------	-----------------------	-------------

Employee signature_____ Supervisor signature_____

2) in addressing the object of the cost analysis; and 3) in the methodology used to calculate the costs (Gross, 1980:33). In terms of who incurs the cost, it may be the client, it may be a third party such as a federal or state agency or an insurance plan, or it may be the human service agency incurring the costs which it tries to recoup through public donations and allocations from community allocation agencies.

The object of the cost analysis may be the client, such as numbers of clients served, it may be some other unit of measurement such as hours of service delivered, or number of meals served and so forth. And the methodology used to calculate the costs may vary tremendously, but tends to be related to the unit of analysis chosen.

The types of costing techniques that will be discussed here are related to costs incurred by the agency in delivering its services. Some common methodological approaches to ascertaining costs incurred by the agency are: average per person costing, unit costing, and average per employee costing.

Per Person Costing

The average cost per person is found by dividing the total program service costs by the number of people being served. For example, a senior citizens center that has a nutrition program may spend $100,000 per year to serve approximately 190 per day. 190 people for five days, 52 weeks a year equals 49,400 people. $100,000 divided by 49,400 people equals $2.02 per person per meal (see Table 6-3).

Table 6-3

PER PERSON COSTING

Source of Data

Total program costs   Budget

Avg Cost Per Person = ----------------------

Number of persons served   Daily Count

Unit Costing

The focus of unit costing is the cost of providing one unit of service (however defined). Defining a unit of service is based on the types of service offered by the agency, for example, if an agency offered counseling services, public education workshops, and home help services, then its units of service might be defined as one hour of counseling, one hour of public education, and one hour of home help. The cost of a unit of service is found by dividing the total amount spent by a cost center or program by the number of units of service provided. For example, in a children's home, if the cost of delivering group therapy 10 hours a week for 52 weeks were $100,000 per year and 520 units of service were provided during the year, then the unit cost would be $192.30 (see Table 6-4).

Average Cost Per Employee

Some organizations want to know how much it costs them per professional employee to provide a service. The average cost per direct service

Table 6-4

UNIT COSTING

		Source of data
Unit Cost =	Total program costs	Budget
	————————————	
	Number of units of service	Program count

or professional employee is found by dividing the total professional salaries in a program by the number of clients seen in that program. The source of information used in this analysis may be the functional budget or the statement of functional expenses for salaries, and the statistics gathered by the program for number of clients seen (see Table 6-5).

Table 6-5

AVERAGE PER EMPLOYEE COSTING

		Source
Average cost of service per professional employee =	Total professional salaries	Budget
	————————————————	
	Number of clients in program	Prog.Stats

Variance Budgets

Variance budgets show the differences between amounts budgeted and actual amounts. The variance budget is an important control tool because it may act as an important feedback or sensing mechanism, helping alert administrators and board members to deviations from anticipated expenditures and revenues. Analyzing the sources of the variances may also be helpful in subsequent budgeting, and information gleaned can result in more accurate forecasts of revenues and expenses.

While the variance in the budget shows how anticipated revenues and expenses vary from actual performance, the variance shown does not necessarily mean that this is an indication of poor or ineffective management. Any interpretation of variances must proceed with caution, for positive or negative variances may be misleading without a look at unforeseen factors, e.g., service volume over or under estimate, a cut in allocation or other public support, etc.

Two types of variance budgets of interest are revenue/public support budgets, and expense budgets, although they may also be combined into one budget for ease of analysis.

Revenue/Public Support

Revenue and public support are resource inputs into the human service organization. Revenue is derived from fees earned due to service delivery efforts, while public support includes allocations, grants, and contracts. In examining the differences between actual and budgeted revenue and public support, a favorable variance is one in which actual amounts exceed budgeted ones. In examining the reasons for a revenue/public support variance there are two components to be examined: volume and rate (Milani, 1982:68-69). Volume refers to the number of units of service offered and/or delivered. Volume could be a factor in variance when the number of clients projected, or the number of service units projected to be delivered fall short of the estimated amount, or exceed it. Rate refers to the amounts charged for services and/or products offered by the agency; in the case of public support, however, it may refer to amount of individual contributions to the agency. Rate could be a factor when client fees or estimated public support fall short of the projected amounts, or exceed it. In looking at these two components of variance, the socio-political and economic factors taken into account in the budgeting process need to be reexamined for possible clues for the variances.

Expense

Expenses are costs incurred by a human service agency in delivering its services. In examining the differences between actual and budgeted expenses, a favorable variance is one in which actual amounts are less than budgeted ones. In examining the reasons for an expense variance, there are two components that need to be examined: volume and cost. Volume could be a factor when the number of items budgeted—for example, office supplies—was used excessively during a period, or not totally used during the period. Cost could be a factor when an item was projected in the budget to cost a certain price, and the actual price is either above or below this figure. Thus, patterns of usage and economic trends need to be examined in analyzing expense variances.

Consistently wide variances, whether positive or negative should be examined by the agency and adjustments made, either in levels of spending, in levels of funds sought, or in subsequent forecasts. Variance budgets should be prepared quarterly and then analyzed for trends at the end of the year when the new budget is being prepared. They should be prepared quarterly in order to show seasonal variations, which in and of themselves may explain some of the variances (see Table 6-6).

Table 6-6

QUARTERLY VARIANCE BUDGET

	Budgeted	Actual	Variance	Comments
Revenue/Public Support	$120,000.	$150,000.	$30,000.	Unanticipated Bequest.
Expenses	$120,000.	$110,000.	($10,000.)	Budgeted item donated.
Total Variance			$ 40,000.	

Budget Summaries

Budget summaries are a compilation and summarization of all the individual budgets of an agency. This summary enables the agency to see service volume, costs, revenue, utilization of capital, investments, and so forth, in their relation to one another. In this way, agency administrators can see how the agency as a whole is meeting its objectives.

In order to best use the budget summary as a control tool, the administrator and budget committee should be fairly comfortable in assuming that total budgets are an accurate reflection of agency plans and goals. The budgets that make up the summary should be scrutinized to ensure that a comparison of budgeted and actual costs really reveal the true nature of any deviations. Minor deviations from budget are not a matter of concern because the purpose of a control system is to draw attention to significant variations from the norm. If the budget summary reveals that the agency is not moving toward its objectives, then the summary provides a way of quickly discovering where the problems are occurring (see Table 6-7).

Table 6-7

BUDGET SUMMARY: ALL PROGRAMS

	1st Quarter	2nd Quarter	3rd Quarter	4th Quarter	Total
Public Support	$ 90,000	$ 93,000	$ 97,400	$136,700	$417,100
Revenue	24,500	16,700	25,350	35,200	101,750
Total	$114,500	$109,700	$122,750	$171,900	$518,850
Expenses	$124,500	$124,600	$123,500	$126,350	$498,950

While the budget is an excellent control tool, it must be kept in mind that budgets do not replace a sound financial management system. Also, budgets are tools to be used by all program managers or others who have responsibility for agency programs and operations. And if budgetary control is to be workable in an agency, the budget committee should receive timely information on actual and estimated performance under budgets by those responsible for the budgets of their departments. Variance from budget must be communicated promptly to program managers to give them feedback as to how they are doing in order for them to take steps to avoid budget deviations.

CONTROLLING CASH AND OTHER ASSETS

Control was defined earlier as a system for monitoring the activities of the agency, providing feedback regarding these activities, and taking corrective action if necessary. While the focus of the preceding discussion was on methods of controlling costs, control of the physical assets of the agency should be an integral part of any such system. Our concern here is in the development of "a system of procedures and cross checking which in the absence of collusion minimizes the likelihood of misappro-priation of assets or misstatement of the accounts and maximizes the likelihood of detection if it occurs" (Gross and Warshauer, 1983:368).

Two of the most important tools of internal controls are the cash flow budget and the monthly budget. These forms were discussed in Chapter Three, they give a quick overall review of cash received and disbursed, and any deviations from the norm for the month. In order for a control system to be effective, however, there must be control over receipt of cash, disbursement of cash, bank deposits of cash, and recording of cash, as well as other physical assets of the agency. Besides budgeting, the other important elements of internal control of assets are: Personnel controls, transaction controls, and physical controls (Gross and Warshauer, 1983:360–369; Leduc and Callaghan, 1980:6-78/6-81; Sorensen, et al, 1983:59–68):

Personnel Controls

Personnel controls really should form the heart of a control system for assets. They involve three main aspects: separation of duties, indepen-dent checks, and bonding of personnel.

Separation of Duties

Ideally, the receiving of cash should be separated from the recording of cash transactions. This may be difficult in small agencies where the receptionist may also be the one who receives money and records the receipt of it. But the principal of separation of duties applies here most of all if the agency is going to have a meaningful control system. Some other person besides the bookkeeper should have the designated respon-sibility of receiving cash and preparing receipts. If cash is received through the mail, two persons should open the mail, one of whom may be the person who records receipt of cash.

Two signatures should be required on all checks in order to have better control over payments. The signers should be the director of the agency and a board member, but not the bookkeeper as the bookkeeper has to record the transaction in the books.

The receipt and reconciliation of the bank statements should be done by someone other than the bookkeeper so as to provide a check on the bookkeeper's activities. Bonding of employees is another type of personnel control. Bonding is a process by which a fidelity company issues an insurance policy that protects the agency in case of loss or embezzlement. If assets are lost due to dishonest employees, the bonding company ensures that the agency can recover its loss. Bonding is seen as a deterrent to dishonesty, because in some cases bonding companies may screen employees for a company before they will cover them in a bond.

Transaction Controls

Transaction controls are concerned with ensuring that transactions are executed and recorded properly. Some methods of transaction control involve using prenumbered documents, controlling the access to documents, making permanent indications on documents, and requiring cash received or disbursed to be made by check only.

Prenumbered documents help the agency keep track of every transaction in some chronological sequence. For example, with prenumbered receipts, it is simple to notice if a receipt is missing. Even voided receipts should be kept and filed so as to account for every prenumbered document.

Controlling access to documents means that not just anyone in the agency should be able to take petty cash slips to fill out, or even sign authorization documents for receipt or disbursement of funds. In small agencies this is sometimes again a problem, especially if there is a shortage of staff on occasion and some cash transactions need to take place. But the agency should have a standard set of policies and procedures to handle these contingencies and a clear line of responsibility when it comes to receipt and disbursement of cash.

Making permanent indications on documents in the form of stamping, hole punching, or some other means, ensures that documents cannot be used again. In addition, they provide additional evidence as to date received, sent, disbursed, and so forth. Whatever mechanism used by the agency, having a distinctive logo reduces the risk that the markings will not be duplicated.

All receipts and disbursements should be made by check in order to have a permanent record of how much was paid to whom. This provides documentation to an auditor who will be able to trace the financial transaction. It also reduces the risk of loss when there is little or no cash in the agency.

Physical Controls

Along with personnel and transaction controls, there are physical control measures that can be taken by the agency. The objective of physical control measures is the safeguarding of assets and records. Equipment and other physical assets of the agency should be kept secured, with records of model numbers, identification numbers, and other such information on file. Supply rooms should be supervised, and periodic inventories made and recorded to determine patterns of usage as well as possible pilferage. Important documents relating to property and assets of the agency should be kept in a fireproof safe. Duplicates could be filed in a safe deposit as well as with the agency insurance company.

The internal control policies and procedures adopted by the human service agency help assure that its accounting data are accurate and reliable, that its assets are safeguarded, and that it is moving forward in promoting organizational efficiency to better serve its client population.

Chapter Six
Questions and Topics for Discussion

1. What is control in the human service agency?
2. What are some components of an effective control system?
3. Of what value is a chart of accounts?
4. If an agency had chart of accounts based on the UWAACS schema, what would the following account codes mean: 1-2000, 2-3000, 3-4000?
4. What are some means of allocating costs?
5. What is the formula for determining unit costs?
6. What is the formula for determining cost per person?
7. How can you determine cost per employee?
8. What are the advantage of using a variance budget?
9. What are some steps the human service agency needs to take in order to have an adequate control of cash?

Exercise 6-1: Cost Analysis

Using your field placement or job as the unit of analysis, find out what methods of costing are used by the agency, e.g., unit costing, per person costing, etc. Then try to determine how this information is used by the agency.

What is your assessment of the costing approach used, that is, would alternative methods might be used?

What other uses could the agency have for the data it collects for costing?

Case 6-1: The Murray Children's Home*

The Murray Children's Home is a 24-hour residential care facility for boys and girls under the age of 18 who are suffering from emotional or situational problems that necessitate their removal from the home. It is a 50-bed facility that offers the following services:

- Room and board (i.e., a bed, meals, and basic supervision);
- Educational services (an on-campus school as well as transportation to community schools and tutorials);
- Counseling.

A variety of staff are employed within departments corresponding to each of the above service components. In addition, the following organizational units are necessary to operate the facility: general administration, training, maintenance, kitchen, and housekeeping. The kitchen and housekeeping units report to the supervisor of the room and board department. The resulting organizational chart is shown in Figure 6-2.

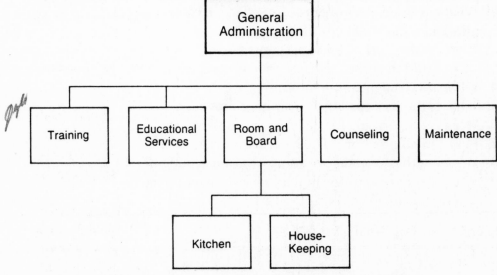

Figure 6-2: Organizational Chart of Murray Children's Home

*Adapted from Richardson, David A. Jr.: *Rate Setting in the Human Services: A Guide for Administrators.* Human Services Monograph Series, No. 24. Project Share, Dept. of Health and Human Services. Rockville, 1981.

The agency has established a chart of accounts that is divided into three components. The first component lists the names of the primary expense accounts. To facilitate budgeting and fiscal control, the home has adopted the primary account directly from the organizational chart. Hence, account number 01 is the general administration account, 02 is the maintenance account, etc. An additional primary expense account, the plant account, does not relate to the organizational chart. This account is used to record expenditures for depreciation and mortgage payments for the buildings and grounds. The primary accounts provide for the accumulation of the home's expenses by each of its major organizational units and for its facilities and grounds.

The second component is the objects of expense, that is, the general categories of expenditures made by one or more of the agency's organizational units. To simplify this presentation, the hypothetical objects of expense are limited to the following:

01	direct salaries
02	fringe benefits
03	equipment
04	goods and services

The third component is a detailing of the types of expenditures that can be made within each of the preceding four objects of expense. For example, within object 01 (direct salaries), the expenditures could be specified by type and grade of employee:

.01	clerical trainee
.02	clerical (senior)
.03	clerical (supervisor)

. . . This component (expenditure by type) is used simply to add detail to the accounting system and to its expenditure reports. . . .

With the omission of the "type of expense" detail, the structure of the hypothetical chart of account for the Murray Children's Home can be viewed as a matrix (see Table 6-8).

The same matrix can be used to exemplify the expense account reports provided by the traditional accounting system. Hence, Table 6-8 shows hypothetical expense data for a 1-year period. These data can be interpreted as a unit by unit expense report for a prior year, as well as an agencywide total for the Children's Home. The same method of presentation might be used to summarize the home's budget for the upcoming year.

In either case, this report form exemplifies the final "output," or definition, of . . . agency costs provided in a traditional accounting system. The

Table 6-8

EXPENDITURES BY ACCOUNT AND OBJECT OF EXPENSE
FOR MURRAY CHILDREN'S HOME

Expense Objects →						
Primary Account Titles ↓	.01 Direct Salary	.02 Fringe Benefits	.03 Equipment	.04 Goods and Services	.05 Facility Mortgage	*Total by Account*
01. General Administrative Unit	100,000	20,000	5,000	10,000	—	135,000
02. Training Unit	26,000	5,200	500	1,000	—	32,700
03. Maintenance Unit	30,000	6,000	8,000	4,000	—	48,000
04. Educational Unit	60,000	12,000	2,000	1,000	—	75,000
05. Counseling Unit	40,000	8,000	500	10,000	—	58,500
06. Room and Board Unit*	120,000	24,000	5,000	26,000	—	175,000
07. Plant Expense	—	—	—	—	90,000	90,000
Agency Totals	*376,000*	*75,200*	*21,000*	*52,000*	*90,000*	*614,200*

Note: Matrix does not show revenue accounts or detail of "type of expense" within each object of expense.
* Includes kitchen and housekeeping units.

distinguishing characteristic of the traditional accounting cost definition is observed on this form: Expense is defined in terms of the costs the agency incurs for goods and services that are utilized inputs to its program. The home's "output" of services (e.g., number of each service provided) is not depicted on the traditional accounting report. Nor does the format define the total costs incurred for each type of service or for each unit of service.

Unit Costing

Unit costing employs the expense data found in traditional accounting reports. However, cost finding (or unit costing) does not define costs in terms of "types" of . . . agency expenditures. Rather, cost finding defines expenses in relation to the types and quantities of client services actually delivered by the . . . agency. In other words, this approach finds the total amount of dollars the . . . agency expends for the delivery of each service in its program.

In Table 6-8, the direct costs of room and board were given as:

Room and Board Expense Object	Amount
Direct salaries	$120,000
Fringe benefits	24,000
Equipment	5,000
Supplies and service	26,000
Total	175,000

In the children's home, a cost center structure has been set up. The following classification of final service-providing centers and support cost centers is used:

Support Cost Centers	Final Service-Producing Cost Centers
Administrative unit	Room and board unit
Training unit	Educational unit
Maintenance unit	Counseling unit
Plant expense	

In order to be able to allocate costs to the appropriate unit, the agency has to be able to base its allocation on some criteria. Table 6-9 describes the nature and use of the allocation bases used by the agency. Note that each allocation base has a rule for valuing a particular service provided by a support unit to a receiving unit.

This agency uses the direct allocation method of finding indirect costs. Based on its findings, it has come up with the following amounts of indirect costs for its programs as seen in Table 6–10.

In order to ascertain its unit costs, the agency has also defined its service units as follows:

Service	Unit Definition
Room and board	Day of care
Education	Credit hour
Counseling	Hour of service

It has analyzed its utilization rates and come up with the following data for the last fiscal year:

Days of care provided	=	10,000
Credit hours provided	=	800
Counseling hours provided	=	5,000

Table 6-9

EXAMPLES OF BASES OF ALLOCATION
FOR MURRAY CHILDREN'S HOME

Good or Service Provided by Support to Other Unit (Cost Center	*Type of Expense to be Allocated**	*Examples of Allocation Basis*
Office Space	Rent, depreciation, mortgage payments	Percentage of total agency office square footage occupied by unit
Equipment (e.g., copier)	Rental costs, depreciation, paper, and supply costs	• Percentage of total copies made • Percentage of benefiting unit direct costs to total agency costs
Employee Fringe Benefits	Agency FICA payments, agency payments for health, life insurance	• Actual expenses recorded for each employee • Percentage of unit's payroll costs to total agency costs
Maintenance (e.g., repair of facilities)	• Direct costs of maintenance unit (salaries, benefits, etc.) • Indirect costs allocated to maintenance (e.g., plant)	• Percentage of total hours maintenance staff work on benefited unit • Percentage of work orders from benefited unit
Travel	• Employee personal auto mileage charges • Air fares • Conference fees • Hotel and meals	• Itemized charges per employee • Percentage of unit's charge for administration or training
Training	• Training consultant fees • Training staff salaries and indirect costs	• Itemized costs per employee trained • Percentage of staff hours spent on benefited unit

* For certain examples, the types are mutually exclusive alternatives.

Based on this information, you are to do the following:

1. Compute the total of direct and indirect costs for each direct service center and complete Table 6-10 on next page.

Table 6-10

SUMMARY OF COST FINDING
FOR MURRAY CHILDREN'S HOME

Direct Service Centers	Allocations by Support Unit $				Total of Indirect $	Total Direct $	Total Service Costs
	Plant	Admin.	Maint.	Train.			
Education	30,000	40,000	18,000	12,700			
Counseling	10,000	15,000	5,000	15,000			
Room and Board	50,000	80,000	25,000	5,000			
Agency Total	90,000	135,000	48,000	32,700			

Note: Presentation assumes direct allocation method of cost finding.

2. Compute the unit costs per service unit.
3. Analyze your results by answering the following questions:
    a. Of what use is this information to the agency?
    b. What other methods of allocating costs could it use?
    c. Does it have enough information to determine the break-even point? If not, what other information does it need?

Reading 6-1: "The $35.50 Solution"*

TDMHMR [Texas Department of Mental Health and Mental Retardation], presented with the challenge of achieving court-ordered staff-to-patient ratios in state hospitals while facing a long-existing shortage of funds, molded a plan that not only fulfills the court's requirements. It also propels the department toward its goal of caring for patients in the community when it is in their best interest.

The court-ordered ratios were established in 1984 based on a 1981 federal court agreement in the RAJ v. Miller lawsuit, a class action brought against the department by state hospital patients.

---

*Reprinted from: *Impact*, Texas Department of Mental Health and Mental Retardation, September/October 1984.

The solution calls for TDMHMR to pay mental health authorities $35.50 for each patient day reduced from the state hospital census.

Where does this figure come from? Where will the money go, and who will be accountable for it? Why doesn't the department instead hire more hospital direct care workers to correct the ratios?

Impact discussed this with Jaylon Fincannon, deputy commissioner for management and support services and one of the main architects of the solution. Following is an explanation of the plan to comply with staffing requirements of the court agreement.

To bring state hospital staff-to-patient ratios into alignment with requirements of the 1984 court order, TDMHMR adopted a plan that will reduce the population of those facilities by 1,288 patients over a one-year period.

According to the plan, the department will provide financial assistance for community care of patients, including those who have been discharged from state hospitals or whose hospital admission has been averted through services in their home communities.

"The simplest way to correct the ratios would have been to hire more direct care workers," says Fincannon, "but we wouldn't be meeting the goal of the department by doing that. The goal is to care for patients in the community whenever appropriate and feasible."

Staff-to-patient ratios must be 1 to 5 during the 7 a.m. to 3 p.m. and 3 p.m. to 11 a.m. shifts; they must be 1 to 10 during the 11 p.m. to 7 a.m. shift. The ratios apply to general psychiatric units and some specialty units.

Each of the state's 60 mental health authorities will receive the $35.50 per-patient-per-day payment for individuals from their local service area who otherwise would be in state hospitals. The MH authority, responsible for coordinating services at the local level for people with mental illness, will use the funds to provide additional community services.

If the state hospital census cannot be sufficiently reduced to meet these ratios, the department will hire additional MHMR series personnel to augment the direct care staff.

Fincannon explains how he arrived at the $35.50 figure.

First, though, he points out that the department has the option of meeting ratios by reducing the state hospital census by 1,288 patients, by adding 1,095 MHMR series personnel or by implementing an equivalent combination of both approaches.

The cost of hiring 1,095 direct care workers would be $16,687,800 benefits.

Since the department intends to reduce the state hospital rolls in lieu of hiring staff, Fincannon divides the $16,687,800 by 1,288, the number of patients by which [the] state hospital population will be reduced. The resulting amount, divided by 365 days per year, equals $35.50 per patient per day, or $35.50 per bed day.

"This is not to say that we think it costs $35.50 to serve someone in the community," says Fincannon. "But," he adds, "this approach is an equitable way of distributing the limited funds we have to work with."

Since it is not feasible to expect the staff-to-patient ratios to be immediately accomplished, the court has granted the department a year to do it. In FY 1985 the adjustment will be phased in quarterly increments, thus requiring approximately $10.4 million, considerably less than the nearly $16.7 million that will be needed annually once the program is in full operation in FY 1986.

As salaries increase yearly, so will the amount needed by the department for this effort. TDMHMR has requested the additional funds from the legislature for FY 1986 and FY 1987 to keep pace with increasing salaries and allow the per-bed-day amount also to increase.

Reading 6-1 Questions:

1. What method was used by this agency to determine cost-per-patient?
2. What do you think of this agency's method for determining cost? Have they really determined cost-per-patient? If not, what does the $35.50 represent?
3. What other methods could this agency have used to discover cost-per-patient?
4. What factors impact on this agency's costs?

Chapter Seven

INVESTMENTS

After reading this chapter you should be able to:

1. Describe the major types of investments;
2. Discuss the advantages and disadvantages of different investment strategies;
3. Understand the varying degrees of risk involved in investments;
4. Develop an investment plan;
5. Know how to choose an investment consultant.

INTRODUCTION

Financial investment may be defined as the current commitment of funds in order to receive a future financial gain. In systems terms, the agency may have a need for a secure, continuing source of funds. It receives inputs in the form of endowment or surplus funds. Through a planning process it develops an investment strategy suitable for the agency within a legal, political, social, economic climate in which non-profit organizations interface with investment markets. The output of this investment process is an investment mix tailored to the special needs of the nonprofit human service agency (see Figure 7-1).

While some human service agencies barely have enough revenue and public support to go from one fiscal year to the next, some agencies are fortunate enough to have surplus funds that can be used for investment. At times an agency may receive restricted funds in the form of an endowment. An endowment is a monetary gift that can be invested and the earned interest used by an agency for designated purposes or just general operating expenses. Other sources of funds for investment may be temporary excess resources from the Current Unrestricted Fund, or excess monies from the more permanent Land, Building, and Equipment Fund. Restrictions mandated by the donor are a factor in investment decisionmaking, as are any legal restrictions that may apply. While the nonprofit agency may not be bound by legal restrictions as to types of

159

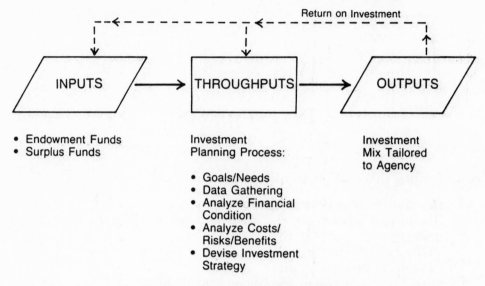

Figure 7-1: The Investment Subsystem

securities it may purchase, it may be bound by restrictions in its own charter.

When it comes to purchasing investment vehicles, the nonprofit human service agency is in a very different situation than the average investor. This is mainly due to Section 501(c)(3) of the Internal Revenue Code, which classifies most nonprofits as tax-exempt (see Appendix). One implication of this tax-exempt status is that the human service organization may not be motivated by some of the same considerations as other investors, such as the search for tax shelters, or the worry over capital gains taxes, etc. (Powell, 1978:131).

The purpose of this chapter is to familiarize human service professionals with some of the basics of investing. There are many different types of investments, the main types to be discussed in this chapter are the more conventional. There are other, somewhat more sophisticated, types of investments such as convertible securities and options that will not be discussed here. Also, other forms of investments such as art works, stamps, and coins will not be discussed; They take specialized knowledge that is beyond the realm of the typical human service agency. As with much of the subject matter of this book, investing is an art—not a science. Many people have developed their own approaches to analyzing and choosing investments. The important thing to understand is the element of risk, for after all, the money to be invested has been given in trust that the human service agency will use it wisely to further its humanitarian goals.

In this chapter investing by the human service agency will be viewed within the context of risk and long-range planning. Different types of investment vehicles will be described, as well as the advantages and disadvantages of each investment type. Since the aim of this chapter is to make human service agency staff informed investment clients, a discussion of factors to be considered in choosing an investment counselor will be presented. Reading 7-1 will hopefully facilitate an understanding of how investment information is presented to investors and the general public in the financial pages of the newspaper.

There are two main types of investments: fixed-income and variable income. Fixed-income investments, as the name implies, guarantee a given rate of return no matter how the economy fares over the life of the security. Variable-income investments, on the other hand, vary in their rate of return according to how well the company and the economy are doing. All these investments vary in their degree of safety, an important consideration for nonprofit organizations.

FIXED-INCOME INVESTMENTS

Bonds

A bond is a debt instrument, that is, a form of a loan by the person or organization that buys the bond to the issuer of the bond. These debt securities, or bonds, are issued for the purpose of raising money for the issuer. The major types of entities that issue bonds are corporations, the federal government, state, and local governments.

Bonds are considered fixed income securities because the bondholder's return is limited to the fixed interest and principal payments that the issuing organization agrees to pay. If bonds pay only a fixed amount, why would anyone invest in them? First of all, bonds do represent a stable source of current income for investors with that goal. It is a stable source of income precisely because the rate of interest is fixed. The second reason that investors buy bonds is for the possibility, for the more aggressive investor, of earning capital gains. Capital gains are earned because interest rates and prices of bonds tend to move in opposite directions, that is, bond prices rise when interest rates drop and when interest rates go up, bond prices fall (Gitman and Joehnk, 1981:292). This inverse correlation between bond prices and interest rates is the second reason that investors buy bonds.

Corporate Bonds

As you will recall, bonds are debt instruments and investors who buy them become creditors of the issuing institution. Corporations issue bonds to finance their investment projects. Issuing bonds can help the company reduce the cost of financing its projects and use the money it receives as leverage to improve its rate of return on equity capital (Khoury:254). Debt for the company occupies an advantageous position in relation to equity because of the tax deductibility of interest expenses for the issuing company. All types of corporations issue bonds. There are many different types of corporate bonds, but they will not be discussed here. For further discussion of these and other types of investments, the reader is referred to the bibliography at the end of this book.

Advantages and Disadvantages of Corporate Bonds

Advantages: Corporate bonds provide stability of income for investors with this goal, and the yield on corporate bonds is usually higher than for governmental securities. There is a high degree of safety of principal, another important goal for some investors. The degree of safety on high quality bonds is comparable to government bonds.

Disadvantages: There are no capital gains with corporate bonds, that is, the investor does not make money from appreciation in the value of the bond. There is also no buffer from inflation, because the investor is locked into a fixed rate of return with the bond (Amling, 1984:128–129).

Government Bonds

Government bonds are used by all types of federal, state and local authorities.

The United States Treasury issues three types of securities, they are called bills, notes, and bonds. A bill is a short-term type of debt instrument. In effect, this means that the buyer of the bill is lending money to the government. T-bills, as they are called, usually have a maturity of 13 or 26 weeks. They are sold at a discount from face value in denominations of $10,000. The investor receives a return in the difference between the purchase or discount price and the value of the bill at maturity. T-bills are purchased because they are considered to be a safe, secure investment as they are issued by the government. Notes are government coupon obligations with a fixed interest that is payable semiannually. These notes are medium-term debt instruments with a maturity of one to seven years. Treasury bonds are long-term debt instruments with a maturity of ten to twenty-five years. Notes and bonds are usually sold in denominations of $1,000 (Huang, 1981:11).

State and local governments also sell bonds. "All government debts issued by nonfederal agencies or the U.S. Treasury are called municipal bonds" (D'Ambrosio, 1976:89). Many government entities, such as cities, counties, water, and school districts issue bonds to raise money. One feature that makes municipal bonds so attractive to some investors, even though they pay lower rates of interest, is that interest income from these bonds is exempt from federal income taxes. Even though capital gains are taxable, bonds are exempt from federal income taxes and most states also do not tax income from their own bonds or those of their local governments. Probably because of these features, most municipal bonds have yields that are much less than prevailing interest rates. One draw-back to municipals is that some of them may have limited marketability, and thus this may mean lower liquidity for the agency (D'Ambrosio, 1976:92).

Advantages and Disadvantages of Governmental Securities

Advantages: There is minimal risk in acquiring governmental securities. This low market and business risk is due to the high safety of principal and stability of income attached to the securities. Governmental securities have high marketability, they can be acquired and disposed of easily and quickly. Long-term government bonds are not callable, this means that an investor can lock in a high rate of return and keep it, even if interest rates go down.

Disadvantages: One disadvantage of buying bonds is related to the fixed yield, that is, return will not fluctuate with the market rates or inflation. Thus, they provide no buffer for the investor. There is no capital gain with governmental securities unless a bond is selling below par when purchased (Amling, 1984:92).

Preferred Stocks

Preferred stocks possess characteristics of both common stocks and corporate bonds, thus they are considered a sort of hybrid security. Some of the characteristics they share with common stocks are that they represent equity ownership and are issued without stated maturity dates as bonds are. They also pay dividends as common stocks do. Preferreds are like bonds in that the owners or investors have a claim on the income and assets of the company that supersedes that of the common stockholder. Like bonds, they provide a fixed level of current income for the life of the issue, and they are competitive with bonds because they are viewed as fixed income obligations (Gitman and Joehnk, 1981:327).

Certificates of Deposit

"Money market certificates of deposit (CD's) are negotiable time deposits issued by a large commercial bank. They can be issued with virtually any maturity, but most frequent maturities are in units of 30 days with some 180-day maturities. When issued by a commercial bank, they cannot be redeemed until maturity. However, since they are negotiable, the investor can sell the CD as any other market instrument could be sold. The market for CD's is quite liquid, with several large banks actively making a market in CD's. As with commercial paper, the risk is only slightly higher than that of treasury bills" (Stevenson and Jennings, 1984:323–325).

VARIABLE-INCOME INVESTMENTS

Common Stocks

Common stocks represent shares of ownership in a corporation. If a corporation has 10,000 shares of common stock outstanding and your agency buys ten shares of that stock, the agency owns 10/10,000 of equity in the company. As owners, stock-holders have the right to vote on decisions affecting the company. Stockholders are also entitled to earnings and dividends of the company.

Advantages and Disadvantages of Common Stocks

Advantages: Common stocks have the most potential of many investments for profit through price appreciation and/or capital gains. Many investors are attracted to common stocks for the possibility of sharing in the growth of earnings of companies over time. While many common stocks pay little or no dividends, some companies have a continuous record of paying dividends that go back fifty years and more. So, for investors interested in income, there are some common stocks that will fit the need for current income through quarterly dividends.

Disadvantages: While common stocks represent the highest potential for gain, they also represent the most risk. The price of common stocks fluctuates, at times without logic or reason, and there is no guarantee of return in the form of principal or even dividends. Thus common stocks lack stability or safety of principal, as well as stability of income in the form of dividends. Investors who invest in common stocks should be willing to assume the market and business risks associated with such an investment; therefore, most but not all, common stocks may be inappropriate for the majority of human service agencies. Even the less risky stocks, such as utilities or the so-called "blue chips" (major corporations with a long history of growth and steady earnings), should only be considered as a small part of an agency's investment portfolio.

MUTUAL FUNDS

Mutual funds are investment companies which sell their own shares or securities to the public and use the proceeds to invest in other securities. The managers of the investment company decide on the goals of the fund, the level of risk they will assume, and the types of securities to be bought. Buyers of the fund must evaluate whether their goals, needs, and risk factors mesh with those of the particular fund as reflected in their perspectus.

Mutual funds were not included in either the fixed or the variable income categories because there are a wide variety of mutual funds which fit in both categories. There are funds available to meet any possible type of investor goal or combination of goals. Many mutual funds offer a number of different type of funds by one company, such as money market funds, bond funds, growth funds, and so forth, and usually the investor is given the option of being able to switch back and forth between funds depending of market conditions. Investors are also given the option to reinvest their dividends rather than having them distributed. This helps accumulate more capital for investment.

Advantages and Disadvantages of Mutual Funds

Advantages: Mutual funds are managed by financial professionals whose knowledge and expertise may give them an advantage over the lay investor. Professional management also reduces commission costs on the buying and selling of securities as well as the costs incurred in information gathering. It is assumed that the professional manager will be able to outperform the investment amateur, but some have said that this is an unwarranted assumption based on the record of most mutual funds (Khoury:228). The pooling of funds with other investors is the most cost-efficient way for the small investor to diversify and minimize risk. One of the problems of the small investor is that excessive transaction costs are incurred in trying to buy a sufficient number of different securities for diversification, this is taken care of with mutual funds because the fund managers are able to buy large quantities at one time and therefore minimize costs.

Mutual funds may be redeemed or sold at any time by the shareholder, thus they have high liquidity. There is a small transaction fee, but orders are processed quickly and this is an advantage for agencies who do not want to have their money tied up in investments that take longer to liquidate. For example, real estate is not as liquid an investment because the seller has no idea if, when, and how long it will take to sell a property (Khoury, 1983: 228–233).

Disadvantages: It is often difficult for an investor to determine the quality of a mutual fund and its management. It is often necessary to consult financial publications which periodically assess and rank mutual funds based on their current and past performance compared to the stock market. Over time, a number of mutual funds have not performed as well as the stock market. Thus, in some cases, an investor would have been better off to have looked to other vehicles for investment.

The cost of buying and selling mutual funds may in some cases be higher than purchasing stock, this is mainly due to the "load" or commission charged by some mutual funds (Amling, 1984:208–209). The human service agency must remember that mutual funds are as safe or as risky as the securities they invest in. Investing in a mutual fund, as with any investment, should only be done after an analysis of the track record of the fund over time and its fit with agency investment goals.

INVESTMENT PLANNING FOR HUMAN SERVICE AGENCIES

An effective investment plan for the agency must reflect critical thought on the part of agency staff and board members. Such a plan should be the result of a process that includes the following steps: (1) an analysis of long-term organizational goals and needs; (2) data gathering of critical agency financial reports as well as information seeking about suitable investments; (3) an analysis of agency financial condition; (4) an analysis of costs/risks/benefits; (5) development of investment strategy which involves an understanding and clarification of investment goals; (6) periodic review and evaluation of investments and investment plan.

Analysis of Long-Term Organizational Goals and Needs

Key elements in investment planning are the goals of the investment within the context of the human service agency's needs and the restrictions of the endowment gift. The agency needs to have a clear idea of its goals before it embarks on an investment program, since its investments should be an integral part of its long-term agency plan. If the agency is not clear and explicit about its goals, what it does with its assets may result in disappointment for the agency. Without understanding what it is doing, it may allow an investment advisor to assemble an inappropriate portfolio of investments that will not be in the agency's best interest.

If the agency's long-range plans include the initiation or expansion of programs, the renovation or building of facilities, then the agency may want to target investment income to these ends. The key question for the agency with funds for investment is—where is the greatest need for the extra income that could be generated with the prudent investment of this money?

Data Gathering

The persons responsible for the investment decisions in the agency should assemble the agency's budgets, financial statements, cash flow charts, program reports, needs assessments, and any other pertinent data that could be helpful in analyzing the financial condition of the agency. Other information that needs to be gathered includes information about various types of investments, and competent financial consultants in the area, their fees and services.

Analysis of Financial Condition

Before the agency embarks on an investment program, it must be sure that it has a financially secure enough base in case of emergency; for example, the loss of a major grant or large cut in allocation. Financial spots to check internally may include sufficient insurance on building and property, professional liability insurance for staff, low debt ratio, a satisfactory credit rating, sufficient cash flow, and an adequate, consistent source of public support from allocations and fundraising. Any shortcomings in these areas must be attended to before an investment program has begun, for there are some risks associated with any investment.

Analysis of Costs/Risks/Benefits

As in any financial endeavor, there are risks involved. The human service agency has to be more cognizant of the risk factors because of its stewardship function; it is not investing its own money. Risk may be defined as "uncertainty regarding the expected rate of return from an investment" (Reilly, 1979:7), although risk also involves the degree to which your principal itself is in danger of being decreased. The degree of risk in investments is related to the types and grades of securities involved. There are five major categories of risk: 1) business or financial risk; 2) price-level risk; 3) interest rate risk; 4) market risk; 5) psychological risk (Huang, 1981:5–6).

Business or Financial Risk

Most businesses finance their operations by borrowing money. The larger the proportion of debt used by the organization, the greater the risk is. The reason for this is that large debt financing means that the company has to not only repay the debt, but the interest as well before it can distribute any earnings to investors. If the company cannot meet its debt repayments, it may go out of business and this would mean financial loss for investors and creditors alike.

There is no guarantee of how long any organization will remain in business; thousands of enterprises go out of business each year. In economic hard times, or periods of rapidly changing technology, businesses need to keep highly competitive to survive and make a profit. When a business does not make a profit over a period of time, it may eventually go bankrupt. In this case, the investors or shareholders of the business will lose their investments. The creditors of the business may receive something, but usually only a fraction of what they are owed. Thus business risk is "concerned with the degree of uncertainty associated with an investment's earnings and ability to pay investors interest, dividends, and any other returns owed them" (Gitman and Joehnk, 1981:120).

Price-Level Risk

"This refers to the risk of losing purchasing power from returns of fixed income securities because of inflation" (Huang, 1981:5). For example, the Consumer Price Index, which measures changes in the cost of living, rose from a base of 100 in 1969 to 218 in 1979 (Huang:5). Thus, an investor who purchased a bond at par value of $1000 would find in cashing it in ten years later that it had lost about 54% of its original value due to inflation. Because of the constant loss in the value of the dollar and the constant rise in the price of living, this investor suffered from price-level risk.

Interest Rate Risk

Interest rate risk is usually borne by those who invest in fixed-income securities. Because interest rates change over time, due to a large extent to federal monetary policies, the prices of securities fluctuate. When interest rates are high, the prices of fixed-income securities tend to go down; when interest rates go down, the prices of fixed-income securities tend to rise. Common stocks are also affected by changing money rates, but to a lesser degree. The reason for the fluctuation in price is an attempt to create attractiveness and competitiveness of yield. For example, when interest rates are 10% why would anyone want to buy a bond only paying 5%? In order to make the fixed-income bond more attractive to buyers, its par value of $1000 will decrease in price and be sold at a discount in the marketplace.

Market Risk

External factors such as political, social and economic occurrences, changes in consumer preference or taste can influence the market for investments and their rate of return. These external factors thus cause market risk; that is, the fluctuation in the price of securities because of events perceived to be related to the earning power of the issuing corporation. For example, when one computer company recently announced reduced earnings, the prices of all micro-computer company stocks went down because of investor perceptions of weakness in the home computer market as a whole.

Psychological Risk

Psychological risk refers to the investor's emotional instability (Huang, 1981:6). When the market is up, investors become very enthusiastic; when it goes down, some investors panic and fear loss. They begin to sell their securities without regard for their real and potential earnings. This type of irrational behavior is due to the fact that the vagaries of investment markets are too stressful for some people to deal with. This type of person should not be in charge of the investment function in your agency.

These, then, are the major types of risks associated with investing. There are other, more specific, risks that are related to the type of investment itself. Some of these risks have been described along with each particular type of investment mentioned previously.

Development of Investment Strategy

The best investment approach for any given human service agency depends on many factors, some of these are (Huang, 1981:528):

Degree of Risk

The agency must decide how much risk it is willing to assume on such things as loss of principal, fluctuation in price of security and in rate of return on investment.

Expertise of Agency Staff

The agency must decide whether someone in administration has sufficient knowledge, training, and expertise to be able to take the responsibility for the investment function. If there is no one able to meet the necessary criteria, the agency must depend on a professional investment planner/consultant to make the investment decisions.

Assessment of the Investment Environment

The agency's administrative staff and board need to discuss with a competent professional his or her assessment of the investment climate at the present time and in the near future. There are, of course, a number of factors of a socioeconomic political nature that impinge on the investment environment at any given time, try to evaluate your consultant's estimation of the importance of these factors for your agency. Obviously, in economic downturns the agency will want to be even more prudent with its money than it normally would be.

Agency Investment Goals

Obviously, the agency wants maximum return on its investment in the safest way possible. At times, an agency may be willing to take small risks in order to get a higher return on investment. Some investment goals that the agency must consider are: 1) safety of principal; 2) protection of purchasing power; 3) current income; 4) capital appreciation; 5) liquidity; and 6) ease of management (Huang, 1981:3; Stevenson and Jennings, 1984:4–6).

Safety of Principal: Principal is the amount of money originally invested. Because of the stewardship function of the human service agency, in most cases the first objective of any investment strategy should be safety of principal. This means that the agency should not engage in speculation, that is, high risk ventures. Rather, the human service agency should try to avoid unsound and unnecessary risks. In attempting to meet the priority of safety of principal, the agency should turn first to low-risk, highly rated corporate and government bonds, money market funds, and certificates of deposit. Diversification of portfolio is a strategy that can help the agency toward attaining safety of principal as well as stability of investment income. However, safety of principal should be viewed within the context of the constant spiral of upward prices. So, the constantly diminishing value of the invested dollars due to inflation needs to be taken into account in investment strategy and accounted for by attempting to protect purchasing power. Table 7-1 shows the association between some investment goals, types of investments, and risk.

Protection of Purchasing Power: Constantly rising price levels have diminished the value of the dollar over time. Another goal of investment should be to try to hedge against inflation by investing in equities and tangible properties that will increase in value at a higher rate than inflation. The uncertainties of politics, the market place, and future price trends again would dictate that the agency diversify holdings as much as possible. In making decisions about the proportion of holdings between different investment types, the agency and its investment advisor should carefully study economic trends and try to project: 1) the

Table 7-1

INVESTMENT GOALS AND RISK*

| | | Risk Factor of Goal | | |
Type of Investment	Goals: Safety of Principal	Stability of Principal	Liquidity	Stability of Income
Fixed-rate CD	high	high	low	high
Variable-rate CD	high	high	high	low
Money-market mutual fund	med.-high	high	high	low
Stock mutual fund	variable	low	high	variable
Bond mutual fund	variable	medium	medium	med.-high
Treasury receipt	high	medium	medium	high
Stocks	variable	variable	high	variable

*Adapted from: Consumer Reports, January 1984.

degree of price-level inflation expected; and 2) the possibilities of gain or loss in the investments available to the agency, all within the limitations imposed by legal, moral, donor, and agency-imposed restrictions.

Current Income: Current income refers to the goal of ensuring that an investment pays a regular amount of interest or dividend so that the agency can project its cash flow. For the nonprofit human service agency, the goal of income should be subordinate to the main goal of safety of principal. Income, and the assurance of the regularity of income, is related to safety. Income and safety are related because those investment vehicles with a guarantee of income, or those companies with a stable, long-standing record of dividend and/or interest payment tend to be the safest. Nonprofit agencies, for whom stableness of investment income is crucial, must view carefully the history, ratings, and prospects of any issuer of securities they consider purchasing. Those companies with long records in the payment of interest or dividends are the safest, and most likely to fulfill the goal of current, stable income.

Investments with a guaranteed stable rate of return include bonds, treasury notes, certificates of deposit, and preferred stocks. However, in looking for a fixed rate of return the agency must also take into account the factor of inflation. For example, an investor must think in terms of "real, or constant-dollar, returns rather than of conventional ones expressed in current dollars only" (Christy and Clendenin, 1978:91). In inflationary periods, returns measured in terms of purchasing power are always lower than those expressed in terms of money. For example, if an investment was paying 10% and the inflation rate was 7%, the real rate of return would only be 3%. In order for the investor to make the 10% return during this period of 7% inflation, the return would have to be 17%.

Capital Appreciation: Capital appreciation refers to the increase in the price paid for an investment. If an investment appreciates in value, then some profit will be made when the investment is sold. Some investors are more interested in capital appreciation than anything else, their motto is, "buy low, sell high." The difficulty for them is to know when the lows and the highs of the cycles have been reached. Many investors combine goals such as capital appreciation with others such as high yield and stability of income. But for the conservative investor such as the human service agency, capital appreciation should be considered a secondary benefit if it happens.

Liquidity: Liquidity is the ability to convert an investment into cash quickly at a value similar to the original amount of the principal invested. This may or may not be an important investment goal for an agency. It depends on the purpose of the investment, that is, whether the investment is to generate operating monies, monies for the capital fund, or some other purpose. If they are to generate extra operating monies, then the agency may want its investment, or part of it, to be liquid in case of emergency. On the other hand, investment for a capital building fund may not have to be as liquid.

Ease of Management: Most human service agency staff have neither the time nor the expertise to manage investments. However, there are some simple types of investments, such as fixed-income investments, that a designated agency staff person could be responsible for with minimum trouble. If ease of management is an important goal, then wisely choosing an investment counselor is the best route for the agency. Factors involved in choosing such a person or institution will be discussed later in this chapter. If the agency has a small amount of money to invest and wants more control of the investments, a mutual fund might be the best choice.

Periodic Review and Evaluation

Nothing remains constant except change, and this is no where more true than the world of investments. Therefore, it is imperative that the agency administrators and board periodically review the agency's investment plan—at least annually. Not only can the investment climate change due to economic and political events, but so can the financial situation of the agency change. A periodic review involves a look at the current status of the investments and an evaluation as to their current suitability given the immediate and forseeable goals of the agency.

SELECTING AN INVESTMENT COUNSELOR

Analyzing investments and managing portfolios are specialized fields requiring the kinds of skill, training, and experience that most human service administrators do not have. While this chapter has tried to present a brief overview of investments, the safest and most prudent course of action is to seek professional advice. Granting this, how does one go about finding a competent financial consultant?

The financial planner or consultant used by the agency should be familiar with nonprofits. He or she should be able to look at the financial statements, cash flow, and budgets, and be able to mesh this information with the needs and goals of the agency. In selecting such a person, it may be helpful to use criteria such as the following (O'Toole, 1984: 131–138):

Credentials

What is the educational background of this person? Is the person a lawyer who is board-certified in tax law or estate planning? If an accountant, is the person a Certified Public Accountant (CPA)? If a planner, is the person a Certified Financial Planner or Chartered Financial Consultant? Does this person belong to the Institute of Certified Financial Planners or the International Association for Financial Planning? While the Certified Financial Planner or Chartered Financial Consultant designations are earned through a correspondence course, the participants must pass tests, and usually have experience in the financial field as insurance agents, stock brokers, or other related occupations.

What kinds of experience does this person bring to financial planning? Can this person furnish verifiable references from other clients, as well as other professionals such as bankers and lawyers with whom this person may have worked? Is this person willing to show sample financial plans that have been done for others (without breaking confidentiality)? It is also important that the person have experience and/or extensive knowledge of the nonprofit area, since nonprofits have unique characteristics that make their goal setting, planning, and needs different from other types of organizations.

Compensation

Financial consultants, planners, or investment advisors make money in a variety of ways: 1) They may charge a fee for their advice. The fee is usually reasonable, and you are not obligated to purchase anything else from them but what you are paying for—advice. 2) They may give free advice, but receive a commission on whatever products they sell you. So if you buy a mutual fund, stock, or bond through them they will earn a commission. This sort of advisor can give you unbiased opinions if he or she is not working for just one company, but rather can sell anything on the market. 3) They may have some combination of fees and commissions. In most cases, you will be encouraged to invest funds or purchase securities through the consultant. In this way, the investment counselor's services may cost from zero to $5,000.

The agency should ask how much the consultant will make on any product he or she tries to sell. What should be avoided are those kinds of arrangements in which the consultant has a conflict of interest because he or she may in fact be employed by a parent investment company and therefore it is in the consultant's best interest, rather than the agency's, to sell the product they are recommending. This is not to say that all commission consultants should be avoided, rather be on guard if the person is trying to sell a specific product rather than fit agency needs to its long-term goals.

Content

What should the agency expect for the money it pays an investment counselor? The result of the agency's discussions with the consultant should be a written financial plan, with explanations of all assumptions made in the writing of it—such as estimated rate of inflation used, rate of assumed rate of return on the investments, agency goals and tolerance for risk. Using the financial statements, budgets, and other cost data made available to him or her, the consultant should be able to pinpoint trouble spots or special areas of concern. The last part of the plan should present alternative strategies, along with advantages and disadvantages of each approach, for the attainment of agency financial goals. The planner may recommend types or categories of investments rather than specific investments. A well thought out financial plan should have the following components (Consumer Reports, January 1986, P. 38):

- a statement of agency goals, objectives, and tolerance for risk
- an examination of the agency's current investment portfolio, with suggestions for revising, if appropriate
- an examination of the current debt ratio of the agency
- a cash flow analysis, before and after investment
- recommendations that are clear and unambiguous
- language that the users of the plan can understand

Commitment

The agency needs to clarify how much time the planner will spend with key agency people and who will write the final report. In some firms the planner spends time in consultation, but the final plan is written by a junior staff person. This may not matter to your agency, but you may want to know this in advance. When the plan is ready, it should be presented to administrative staff in person so that any questions can be answered at that time. Final decisions on alternative courses of action should be deferred until staff have had time to study and analyze the plan and discuss it in private.

The agency should also clarify what support from other professionals will be used in the drawing up of the financial plan. Since it is almost impossible to be an expert in all areas of insurance, tax laws, banking, and investments, the planner may consult with others on these matters. The agency may want the planner to meet with its accountant and lawyer as well. Some large planning firms have accountants and lawyers on staff whom they will consult with.

If an agency does have money it wishes to invest, a competent financial planner, tax accountant, and lawyer should be consulted. A board member may be able to recommend someone competent who understands nonprofit organizations. Remember that a financial plan is not an end, it is a beginning. It is the beginning of some hard-decision making on the part of the agency as to the best avenue to use in investing money given for the public good.

Chapter Seven
Questions and Topics for Discussion

1. What are the major types of fixed securities?
2. What are the major types of variable-income securities?
3. What are mutual funds?
4. What are the major categories of risk?
5. What should be the major investment objective of the nonprofit human service agency?
6. How often should a portfolio be reviewed?
7. What factors should be considered in portfolio selection?
8. What factors should be considered in selecting an investment advisor?

Exercise 7-1: Developing an Investment Strategy

Select a human service agency that you are familiar with, perhaps a field placement or agency where you have worked. Assume that this agency has $50,000 to invest.

1. Develop an investment strategy for this agency.
   a. Describe this agency, its investment goals, and your rationale for choosing the investment instruments that you have.
   b. If you have chosen variable-rate securities, chart their price over the length of this course.
   c. If you have chosen fixed-rate investments, calculate how much interest income has been earned by the agency in the period under review. For example, if an investment were paying 8% a year (not compounded) and the agency only had it for a quarter of the year, then it would receive a quarter of 8% or 2%.
2. Report on the results of the investments for the agency, that is, how much money has been made or lost over the interim period for the agency by these investments? Has the investment appreciated in value? How much interest income has been made for the agency?
3. Evaluate the suitability of the investment(s) in relation to the goals of the agency and the investment outcome.
4. Please present your results in a 2–3 page memo along with appropriate attachments, charts, etc. Be prepared to discuss this in class.

Case 7-1: Senior Citizens Centers of Metro County, Inc.

Senior Citizens Centers of Metro County, Inc. is an agency whose goals include the following:

1. To help older adults improve the quality of their lives;
2. To maintain the self-esteem of older adults;
3. To enable older adults to remain as independent and mobile as possible;
4. To make the community and society aware of the contribution of older adults;
5. To change negative attitudes about older adults.

The organization consists of a board of directors whose function is to establish goals, develop policy and procedure guidelines; an executive director; an assistant to the director who also functions as the agency bookkeeper, and four program heads for the following programs: Individual and Family Life Advocacy, Social Development, Comprehensive Volunteerism, and Home Bound Employment. The agency has a number of programs under Comprehensive Volunteerism such as a foster grandparents program and a retired senior volunteer program (RSVP) in which a large number of senior citizens participate. In its advocacy program, the agency has volunteers who become "friendly visitors" for homebound elderly as well as ombudsmen for their needs. The social development program initiates and sponsors a number of social activities for seniors at the various sites in Metro County. The home bound employment program provides avenues for home bound elderly to become self-employed.

The agency receives the majority of its funds from governmental grants. Its second largest source of funds is a United Way allocation which accounts for approximately one-fourth of its total budget. Comprehensive volunteerism receives the largest portion of the total budget because it is perceived that this program helps the older person remain independent and active, thus enhancing the quality of their lives and their self esteem. The agency has a small amount of investment income from CD's, this income is used for support services exclusively.

Recently, a former senior volunteer who was very active at the Centers passed away and left $25,000 to the agency with the stipulation that the principal be invested and the interest used for providing needed equipment for the Social Development activities. The administrator has called a meeting of the board and administrative staff to discuss what approaches the agency should take with the endowment gift and its investment.

1. What factors should be taken into account in deciding on invest-ment strategy?

2. If you were the administrator what would you suggest to the board in terms of investments?

Reading 7-1: How to Read the Financial Pages of the Newspaper.

The figures below illustrate a typical New York Stock Exchange quota-tion from a daily paper, along with an explanation of the common symbols used by the Exchange. To understand exactly what is being reported, let us look more closely at one stock, Bell South, one of the companies created by the break-up of AT & T. This day showed the following for Bell South:

52 Weeks					Yld	P–E	Sales	Week's			Net
High	*Low*	*Stock*	*Div.*	*%*		*Ratio*	*100s*	*High*	*Low*	*Last*	*Chg.*
32¾	27¼	BellSo	s2.60	8.5		8	16792	31½	29¾	30⅝	−⅜

The first two columns show how the price of this stock varied over a period of 52 weeks by showing the highest and lowest price it was sold for during this period. As you can see, the highest price of Bell South during the last 52 weeks was $32.75. The lowest price it sold for was $27.25.

In the next column is the name of the stock, this is often abbreviated, in fact every company is assigned initials that represent it on all stock market quotations. Following the name is the amount of dividend paid by the company to its shareholders. In this case, one can see that there is the letter 's' before the amount of $2.60. One must look at the footnotes that accompany the stock reports, each letter represents something. In the footnotes, the letter "s" means that this dividend amount includes a "split or stock dividend of 25 percent or more in the past 52 weeks. The high-low range is adjusted from the old stock" (N.Y.Times).

The yield column translates the dividend amount into the percentage the investor is making on the money he or she has invested. In this case, the investor is earning a yield of 8½%, more than he or she would earn if the money were in a regular savings account.

The P–E Ratio stands for Price-Earnings Ratio, it tells the investor the proportion the stock is selling for in relation to its earnings. In this case, BellSo is selling at 8 times its earnings. This is considered a low ratio. A low ratio (under 13) is often considered a "bargain" buy, while a very high ratio, say 35, is not.

Sales in 100's means that 1,679,200 shares of BellSo were traded on that day. The "High" and "Low" columns show the highest and lowest amounts that BellSo was traded for that week; while the "Last" column contains the closing or final price of the stock on that day of trading.

The "Net Change" column shows the net change in price between the current day's closing price and the previous day's closing price. As you can see, BellSo's price declined by ⅜ from the day before. This means it must have closed at $31 on the preceding day.

You are to do the following:

1. Take a look at the financial pages of your local newspaper, or go to your local library and get a copy of the New York Times or the Wall Street Journal. Look at the New York Stock Exchange listings for the day, pick one company, and describe what each column means for that stock.

2. What other kinds of financial reports are listed in this section of the newspaper?

3. Which reports do you think would be most relevant for the human service agency and its investments?

Reading 7-2: "Investing for the Ford Foundation"

The next reading, "Investing for the Ford Foundation," gives an inside view of one of the largest charitable foundations and its investment strategies and philosophy. The Ford Foundation invests its funds and must not only keep ahead of inflation, but must generate an average annual return at least equal to its spending level—5%. The Foundation obviously has at its disposal a plethora of expert financial and legal help to advise it on portfolio acquisitions and tax implications of its actions. Small human service agencies do not have the advantages of such help, but they may have persons on their boards who can give guidance in selecting an investment counselor. Again, remember that investment goals must first be determined by the agency board before any investment decisions are made.

"Investing for the Ford Foundation" by Ed Doherty*

On a trip to the African nation of Kenya last September, John W. English and his colleagues were ceremoniously regaled in a poor village near Kenya's capital, Nairobi. "Eat, eat, urged the beaming villagers as they served each visitor two nearly rotten boiled eggs, without plates or utensils. English bravely downed the eggs, as well as subsequent courses—two ears of seed corn, two green bananas and some bitter corn wine. Finally, with great pride, the villagers served the "piece de resistance"—a bottle of warm Sprite. "They gave us just about everything they had," recalls English, his eyes glistening with emotion. "I've never seen so much love. They would have given us the ragged shirts off their backs and then some more—if we'd asked."

Such an experience might seem unrelated to Wall Street or to the bull market that was then gathering momentum in the United States. But for English, now 50, the connection is both obvious and important. As vice president and chief investment officer of the Ford Foundation, he manages the $3.5 billion of assets that are the sole source of income for the nation's largest private foundation. If those assets grow, then so do the size and number of grants that the foundation can make to what it deems worthy causes and organizations in the United States and abroad. In Kenya, Mr. English experienced vividly the difference that such philanthropic donations can make to lives that, by American standards, are deprived indeed. The villagers' feast was an expression of gratitude to the trustees and officers of the Ford Foundation, gathered in Nairobi for a board meeting, for financing the construction of a diesel pump that brought water directly into the village from the bottom of a nearby mountainside. Multiply the evident elation of the villagers a thousand-fold or more—and you see why English is feeling pretty good about his work these days. Back in his elegant and spacious office in the Ford Foundation's Manhattan headquarters, he is obviously more enthusiastic about narrating his experience in Kenya—and showing all the photos he took there—than in talking about his approach to investments. But he does get up frequently to check the market action on his computer screen.

Until two years ago, English, who speaks with calm deliberation in

---

*Reprinted by permission of *Financial World,* August 31, 1983, Copyright 1983.

witty epigrams delivered in a Midwestern twang, was a loyal corporation man. But he was intrigued when a headhunter called him in early 1981 about the Ford Foundation job. So, after what he calls an "agonizing" reappraisal of his goals, he joined the Ford Foundation in November, 1981.

The marriage has been a happy one for both partners. Since his arrival, English has helped push the market value of the Foundation's investments up by 43%, from $2.4 billion to $3.5 billion now. The portfolio's total return—including dividends, interest income, and capital gains—was a healthy 19% for the fiscal year that ended in September 1982. And the return has jumped to 46.3% for the nine months of fiscal 1983 through last June. Compared with some of the best mutual funds, that return may seem modest. But for an institution that spent the past decade slowly recovering from a major fiscal crisis, it is spectacular. There has been nothing like it at the Ford Foundation since the go-go years of the 1960's. English, modest to the core, disclaims the credit. "We were incredibly fortunate to be here when the capital markets exploded into the most robust activity since World War II." He exploited that market without taking excessive risk.

For most of its life, the Ford Foundation seemed to acquire wealth faster than it could spend it. Henry Ford I and his son Edsel founded it with a $25,000 donation in 1936 to "promote human welfare." Until 1947, the Ford family periodically bestowed on it large blocks of the then-private Ford Motor Co. The Foundation flourished on a diet of Ford dividends—and began to support an unprecedented range of domestic and international projects and services. But in 1956 the Foundation, which then owned 88% of Ford's shares, gradually began selling them to the public, using the proceeds to amass a portfolio of diversified stocks and bonds. These holdings prospered too, pushing assets to a peak of nearly $4 billion in 1964. By 1966, when McGeorge Bundy, national security advisor under President Kennedy, became its president, the Ford Foundation had become a byword for liberal commitment and philanthropic generosity. Under Bundy, the Foundation poured cash into such causes as the arts and civil rights, international understanding and world population control.

But, unfortunately, in 1974, with the Foundation spending faster than it could earn money even in a relatively healthy market, the stock market fell to pieces. That year the Foundation's assets plummeted to $1.7 billion—from $3 billion in 1973. Fighting for survival, the foundation gradually cut its grants and expenses from $245 million in 1974—or over 14% of assets—to as little as $119 million, or 5% of assets in 1979. Since then, the Foundation has been keeping its expenditures at around the 5% level—the minimum amount that a private foundation must give annually, according to Federal law.

That discipline, combined with gains in the market value of the portfolio, enabled the institution to increase spending. This year, the portfolio's current market value suggests a level of funding of approximating $175 million. Meanwhile, of course, inflation has made terrible inroads into the real value of the Foundation's grants. But the retreat seems to be over. Franklin S. Thomas, a black lawyer and former head of the Bedford Stuyvesant Restoration Corp., replaced Bundy as president in 1979. While continuing many of the foundation's previous commitments, Thomas has used some of the Foundation's hard-won gains to focus increasingly on such critical problems as urban poverty and the plight of refugees around the world.

John English has also made some significant changes of his own. Essentially, he has reworked the managerial methods he learned in the Bell System, adapting them to the foundation. He views himself not as a stock picker or a fund manager, but as the captain of a team of both inside and outside money managers. While he provides general guidelines, he lets his managers call their own shots.

Before putting his approach into action, English had to learn the ropes of foundation investing. Unlike pension funds, for example, foundations pay a 2% Federal excise tax on net income. Also, the Ford Foundation holds itself to canons of "social responsibility." This does not necessarily mean that it won't invest in companies that do business in, say, South Africa or Chile. But it would first make sure that the firms do not in its judgment lend support to apartheid in the one country or violate human rights in the other. But neither taxes nor social concerns greatly affect the Foundation's overall investment strategy. Much more important was the Foundation's financial vulnerability. "At AT & T one of my biggest problems was deciding how to invest the money that flowed into the pension plan at the rate of $1 million an hour," recalls English. "So on my first day at Ford, I asked my staff when we received our monthly contributions from the Ford Motor Co. After an embarrassing silence, one person piped up and told me the last time the company had given us anything was in 1947. Right then I knew this would be a different ball game." He decided that he would have to put a premium on capital preservation and take a more conservative investment approach than he did at AT & T. Decisions on how to allocate assets would also be harder to make—since he would have to sell one security to raise money to buy another. Yet he couldn't be too cautious. Simply to sustain the Foundation's present philanthropic clout, he would have to generate an average annual return of at least 5%—the minimum legal spending level —plus the inflation rate. Otherwise, the portfolio would dwindle away.

To maintain the proper balance between the need to preserve capital and to maximize gains, English relied on the prime principle of modern portfolio theory—diversification. For him, this meant not only spreading his bets, but also multiplying the number of bettors and the total pool of power and talent available to him. One major plus was the star-studded roster of the Foundation's board of trustees. At the three-day quarterly board meetings and on other occasions, English says he's benefitted from the advice of trustees such as Robert S. McNamara, former president of the World Bank; Irving S. Shapiro, former chairman of DuPont; and Paul Miller Jr., a Philadelphia investment advisor and chairman of the Foundation's investment committee.

To achieve diversification in day-to-day portfolio management, however, English has increased the proportion of assets managed by external investment firms from about 15% to 36%. "Outsiders have different approaches and areas of expertise that supplement our in-house talents," he explains. In May 1982, English transferred $500 million of the domestic equities portfolio to six outside money managers. He also boosted from two to four the number of outside firms managing international equities. How have these external managers performed? "So far, they've done terrifically," says English. "The managers of domestic stocks, in particular, have provided a valuable supplement to the foundation's in-house portfolio of high-capitalization household name companies," he adds.

. . . . Each week English holds what he calls an "investment cabinet meeting" with his four top managers to discuss all key economic factors and to reconsider the overall asset mix. . . .

In retrospect, the major strategic moves made by English and his "cabinet" look like sound ones. When he arrived at the foundation, he found that 80% of its assets were invested in domestic and international equities—much too high a proportion for his comfort. Even pension funds that get regular corporate contributions generally average a mix of 60% stocks and 40% bonds, he points out. With the prime importance of capital preservation in mind, he gradually sold off equities until, by January, 1982, they represented a bit less than 50% of all assets. At the same time, English used the proceeds to increase the foundation's holdings of Government and corporate bonds from 20% to nearly 50% that same January.... The net result was that the foundation got considerable mileage out of the bond rally that started in June, 1982. And the shift to bonds minimized the damage from the bear market in equities that lasted until August.

Currently, English has 54% of the foundation's assets in domestic stocks and 7% in international equities. And the bond portfolio represents 30% of assets.... English is reluctant to name stocks he likes, for fear of seeming to tout them. But the records show that at the end of March the foundation's largest in-house domestic holdings included IBM, AT & T, General Motors, General Electric, Philip Morris, Exxon, and Schlumberger. [See Table below]. English is now considering increasing the foundation's stake in equities.

.... Despite his promising start, English insists that "the jury is still not in" on his performance or on that of his outside money managers. "It takes a complete market cycle—usually three to five years from bottom to bottom or top to top—to evaluate investment performance," he says. Yet his performance has been good enough to discourage any meddling from top brass.... For English, it would seem that the honeymoon with his new employer is not over. For the foundation, it seems likely that a fortunate combination of factors—the bull market and the economic recovery, disinflation and the managerial finesse of John English—may herald a new era, one combining the hopefulness of the 1960's with the financial discipline of the 1970's.

Reading 7-2 Questions:

1. What is your opinion of the Foundation's portfolio mix?
2. Do you think its 10 top holdings are suitable for a small human service agency? Why or why not?
3. What type of investment goals are reflected by such holdings?
4. What kind of a team could a human service agency put together to help with investment decision-making?

Table 7-2

THE FORD FOUNDATION'S TOP 10 HOLDINGS

		Recent No. of Shares Held (thds.)	Recent Price	Portfolio Value (thds.)
1.	IBM	724	126	$91,224
2.	AT & T	805	62	49,910
3.	General Motors	399	75	29,925
4.	Schlumberger	464	57 1/2	26,680
5.	General Electric	440	53 1/2	23,540
6.	Philip Morris	370	60 1/2	22,385
7.	Exxon	617	35	21,595
8.	Hosp. Corp. of Amer.	365	54	19,710
9.	Melville Corp.	456	42 1/2	19,494
10.	Digital Equipment	150	112	16,800

Chapter Eight

THE BASICS OF ACCOUNTING

After reading this chapter you should be able to:

1. Explain basic accounting principles and concepts;
2. Understand accounting differences between for-profit and nonprofit organizations;
3. Demonstrate effects of agency transactions on the accounting equation;
4. Follow simple transactions through the accounting cycle.

INTRODUCTION

Accounting is the art of analyzing, recording, summarizing, and reporting the financial activities of an agency. In systems terms the agency is taking in resources and converting them into usable goods and services. Therefore, the accounting subsystem in the human service agency is concerned with analyzing and recording these activities in a consistent, generally accepted manner so that the accumulated information can be used by management as well as interested outsiders (see Figure 8-1). As an art, accounting is a dynamic process that is evolving to meet the changing needs of economic organizations, regulatory agencies, and the general public. This is especially true in the area of nonprofit accounting because it is only quite recently that the accounting profession has taken note of the peculiar characteristics of nonprofit human service agencies, and therefore, their special accounting needs.

The art of recording business transactions is as old as civilization itself (Henderson and Peirson, 1977). Ancient Babylonia, Greece, and Rome all had some sort of bookkeeping systems. Though different than the kind of system we are familiar with today, they were still forms of business recording. The present cost-based system of double-entry bookkeeping was developed in Italy in the twelfth and thirteenth centuries. This bookkeeping method spread across Europe, and the first printed book describing this system was printed in 1494. There were virtually few changes in the basic system for three hundred years after. In the nineteenth century, some writers began to try to formulate general theo-

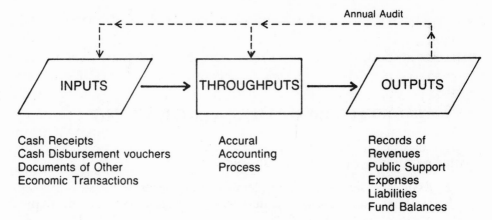

Figure 8-1: A Systems View of Accounting

ries of accounting. These formulations laid the cornerstone for some of the commonly accepted accounting principles of today. In the 1950's, efforts moved toward more research on improving accounting practice. After the 1970's, attempts to provide a general theory of accounting were to some extent abandoned and energy directed toward applying the scientific method to problems of the discipline (Racek, 1982).

While all this had gone on, however, very little attention had been directed toward the nonprofit side of accounting. Until recently, financial reporting by nonprofit agencies was not considered very important by the general public or even contributors. The prevailing attitude was that as charities, human service agencies provided the kind of help difficult to quantify or measure. Thus many times nonprofit human service agencies issued confusing, misleading, and inconsistent financial reports. There were very few laws regulating nonprofits. There was also a lack of clear direction from the accounting profession, which tended to overlook the specific differences between for-profit and nonprofit organizations. At times, nonprofits were treated as special cases in which certain accounting principles did not apply (Racek, 1982).

During the 1950's, awareness developed for the need for guidelines and regulations for nonprofits. A well-publicized case of fraud by a charitable organization in the 1950's was the impetus for some states to pass legislation requiring nonprofit organizations to file certain types of financial information with their state governments on an annual basis. The nonprofit sector itself also took steps to regulate itself. In 1964, STANDARDS OF ACCOUNTING AND FINANCIAL REPORTING FOR VOLUNTARY HEALTH AND WELFARE ORGANIZATIONS was published by a joint committee made up of the National Health Council and the National Social Welfare Assembly. This was the first time that an attempt had been made to establish uniformity in accounting principles and financial reports for nonprofit organizations. The agencies that were members of the National Health Council agreed to voluntarily follow the guidelines set forth in the STANDARDS.

The American Institute of Certified Public Accountants (AICPA) is the body, along with the Financial Standards Accounting Board (FASB), which sets standards for the accounting profession. Generally accepted accounting principles are adopted through usage, but they are not strictly binding unless given sanction by the professional regulatory bodies, very much the way standards are set in the human service professions. In the mid-1960's, the AICPA began to provide some direction for human service accounting by issuing "audit guides." The first one was entitled AUDITS OF VOLUNTARY HEALTH AND WELFARE ORGANIZATIONS; it was published in 1967. Although this guide was useful in providing information regarding auditing procedures, it did not go far enough in helping to develop uniformity in accounting practices in the nonprofit field.

Thus, at the beginning of the 1970's, the nonprofit sector was being provided with very little guidance from the accounting profession. Nonprofits tended to be excluded from most accounting principles, and their financial reports were viewed as "special-purpose reports" (Racek, 1982). But pressure had been mounting during the 1960's for some more definitive guidelines due to the need for greater accountability on the part of human service organizations as well as the increased federal involvement in the health and welfare field.

Early in the 1970'a number of significant measures were taken. The AICPA's 1967 audit guide was revised and reissued in 1974. Also in 1974, the United Way published ACCOUNTING AND FINANCIAL REPORTING—A GUIDE FOR UNITED WAYS AND NOT-FOR-PROFIT HUMAN SERVICE ORGANIZATIONS. The same year a revision of the 1964 work by the National Health council and the National Social Welfare Assembly was also published with the United Way. In 1980, the FASB published OBJECTIVES OF FINANCIAL REPORTING BY NONBUSINESS ORGANIZATIONS, trying to delineate fundamentals and objectives that could be used as a basis to develop financial accounting and reporting standards (FASB, 1980). At the present time the Financial Accounting Standards Board is working on a project to determine and resolve some of the issues related to accounting for nonprofit organizations. But at the present time, the guidelines for helping the nonprofit agency report its financial activities are provided by the above mentioned publications. And most state laws regulating nonprofits base their codes on the Audit Guide. It is imperative that human service staff develop the capability for fiscal credibility if their agencies are to survive in an era of scarce resources. In developing this capability, some understanding of the basics of accounting is essential. In this chapter, basic accounting principles and practices as they apply to the human service agency will be reviewed. These practices and their relationship to the accounting cycle and the financial reporting of the agency will also be explained.

TYPES OF ACCOUNTING SYSTEMS

There may be one of three types of accounting systems used in a nonprofit human service agency: a cash basis accounting system, an accrual accounting system, or a modified accrual accounting system. Cash basis accounting records only those transactions in which cash is received or disbursed. Thus, in this system revenue and expenses are only recognized or realized when money is paid to the agency or paid out by the agency. While a very simple method of accounting, the cash basis method has many disadvantages. First of all, it does not provide an accurate picture of the agency's financial condition at any point in time. Secondly, in any but the simplest fee-for-service agency, it compounds the possibility of error and manipulation of records. Some agencies may use a cash basis of accounting, but then convert their records to the accrual basis to prepare financial reports (Listro, 1983:96).

Accrual basis accounting records not only transactions involving the receipt and disbursement of cash, but also transactions in which the agency incurs obligations or others incur obligations to the agency. Most business organizations keep their records on an accrual basis, while more and more of the medium to large nonprofits have moved toward the accrual basis as well. Actually, the distinction between profits and non-profits based on accounting methods is tenuous inasmuch as most small commercial "mom and pop" enterprises use the cash basis of accounting, just as small nonprofits do. Therefore the distinction is really based on size, not the profit/nonprofit dichotomy.

A modified accrual accounting system has characteristics of both the accrual and cash bases. That is, an agency may record certain transactions on a cash basis, usually uncollected income, and record other transactions on an accrual basis, usually unpaid bills (Gross and Warshauer, 1983:23). However, there may be many variations as to what is kept on a cash vs. accrual basis. One reason this system may be used in small to medium-sized agencies is so that a complex set of books does not have to be used, but it is not generally considered an appropriate system.

According to the Audit Guide, "The accrual basis of accounting is required by generally accepted accounting principles for a fair representation of financial position and results of operations" (1974:33). If an agency uses a cash or modified accrual basis, its reports may be acceptable only if they do not differ materially from reports prepared on an accrual basis. An agency's reports will also be acceptable only if they are prepared using generally accepted accounting principles.

BASIC ACCOUNTING PRINCIPLES AND CONCEPTS

While no definitive list of basic accounting principles and concepts has yet been published, there are generally accepted principles in use in the accounting profession. Not all of them may apply to human service agencies, so the principles discussed here are the ones that appear to be the most applicable.

The Accounting Entity Concept

Accounting is concerned with data gathered from a discrete economic unit. An accounting or business entity is any economic unit that takes in resources and engages in some form of economic activity. For our purposes the accounting entity in the human service agency is the agency itself or possibly each of its separate programs or funds. But it does not include any of the economic activities of any of its employees that are unrelated to, or take place outside of, the main objectives and tasks of the agency. This book will review the accounting activities of two types of human service agencies. The first type is the simplest in structure and has only one source of revenue—fees from clients. The second type is a human service agency with multiple funding sources.

Consistency

It is important that management and interested outsiders have a basis upon which to compare the economic performance of the agency from one year to the next. It would be very confusing if an agency changed its system every other year. So the principle of consistency means that once an accounting system is adopted by an agency it will not be changed from period to period. Obviously, changes in a system can take place when appropriate and they must be pointed out in the notes accompanying the financial statements of the agency.

The Cost Principle

This is the traditional, widely used method of recording the acquisition of assets. The cost principle means that assets are initially recorded in the accounting books of the agency at their actual cost, and no adjustment for inflation or appreciation is made in the books at a later time. The only adjustments made are to allocate a portion of the cost to expenses as the assets expire or depreciate. While there is some debate over the usefulness of this principle because of inflation, it is supported by many accountants as an objective way to value an asset. It is objective because it can be verified by supporting documents such as receipts, bills of sale, and cancelled checks whereas later estimates of asset value are only that—estimates.

Disclosure Principle

Material and relevent facts upon which outsiders can evaluate the economic activities of the agency should be disclosed either in its financial statements or in the notes accompanying them. These kinds of disclosures make the statements less misleading and therefore more useful to readers. While the information does not have to be in great detail, it should include all relevant information.

The Going Concern Concept

Most of the time it is impossible to know how long the life of an organization will be, but most human services agencies are not formed with the intention of closing shop in a year or two. Thus the going concern concept means that an assumption is made that the accounting entity will not be going into liquidation in the forseeable future. This assumption effects the way we record financial transactions and report them in our financial statements. Thus we record assets at the cost we paid for them, not their liquidation value.

The Matching Principle

In order to measure income accurately, revenue from one accounting period is matched or compared with expenses incurred during the same accounting period. The matching principle is important in the accrual method of accounting, which we will discuss later in this chapter.

Materiality

The concept of materiality may be applied to procedures in recording transactions as well as in preparing financial statements. Materiality is the relative importance of any amount, event, or procedure. It is relative because what is material in one agency may not be in another, depending of the size of the agency's budget and the size and nature of the item in question. If an item is not considered important enough to influence the users of the agency's statements, then it is probably immaterial. Materiality is not guided by theoretical principles, but more by the professional judgement of the accountant who makes such a decision.

The Monetary Principle

In accounting the monetary principle states that all financial transactions and statements are reflected in terms of money. There are some shortcomings in this from the point of view of some accountants, however. First of all, because of the cost principle, assets that may have been acquired many years ago and recorded at cost will not reflect the current value of the asset. Secondly, the monetary principle assumes a stability in the value of the dollar that does not exist. So an asset acquired for $20,000 fifteen years ago, such as land, will at the present time be worth much more than that because of appreciation. Also, $20,000 today does not have the same value that $20,000 did fifteen years ago. Some large corporations are now trying to take these factors into account in their financial statements, but most human service agencies have not developed the financial sophistication to be able to do so.

Conservatism

The principle of conservatism is aptly illustrated in the old saying, "anticipate no profits and provide for all losses" (Meigs and Meigs, 1981). This means that accountants often choose among alternative methods or procedures that result in lower amounts of net revenue or asset value being reflected in the financial statements. Today some accountants have moved away from this principle and believe that other principles such as materiality, consistency, disclosure, and objectivity should take precedence (Fess and Niswonger, 1981).

Objectivity

In order to accept the accounting records of an agency as an accurate reflection of its economic activities, the principle of objectivity is used. Objective evidence is necessarily the basis upon which cost and revenue are recorded. Objective evidence is in the form of documents such as receipts, invoices, checks, vouchers, and so forth. They form the bases of the journal entries that are made. Despite the goal of objectivity, however, there will always be judgements made that are open to interpretation.

Time Period Principle

Users of financial reports need some periodic feedback for decision-making purposes. Thus while we assume an indefinite life for accounting entities, this indefinite life is broken into short time intervals for reporting purposes. For example, an agency usually has monthly cash flow reports and trial balances, monthly or quarterly budget variance reports, and yearly financial statements.

The Realization Principle

In accrual accounting, revenue should be recognized when it is earned. However, it is sometimes difficult to judge at times exactly when revenue is earned. Therefore, accountants commonly do not recognize revenue until it is realized. Two conditions have to be met for revenue to be realized. First, there must be objective evidence that this is so. Secondly, the earning process must be essentially complete. In the case of the human services, this usually means that earnings would be realized at the time of the rendering of the services.

The application of these principles and concepts will be illustrated within the context of the human service agency. Before this is done, however, it must be pointed out that just as there are organizational and environmental differences between for-profit and nonprofit organizations, there are also some differences in accounting procedures and functions. There are six main areas of distinction that will be discussed in the next section.

UNIQUE ACCOUNTING CHARACTERISTICS OF NONPROFIT HUMAN SERVICE AGENCIES

(Taken from Gross and Warshauer, 1979:12–15; United Way, 1974:10–11; *Standards*, 1974; *Audit Guide*, 1974.)

Fund Accounting

In fund accounting, separate accounting entities, or funds, are set up to segregate and report on those resources available to be used at the discretion of the board—unrestricted funds; as well as those available to be used for specific purposes only—restricted funds. In business organizations there is no such thing as fund accounting, whereas it is widely used in nonprofits because it reflects stewardship. Fund accounting is the most unique aspect that differentiates nonprofit from for-profit organizations and will be discussed more fully in the next chapter.

Transfers and Appropriations

Transfers are monetary transactions between funds. For example, earnings from investments may be transferred from an endowment fund to the current fund for operating expenses. Excess cash from a current fund may also be transferred to an endowment fund. Appropriations are monies that may be set aside for specific future uses. These transactions are unique to nonprofit organizations because for-profit organizations do not use funds in their accounting systems.

Allocations, Contributions, Grants, Pledges, and Noncash Contributions

For-profit organizations do not receive allocations from community agencies, contributions or pledges from the public, or noncash (in-kind) contributions. They may, at times, receive grant monies, but this is not a major source of income for profit-oriented organizations. Yet these sources of funds constitute a large proportion of the available resources of nonprofit agencies. These sources of funds may constitute unique accounting problems for the nonprofit agency. If a for-profit is owed money, for example, it is recorded as an account receivable. If a nonprofit receives a pledge, the obligation created may not be legally binding, though some may consider it morally so. But most agencies do record these pledges on their books as receivables.

Functional Basis Accounting

Functional basis accounting is required by the *AICPA Audit Guide,* it is an accounting device for separating an agency's expenses into two main categories: program services and support services. This is done by distributing all expenses between these two functions. Since agency staff and other resources may be used by more than one category, this functional separation of expenses can sometimes be difficult as was discussed in Chapter Six.

Treatment of Fixed Assets

While business enterprises usually record fixed assets as assets and depreciate them over their period of expected life, nonprofits have varied tremendously in their recording of fixed assets. According to the *Audit Guide,* generally accepted accounting principles "require fixed assets to be carried at cost and donated assets to be recorded at their fair value at the date of the gift" (1974:10). The *Audit Guide* also states that depreciation should be included as an element of expense in the appropriate financial statements of the agency. Even with these guidelines, there are some nonprofit agencies that neither record fixed assets nor depreciate.

Nature and Purpose of Financial Statements

The purpose of nonprofit human service agencies is service, while the purpose of for-profit organizations is profit. This basic distinction is also the basis of the difference in the financial statements of the two types of organizations. The financial statements of for-profit organizations are concerned with the bottom line—how much net profit was earned? The financial statements of nonprofits are concerned with reflecting stewardship and fiduciary responsibility of public monies, as there is no profit. Financial statements will be discussed more fully in Chapter Ten.

These then, are some of the major distinctions between nonprofit and for-profit accounting. The particular accounting characteristics of nonprofits will be seen more clearly in the next chapter which uses a case to illustrate simple fund accounting procedures in a nonprofit human service agency. In order to understand these procedures and their relationship to the accounting cycle, the financial statements, and the agency as a whole, the fundamental accounting equation will be discussed. The accounting equation is the basis of the double-entry bookkeeping system.

THE ACCOUNTING EQUATION

ASSETS are things of monetary value that are owned by an individual or business entity. EQUITIES are claims on assets. The relationship between assets and equities can by illustrated by the equation:

ASSETS = EQUITIES

There are two components of equities = LIABILITIES are the claims that creditors may have on assets. In other words, liabilities are the debts owed by the firm. These are called ACCOUNTS PAYABLE when merchandise or other goods are bought on credit, while NOTES PAYABLE are debts that are incurred by signing a promissory note to repay the monies owed at a definite future time.

The other component of equities is called CAPITAL OR OWNER'S EQUITY. Capital or owner's equity is the rights of the owners of the assets. Capital represents the residual of the resources of the firm after all the liabilities are satisfied or paid. It is important to emphasize that capital does not equal cash, capital only exists as a concept on a piece of paper. It cannot be put in the bank as it it just the result of a mathematical equation (Solomon, Vargo, and Schroeder, 1983:13). As a result of this residual concept, the basic accounting equation can be expanded as follows:

ASSETS = LIABILITIES + CAPITAL

Traditionally and in law, the rights of creditors have precedence over the rights of owners in regard to the assets. This is mainly because assets are frequently used as collateral in securing loans from creditors to acquire more assets for expansion or maintenance. Thus a corollary to the basic equation is one that illustrates these rights:

ASSETS − LIABILITIES = CAPITAL

Effects of Transactions on the Accounting Equation

In order to illustrate the effects of some simple transactions on the basic accounting equation, a hypothetical human service agency will be set up to see its initial transactions and their effects on the equation. In the following example, the accrual basis of accounting will be used.

Suppose John Jones, M.S.W., decides to open up a private practice to be called "John Jones Counseling Services." The first thing that John does is open a bank account in the name of his new agency with $10,000. The effect of this transaction is to increase the asset, cash, by $10,000 and at the same time to increase capital by a similar amount. Changes in capital are the result of factors such as:

1. Investments by the owner (I): as can be seen here John has taken his personal assets and invested them in this new counseling service. This money is not considered a loan, its effect is to increase assets and therefore it increases capital.

2. Withdrawals by the owner (W): if John were to withdraw assets from the practice for his personal use this would decrease capital.

3. Net Income/net loss: Net income is the excess of revenue over expenses during an accounting period. This is illustrated by the following equation:

Net Income = Revenue − Expenses

Net loss is calculated the same way, except that in the case of a loss expenses exceed revenues. Revenues (R) are amounts earned by an agency for providing a service. Expenses (E) are costs borne by the agency in providing the service. To help us remember these factors as they relate to capital, they will be listed individually next to it. Revenues and Expenses are combined in financial statements later.

This first transaction of John Jones Counseling Services, the depositing of $10,000, would effect the accounting equation as follows:

	ASSETS		=	CAPITAL	
a)	Cash	$10,000	=	John Jones, Capital	$10,000 (+I)

Remember that according to the accounting entity concept, we are only concerned with the entity John Jones Counseling Services, not any other assets that John might have such as a house, car, or any other personal property.

John next secures an office to rent, for which he pays one month's rent of $400. The effect of this transaction is to decrease the asset cash by $400 and to decrease capital by the same amount. The equation would then look like this:

	ASSETS		=		CAPITAL	
b)	Cash	$10,000		John Jones, Capital	$10,000	
	Rent	− 400			− 400(− E)	
	Cash	$ 9,600		John Jones, Capital	$ 9,600	

John now needs to secure office equipment such as a desk, chairs, and a filing cabinet. He finds office equipment that costs $850, and he pays for this on credit. This creates a debt called ACCOUNTS PAYABLE as well as a new asset, OFFICE EQUIPMENT. The accounting equation now looks like this:

	ASSETS	=	LIABILITIES	+	CAPITAL
Cash	+ Office Equipment	=	Accounts Payable	+	John Jones, Capital
c)$9,600+	$850	=	$850	+	$9,600

In actual practice, each piece of equipment would be recorded separately in the agency's books, but equipment has been grouped together here just to illustrate the effects of the transaction. What has occurred is that assets have increased by $850 and liabilities have increased by $850.

By the first two weeks of the month John has started getting referrals for clients. He saw eight clients who paid $480 in fees. These fees are called REVENUES, they are the amounts earned by the agency for providing a service. In this case, these fees increased his asset cash and increased his capital as well.

	ASSETS	=	LIABILITIES	+	CAPITAL
d) Cash +	Office Equipment	=	Accounts Payable	+	John Jones, Capital
$9,600					$9,600
+ 480				+	480
$10,080 +	$850	=	$850	+	$10,080

During the month John pays $250 to his creditors for the office furniture that he purchased. This has the effect of reducing the asset cash and reducing the liability accounts payable:

	ASSETS	=	LIABILITIES	+	CAPITAL
e) Cash +	Office Equipment	=	Accounts Payable	+	John Jones, Capital
$10,080					
− 250			− 250		
$9,830 +	$850	=	$600	+	$10,080

If you will add the assets cash and office equipment you will see that the total of the two is $10,680 and that the equity side of liabilities and capital also is $10,680. Therefore, the amount of assets equals the amount of equity.

During the month John also had some clients who did not pay him at the time the services were rendered. Instead, they agreed to pay him at sometime in the near future. This created a new account called an ACCOUNTS RECEIVABLE. By creating this new account, John is using the accrual method of accounting. John had $725 in accounts receivable, which had the following effect on the accounting equation:

	ASSETS			= LIABILITIES	+	CAPITAL
		Office	Accounts	Accounts		
f) Cash	+	equipment +	receivable =	Payable	+	John Jones, Capital
						$10,080
			+ 725			+ 725(+R)
			———			———
$9,830 +		$850 +	$725 =	$600	+	$10,805

The money due John by his clients increased the asset called accounts receivable as well as increased his capital. When the clients pay there will be no change on the right side of the equation, only the left side will be effected as accounts receivable will decrease and cash will increase.

At the end of the month John paid $300 in expenses. EXPENSES are assets used or consumed by the agency during the course of business. These include such things as supplies, wages, telephone, rent, and so forth. The excess of revenue after deducting all expenses is called NET PROFIT. Since a nonprofit human service agency does not make a profit, this excess is called a surplus. The effect of paying the expenses was to decrease cash as well as capital:

	ASSETS			= LIABILITIES	+	CAPITAL
		Office	Accounts	Accounts		
g) Cash	+	equipment +	receivable =	Payable	+	John Jones, Capital
$9,830						$10,805
− 300						− 300(−E)
———						———
$9,530 +		$850 +	$725 =	$600	+	$10,505

The last transaction John completed during the month was to draw $1000 for himself. The purpose of this drawing was to pay himself a salary. The effect was to decrease cash and capital:

		Office	Accounts	Accounts		
h) Cash	+	equipment +	receivable =	Payable	+	John Jones, Capital
$9,530						$10,505
− 1,000						− 1,000(−W)
———						———
$8,530 +		$850	$725	= $600	+	$9,505

This then would reflect the transactions of John Jones Counseling Services during the month. If you will add all the assets you will find that they equal $10,105 and if you add the liabilities and capital you will note that they also equal $10,105.

There are two points to be drawn from the illustration provided here:

1. In the accounting equation the left side should always equal the right side, that is, assets should always equal liabilities plus capital.

2. The effect of every monetary transaction that takes place in the agency can be stated as an increase or decrease in one or more components of the accounting equation, that is assets, liabilities, or capital.

In the next section will be a brief description of the relationship between the basic accounting equation and one of the required financial statements, the balance sheet.

FINANCIAL STATEMENTS

Financial statements are one of the end products or outputs of the accounting cycle, but they are mentioned here in brief to facilitate an understanding of the accounting process. The purpose of financial statements is to provide a picture of the financial position of an agency at one point in time for management and interested outsiders. Since the financial statements are at the end of the cycle, understanding them and how they reflect changes in transactions will help one appreciate the preceding steps.

While there are three types of financial statements used by human service agencies, the only one we will be concerned with here is the BALANCE SHEET because the balance sheet is essentially a reflection of the accounting equation: assets = liabilities + capital. To illustrate what the balance sheet represents, take the previous example of John Jones Counseling Services and let us see the effect of its transactions on the balance sheet. Briefly, the transactions were:

a) Jan. 1. Began business by depositing $10,000 in a bank account. On Jan. 1 John's Balance Sheet would look like this:

John Jones Counseling Service
Balance Sheet
January 1, 198X

ASSETS		LIABILITIES AND CAPITAL	
Cash	$10,000	John Jones, Capital	$10,000

The balance sheet for January 1 shows that the agency has cash of $10,000. Since there are no liabilities, John also has capital of $10,000 in his practice. Remember that although in this case capital is equal to the amount in the bank, this is rarely the case because capital is just the result of a mathematical equation.

b) Jan. 3. Paid rent of $400 for the month.

c) Jan. 4. Purchased office equipment for $850 on credit.

d) Jan. 15. Received fees of $480.

On Jan. 15 the Balance Sheet of the Counseling Service would look like this:

John Jones Counseling Service
Balance Sheet
January 15, 198X

ASSETS		LIABILITIES AND CAPITAL	
Cash	$10,080	Accounts payable	$850
Office equipment	850	John Jones, Capital	10,080
	$10,930		$10,930

John has cash of $10,080 because while he paid rent of $400, he also received fees of $480. He also increased his assets by acquiring office equipment.

e)	Jan. 17.	Paid $250 on office equipment.
f)	Jan. 20.	Billed clients $725 for services.
g)	Jan. 25.	Paid expenses of $300.
h)	Jan. 30.	Drew $1000 salary.

On January 30, the Balance Sheet of John Jones Counseling Service would look like this:

John Jones Counseling Service
Balance Sheet
January 30, 198X

ASSETS		LIABILITIES AND CAPITAL	
Cash	$8,530	Accounts payable	$ $600
Office equipment	850		
Accounts receivable	725	John Jones, Capital	9,505
	$10,105		$10,105

These then are the transactions of John Jones Counseling Services. All of them affect one or more components of the accounting equation, all of them make up components of the balance sheet. As you will notice, one side of the balance sheet, the assets, equals the other side, the liabilities and capital. The balance sheet shows how these components are distributed, and how much is left over for capital.

In the next chapter an overview of fund accounting and the accounting cycle will be presented, using a multi-funded human service agency as an example.

Chapter Eight
Questions and Topics for Discussion

1. What are the basic principles and concepts applicable to human service agency accounting?
2. What are the basic differences between nonprofit accounting and accounting for profit-oriented organizations?
3. What is accrual accounting?
4. What is the basic accounting equation for nonprofits?
5. What are the components of the accounting equation?
6. What is the balance sheet?
7. How is the balance sheet related to the accounting equation?
8. What factors result in changes in capital?
9. Why is capital only the result of a mathematical equation?
10. How can the effects of monetary transactions in the agency be stated?

Exercise 8-1: Transaction Effects on Cash

Below are a series of transactions of Psychotherapy Associates, Inc. Please indicate what effect each transaction has on the asset cash for this agency. In the column headed "Effect on Cash," indicate increase or decrease and the amount.

Exercise 8-2: Transaction Effects on the Accounting Equation

Below is a series of transactions for Human Services, Inc. for March 1st. This agency uses the accrual method of accounting. For each of the following transactions of this agency please decide which aspect of the fundamental accounting equation is affected and in what way, that is, what is increased or decreased and for what amount? Write your answer in the space provided.

Exercise 8-1 (continued)

Date	Event	Effect on Cash
June 1	Agency pays rent of $500	:
June 2	Agency pays utility bill of $150	:
June 7	Agency deposits fees from clients—$350	:
June 15	Agency records accounts payable of $650	:
June 20	Agency buys new typewriter on credit with $50 deposit, owes $850	:
June 25	Agency receives a bill from plumber for $75	:
June 30	Agency deposits fees from clients—$1800	:
June 30	Agency receives a bill of $50 for books	:
June 30	Agency owes partners $1000 each	:

Exercise 8-2

Human Services, Inc.

Transaction		Effects on		
		Assets	Liabilities	Capital
Mar 2.	Deposited $500 from fees.			
Mar 3.	Paid rent $675.			
Mar 3.	Paid utilities $150.			
Mar 4.	Borrowed $5,000 from bank.			
Mar 5.	Purchased new computer system on credit with $300 down, owe $2800 on balance.			
Mar 15.	Deposited $1500 from fees.			
Mar 15.	Recorded $900 due in fees.			
Mar 20.	Purchased answering machine for $115 on credit.			
Mar 30.	Paid receptionist $800.			
Mar 30.	Received $400 in fees due.			
Mar 30.	Drew $1000 for salary.			

Also shown on page 205 is the balance sheet for the agency for March 1st. After completing your analysis of the transactions, please draw up a new balance sheet for March 30th.

Exercise 8-2 (continued)

Human Services, Inc.
Balance Sheet
March 1, 198x

Assets		Equities	
Cash	$3,450	Liabilities	$2,140
Accounts receivable	850		
Other assets	1,275	Capital	3,435
	$5,575		$5,575

Case 8-1: Metropolitan Family Counseling Services, Inc.

The Metropolitan Family Counseling Services, Inc. is a new human service agency, having been started less than a year ago by a social worker, a psychologist, and a psychiatrist. It provides counseling services to individuals, families, and children on a sliding scale fee basis. Up to this point, payments had to be made when services were rendered. There was no billing, and if clients wanted third-party reimbursement they had to file the claims themselves after paying the Counseling Service. There was no bookkeeper, the receptionist just recorded the fees received on the day of receipt. Each partner in the Counseling service took care of their share of the expenses for overhead by paying into a business checking account which was in the name of the Counseling Service. Each partner had check-signing privileges on the account. The bills to be paid were sorted by the receptionist, who then wrote checks to cover them. The checks were then signed by any of the partners who were available. The receptionist kept a log of the bills paid, the date, amount, and check number.

The Counseling Service has grown tremendously, there is now a waiting list. And as it specializes in group counseling for troubled adolescents, as well as those with alcohol and drug problems, the local school district has been considering contracting with Metropolitan to provide services for emotionally troubled students. The amount of work has become overwhelming to the human service staff. They can no longer keep track of the business side of running a human service organization as they are too busy with clients. In addition, they feel inadequate to deal with the various administrative tasks involved in maintaining high quality counseling services. At the last staff meeting, it was suggested that an administrator and bookkeeper be hired. The agency is especially interested in someone with a human service background who also understands financial management, as one of the first tasks of the new administrator will be to meet with an accountant to discuss what sort of accounting system should be set up for the agency.

You have an appointment for an interview for this administrative position. You know you will be asked your opinion about a new accounting system. You have found a chart that you think may be useful, it may help you appear somewhat knowledgeable.

Case Questions:

1. Based on this chart, what sort of accounting basis do you think this agency should use?
2. What sort of accounting system do they have now?
3. What kind of control system do they have?
4. What other recommendations do you have for this agency that you could discuss in your interview?

Reading 8-1: A Private Group Whose Word is Law*

What's the bottom line? Whatever the Financial Accounting Standards Board says it is. That also goes for anything above or below it, and for "generally accepted accounting principles" as well.

The board comprises seven individuals who meet weekly in Stamford, Conn. They establish standards for financial accounting and reporting. Although the FASB is technically a private organization without governmental authority, its decisions are nearly always accepted by the federal Securities and Exchange Commission, and SEC acceptance gives them the force of law.

Those decisions—which often deal with highly complex accounting rules—can have enormous real-world effects. A current example involves the acquisition of a troubled savings and loan by a healthy one.

The interplay of present accounting rules can cause the combined institution to show much higher income in the first few years after the merger than could be found if each half of the combination were considered separately.

That does not adequately reflect the economics of the transaction,

---

*Reprinted by permission of *Nation's Business,* December, 1982, Copyright 1982, Chamber of Commerce of the United States.

Table 8-1

DETERMINING THE BEST BASIS OF ACCOUNTING FOR YOUR ORGANIZATION*

Organizational Variables	Recording Basis		
	Cash	Modified Cash	Accrual
1. The volume of transactions processed each month:			
a. small	X		
b. large		X	X
2. Bookkeeper knowledge:			
a. little or none	X		
b. adequate to expert		X	X
3. Audits required		X	X
4. Monthly financial reports needed		X	X
5. Only receipt and expense reports required	X		
6. Accurate up-to-date financial data necessary			X
7. Costs involved to maintain system:			
a. low	X		
b. medium		X	
c. high			X

*Adapted from: W.J. Whalen, "The basics of accounting", in T.D. Connors and C. Callaghan (Eds.), Financial Management for Nonprofit Organizations. New York, AMACOM, 1982, p. 276.

especially when a shaky institution is involved, the board holds. It is therefore pondering a rules change to require the amortization of "good-will" over a shorter period than the present maximum of 40 years, which would eliminate the paper earnings increase.

Unfortunately, such a change would also eliminate one of the few inducements to these mergers, which are often shotgun weddings arranged by federal regulators to prevent major failures in the thrift industry. Thus, the FASB may find itself complicating the work of the Federal Savings and Loan Insurance Corporation while furthering the objectives of the SEC.

To minimize problems of this nature, the FASB maintains a Washington office and works closely with numerous federal agencies. Primary among them is the SEC, which has statutory authority under the Securities Act of 1933 and other laws to develop accounting and reporting standards. Board members and the SEC commissioners meet regularly, and there is a continuing liaison between the two staffs.

The FASB is also working with the Internal Revenue Service on accounting standards for safe harbor leasing, with the Labor Department on the treatment of pension plans, with the bank regulatory agencies on thrift problems and with the Small Business Administration on simplification of rules for small enterprises. It interacts frequently with the General Accounting Office, key congressional committees, the Commerce Department and assorted regulatory agencies.

Prior to formation of FASB in 1973, many of its functions were performed by the Accounting Principles Board of the American Institute of Certified Public Accountants. By the end of the 1960's, however, there was much dissatisfaction with this arrangement.

"Whether accurate or not," says Robert Van Riper, FASB's public relations counsel, "there was a widespread perception that the Accounting Principles Board was too dominated by the accounting profession and that its members were overly responsive to the interests of their clients."

Also, there was a feeling that a voluntary organization with a small staff couldn't keep up with the tide of creative accounting and financing in the go-go 1960's.

In 1971 the AICPA appointed a committee to study the problems and recommend a solution. It was headed by a former SEC commissioner, Francis M. Wheat. The FASB, founded by the AICPA and other groups of accounting and financial professionals, is the product of the Wheat committee's deliberations.

The FASB's members must have "knowledge of accounting, finance and business, and a concern for the public interest in matters of financial accounting and reporting." They must sever all connections with firms or institutions they served before taking their full-time, salaried positions on the board.

Backgrounds of the board's present members illustrate the desire of its founders to represent constituencies beyond the accounting profession itself.

Chairman Donald J. Kirk was formerly a partner in Price Waterhouse & Company; Vice Chairman Robert T. Sprouse was a professor of accounting at Stanford University; Frank E. Block was vice president of Bache, Halsey, Stuart, Shields, Inc.; John W. March was a senior partner of Arthur Anderson & Company; Robert W. Morgan was controller of Caterpillar Tractor Company; David Mosso was fiscal assistant secretary, U.S. Treasury; and Ralph E. Walters was director of professional standards, Touche Ross International.

The organization's 45-member professional staff is headed by the director of research and technical activities, a post considered equal in importance to a board member's.

Board members are appointed to five-year terms (they may be reappointed once) by the Financial Accounting Foundation, which also receives contributions from corporations and accountants and approves the board's budget ($8.6 million for 1982).

The foundation's 12 trustees are nominated by six sponsoring organizations: the American Accounting Association (academe), the American Institute of Certified Public Accountants, the Financial Analysis Federation (investors and investment advisers), the Financial Executives Institute (corporate investors officials), the National Association of Accountants (management accountants), and the Securities Industry Association (investment bankers and brokers). A trustee at large is selected by the major associations in the banking industry.

The foundation also appoints the 38-member Financial Accounting Standards Advisory Council, which advises the board on policy questions, project priorities, technical issues and developing problems.

Its membership is broadly representative of the preparers, auditors, and users of financial information. Current chairman of the council is Paul Kolton, a former chairman of the American Stock Exchange.

FASB pronouncements are divided into three categories—statements of financial accounting standards, statements of concepts and interpretations.

The FASB explains:

"Statements of financial accounting standards establish new standards or amend those previously issued. Statements of concepts provide a guide to the board in solving problems and enable those who use financial reports to better understand the context in which financial accounting standards are formulated. [They] . . . do not establish new standards or require any change in existing accounting principles. Interpretations clarify, explain or elaborate on existing standards."

In addition to these three classifications, the FASB staff issues technical bulletins "to provide guidance on applying existing standards to certain financial accounting and reporting problems on a timely basis."

Standards established by the FASB's predecessors remain in effect until repealed or modified by the board.

In developing new standards, the board follows a complicated process intended to give all concerned a chance to have a say. The steps include:

- Appointing a task force of technical experts to make recommendations.
- Studying existing literature.
- Publishing an analysis of the issues involved and possible solutions.
- Holding public hearings.
- Distributing an "exposure draft" of the proposed statement for further public comment.

The board's deliberations are open to the public, as are the records of its proceedings.

One side effect of this elaborate regard for "due process" is that it takes the FASB a long time to act. According to a staff member, adoption of a simple, uncontroversial standard may require six to nine months, while more complicated matters can drag on for a long as three or four years.

One of the more controversial FASB actions of recent years is Statement 33. Published in 1979, it requires large companies to adjust parts of their annual reports for the effects of inflation.

Such reports can dramatically deflate earnings and other statistics to which management likes to point with pride. Further, the index used to represent inflation—the consumer price index—is regarded as inaccurate by many economists.

As one corporation's annual report cautions: "This attempt to illustrate inflation's effect involves subjective judgments, assumptions and estimates to a much greater degree than in financial statements stated at historical costs and must be carefully viewed."

In recognition of the unusual problems it represents, the board is closely monitoring Statement 33 for a five-year period to see if changes are needed.

Questions for Reading 8-1:

1. What is the FASB?
2. What is the composition of the FASB?
3. What is the difference between statements of financial accounting standards, statements of concepts, interpretations, and technical bulletins?
4. What is the process used by the FASB in developing new standards?
5. How does Statement 33 seem to be related to the cost principle and the monetary principle?
6. Should the nonprofit sector have its own equivalent of an FASB?

Chapter Nine

NONPROFIT ACCOUNTING

After reading this chapter you should be able to:

1. Understand fund accounting.
2. Discuss appropriate funds for the nonprofit agency.
3. Follow simple transactions through the accounting cycle.
4. Understand the relationship of accounts to the financial statements.

INTRODUCTION

The example of John Jones Counseling Service was a very simple agency with only one source of revenue—fees from clients. However, as you know, an agency may have a multiplicity of funding sources, all with differing goals, purposes, restrictions, requirements, guidelines, and fiscal periods. For example, one agency may have one or more of the following sources of support all at the same time:

- Federal government
- State government
- County and/or municipal government
- Allocation agency, e.g., United Way, Jewish Federation, Catholic Charities, etc.
- Private foundation grant
- Fees from clients
- Contributions and pledges from donors
- Membership dues
- In-kind donations

These various sources do not always give money for the agency to dispose of at its sole discretion. Many times agencies receive gifts that are restricted by the donor in some way; that is, the agency is not free to use the money for its operating expenses or for just anything it chooses. Rather, it must hold and use the monies as stipulated by the donor if it accepts them. If an agency is not willing to abide by the restrictions as set forth by the donor, the agency must decline the money. Because of the possible multiplicity of funding sources and the problems that ensue in trying to meet agency as well as donor needs and requirements, an agency as public steward, must set up separate accounts called "funds" in order to be better able to account for the monies it has received from various sources.

FUND ACCOUNTING

The "fund" concept is the basis for accounting and reporting in multi-funded human service agencies. "A fund is an entity established to record assets and transactions affecting these assets... The characteristics of a particular fund—the special purposes for which it was conceived and the attendant restrictions—make it necessary to account separately for amounts received, assets, liabilities, and expenses" (Standards, 1974:25). Funds are, therefore, separate accounting entities with their own asset, liability, fund balance, expense and revenue accounts, and even perhaps their own ledgers. Funds are used for two main reasons in nonprofit human service agencies: 1) to control resources that are earmarked for specific programs or projects; and 2) to ensure and be able to demonstrate that the agency has complied with legal and/or administrative requirements (Lynn and Freeman, 1983:8). There is a difference, however, between fund accounting and "funder" accounting. Fund accounting is required by AICPA audit guidelines as well as the *Standards*, 1974, United Way guidelines and the laws governing nonprofits in many states. The mechanism for fund accounting is done by actual separation of sets of books or separation in the chart of accounts for each fund (Whalen, 1982:277).

Funder accounting is a type of accounting by sources and uses of revenue by funding source. For example, if an agency received funds from three different organizations and kept separate books for each funder, it would be doing funder accounting. Funder accounting has no set format or method, there are a variety of way of designing a system to be able to report disposition of funds to funding sources. The agency should be guided by its accountant and funder requirements. In this chapter we will not discuss funder accounting in detail, rather we will concentrate on fund accounting.

The appropriate funds for nonprofit human service agencies include the following (*Standards*, 1974; *Audit Guide*, 1974):

Current Fund—Unrestricted: The Audit Guide defines current unrestricted funds as those resources "over which the governing board has discretionary control to use in carrying on the operations of the organization in accordance with the limitation of its charter and bylaws except for unrestricted amounts invested in land, buildings and equipment that may be accounted for in a separate fund" (1974:2). Current unrestricted funds usually come from program service fees, contributions, membership dues and investments. Decreases in unrestricted funds may be the result of expenses incurred in the carrying out of agency programs. Therefore, current unrestricted funds are usually used for general operating expenses. Even though in acquiring these funds they were unrestricted, the agency board may "appropriate" or restrict part of the funds for specific purposes or projects.

Current Fund—Restricted: Current restricted funds "are often established to account for those resources currently available for use, but expendable only for operating purposes specified by the donor or grantor" (Audit Guide, 1974:2). In other words, the agency may receive gifts, donations, grants, or even income from an endowment fund in which the resource has specified the purpose for which the monies are to be used. For example, a donor may give an agency some money with the stipulation that it only be used to provide services to unwed mothers, or teen-age drug abusers, or whatever special interest the donor might have. Therefore, the agency sets this money aside in a restricted account so that it will not be used for general operating expenses and the agency will be able to account for it properly.

Land, Building and Equipment Fund

This fund is sometimes called the plant fund, it "is often used to accumulate the net investment in fixed assets and to account for the unexpended resources contributed specifically for the purpose of acquiring or replacing land, buildings, or equipment for use in the operations of the organization" (Audit Guide, 1974:2). This means that after an agency has decided to purchase land or a building or major equipment, it would store up its surplus or set aside money in this fund in order to accumulate enough to complete the purchase. It uses this fund in order to be able to account for the money so set aside. Mortgages and other liabilities arising from the acquiring of land, buildings, or equipment are included in this fund as are depreciation expenses and gains or losses from the sale of these fixed assets.

Endowment Fund

An endowment fund is made up of "the principal amount of gifts and bequests accepted with the donor-stipulation that the principal be maintained intact in perpetuity, until the occurrence of a specified event, or for a specified period, and that only the income from investment thereof be expended either for general purposes or for purposes specified by the donor" (*Audit Guide,* 1974:3). In other words, an endowment fund is made up of money that is to be invested. The agency may use the income earned from the investment, while the original amount (the principal) stays intact either to be used indefinitely or to be returned to the donor at some time in the future as agreed. The money earned may be used for general operating expenses unless the donor restricts the money for a specific purpose. If the investment income is available for any general purpose, then it must be included in the revenues of the current unrestricted fund (*Audit Guide:*7).

Custodian Fund

A Custodian Fund is a fund set up "to account for assets received by an organization to be held or disbursed only on instructions of the person or organization from whom they were received" (*Audit Guide:*3). Since the monies in this fund are being held temporarily for someone else, they are not assets of the agency and should not be considered as part of the revenue or support of the agency. A Custodian Fund may be set up, for example, for "pass through" funds. These are funds that are given to the agency to be passed on to someone else as when an agency receives funds to distribute to unemployed youth for summer stipends.

A fifth fund, called the *Loan and Annuity Fund,* may be used if needed. This fund may be used for making loans or paying annuities, but it is not usually an important or common fund in the nonprofit human service agency.

THE ACCOUNTING EQUATION

For the nonprofit human service agency with one or more of these funds, the accounting equation would be basically the same as that discussed in Chapter Seven except that capital is now replaced by the term "fund balances." Capital represents the ownership equity in a business, and is replaced by funds because, by its very nature, the nonprofit human service agency has no owners or stockholders. Therefore, the use of the term capital would be inappropriate. Secondly, since human service agencies must use funds for control and accountability, the balances in the funds must be reported in the agency financial statements. The accounting equation for the human service agency states that assets equal liabilities plus fund balances. Thus, the accounting equation for the human service agency would look like this:

ASSETS = LIABILITIES + FUND BALANCES

Conversely, fund balances represent the residual resources of the agency after all liabilities are satisfied or paid. This is illustrated by the following equation:

ASSETS − LIABILITIES = FUND BALANCES

Fund accounting is unique to nonprofit accounting and, more than anything else, is what distinguishes nonprofit from for-profit accounting. In being able to account for the the disposition of resources by purpose or fund, fund accounting is reflecting the public responsibility and stewardship function of the human service agency. In addition, this type of accounting is reflecting the obligation of human service agencies to separate restricted from nonrestricted funds. Let us now view fund accounting within the framework of the accounting cycle.

THE ACCOUNTING CYCLE

According to the time period principle, the economic activities of the human service agency are divided up into periods of equal length for purposes of recording and reporting. The longest fiscal period is usually one year. The beginning and end of an agency's fiscal year may depend on its major funder. For example, if an agency's major source of funds is a United Way or other federated funder, it may have a fiscal year to coincide with that allocation agency. Other fiscal periods may be divided into shorter periods of time, such as quarters of a year. In any case, in each time period there is a similar cycle of events that take place in all financial subsystems. Some of these are quite routine in nature and make up the accounting cycle. Steps in the accounting cycle include the following (Meigs and Meigs, 1981: 150–152):

1. Occurrence of an Economic Transaction

An economic transaction is any event that occurs in which a representative of the agency and monies are involved. For example, a client pays for casework or counseling services rendered, the caseworker makes a home visit and submits a travel voucher for reimbursement for mileage, the office manager buys office supplies, and so forth (see Figure 9-1).

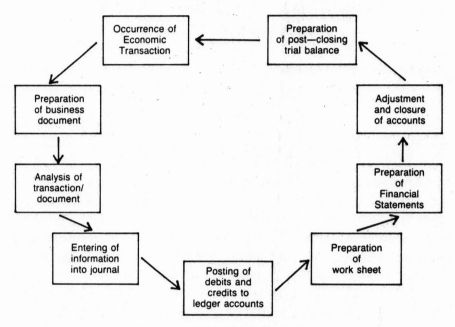

Figure 9-1: The Accounting Cycle

2. Preparation of a Business Document

After an economic transaction has taken place, as in the case of the client paying for services rendered, a business document is prepared. In most cases the business document is a receipt or a voucher. This document represents the objective evidence needed to ascertain the value or cost of the exchange in the economic transaction.

3. Analysis of Transaction/Document

After receiving the document that reflects that a transaction has taken place, the person in charge of the recording function must decide what effect it has on the fund balances of the agency. That is, does the transaction increase them or decrease them? The person in charge, usually a bookkeeper, must also decide what accounts are effected by the transaction. The bookkeeper is helped in this task if a chart of accounts has been established by the agency. You may recall from Chapter Six that a chart of accounts is a listing of the main accounts used by the agency in which every account is assigned a code number. If the agency is a United Way agency, it may use the chart of accounts codes of the United Way (see Chapter 6 for an example). If expenses are involved in the economic transaction, the bookkeeper must also decide how to allocate the costs by program or support service functions. This task is also made easier if the agency has set up a control system which allows for automatic recording by department or function.

4. Entering of Information in Journal

Every monetary transaction that occurs is first recorded in a journal. The journal is called the book of original entry and it is a day-to-day, chronological listing of each transaction and the debit and credit changes caused by each. At periodic intervals in the accounting cycle, the debit and credit entries recorded in the journal are posted, or transferred from the journal to the appropriate accounts in the ledger. The updated ledger accounts then serve as the bases of the financial statements prepared by the agency.

There may be many different types of journals used by an agency, generally, the larger the agency the more specialized journals it may use. Some common journals are the cash receipts and revenue journal, the cash disbursements journal, the voucher register and purchase journal, and the general journal (United Way, 1974:56).

The general journal has the following format (See Figure 9-2):

You will note that the journal has the date, a place for an explanation, a posting number, and columns for debits and credits. The terms debit and credit mean only one thing in accounting. Debit means the left side column and credit means the right side column and that is all. Whether an entry is placed on the right (or credit) side or the left (or debit) side depends on the nature of the transaction and the nature of the account. This is because the normal balance of some accounts, assets and expenses, is a debit, while the normal balance of other accounts, liabilities, fund balances, and revenues, is a credit. Whether a transaction increases or decreases the balance in an account determines whether it will be debited or credited.

Table 9-1 below summarizes the rules for debits and credits. You will

Table 9-1

RULES FOR CHANGES IN ACCOUNTS

Account	Debit		Credit	
	Affect of Entry	Normal Balance	Affect of Entry	Normal Balance
Assets	increase	X	decrease	
Liabilities	decrease		increase	X
Fund balances	decrease		increase	X
Revenues	decrease		increase	X
Expenses	increase	X	decrease	

note, for example, that the effect of debiting an asset account is to *increase* the balance in the account, while crediting an asset account *decreases* the amount in it. You will be able to understand these rules better after the case illustration that follows.

One important point to remember in journalizing is that, because of the accounting equation, debits must always equal credits. So every entry in the journal must be balanced by another entry in the journal.

5. Posting of Debits and Credits to Ledger Accounts

A ledger is made up of the total group of accounts used by the agency. A ledger account is used to record the increases and decreases in every balance sheet item. In a manual accounting system all these separate accounts are kept in a loose-leaf binder and collectively called the ledger. In a computerized accounting system, ledger accounts are stored on computer disks or tapes. Computerized accounting systems will be discussed in Chapter Eleven.

The general ledger is the heart of an agency's accounting system.

HUMAN SERVICES AGENCY, INC.
GENERAL JOURNAL

Date	Description	Chart of Acct. No.	Debit	Credit
July 5	Cash	1-1001	35000 00	
	Public Support	1-4001		35000 00
July 17	Cash	1-1001	4725 00	
	Revenue	1-6004		4725 00
July 28	Cash	1-1001	16000 00	
	Pledges Receivable	1-4002		16000 00

Figure 9-2: Sample General Journal

While the journal is the book of original entry, the ledger is the book of final entry in which all the financial transactions of the agency are summarized by account title and number. A general ledger may have subsidiary ledgers for handling specific types of transactions, for example, an agency may use an accounts receivable ledger, a pledges receivable ledger, an accounts payable ledger and a land, building and equipment ledger (United Way, 1974:61).

The simplest form of a ledger account is called a *T-account* because it resembles the letter T and contains the following information:

- Title of account
- Left or debit side
- Right or credit side (see Table 9-2).

In posting, the bookkeeper transfers the debits and credits from the journal and records them in the general ledger in their proper account. This facilitates the identification and isolation of specific information regarding any particular account. For example, if an agency director wanted to know the balance in the Revenue from Fees Account, rather than having to go day-by-day through the general journal, the bookkeeper can go straight to the appropriate account in the ledger (see Figure 9-3 for an example of a ledger entry).

Table 9-2

T-ACCOUNT

Title of Account

Debit	Credit

6. Preparation of Work Sheet

The work sheet is a multi-column form that helps in making adjust-ments, in preparing the trial balance, and in the construction of the financial statements. A sample worksheet may be seen in Table 9-4. You may note that the worksheet has columns for the unadjusted trial balance, any necessary adjustments, the adjusted trial balance, the Statement of Support, Revenue and Expenses and Changes in Fund Balances (SRECFB) and the Balance Sheet.

HUMAN SERVICES AGENCY, INC.
GENERAL LEDGER

Date	Cash Account No. 1-1001	Debit	Credit	Balance
July 1	Beginning Balance			23250 00
July 5	Gen. Journal, pg. 7	35000 00		58250 00
July 17	Gen. Journal, pg. 7	4725 00		62975 00
July 28	Gen. Journal, pg. 7	16000 00		78975 00

Figure 9-3: Sample Ledger Entry

There are a number of steps in using a worksheet (NIMH, 1983:125):

a. enter all end of period unadjusted account balances;

b. check to make sure that total debit balances equal total credit balances (preliminary trial balance);

c. make all necessary adjusting entries in the adjustments columns;

d. obtain new adjusted trial balance;

e. transfer account balances to balance sheet or SRECFB. The excess of revenue over expenses or vice versa is found by noting the difference on the SRECFB between total credits and total debits. The amount needed to balance is entered in the appropriate column of the SRECFB.

f. next the balance sheet debit and credit totals are determined. Then the amount needed to balance the totals is entered. This amount should equal the amount needed to balance the SRECFB totals, but should be of the opposite type, i.e., a credit if there is an excess and a debit if there is a deficit.

g. if all sets of columns are now balanced, and excess or deficit is found, then the financial statements can be prepared.

7. Preparation of Financial Statements

All of the required financial statements of the human service agency can be prepared from the information in the worksheet. The required statements are:

The Statement of Revenues and Expenses and Changes in Fund Balances (SRECFB);

The Balance Sheet;

The Statement of Functional Expenses.

There will be a complete discussion of financial statements in the next chapter, but Figure 9-4 illustrates the relationship of the agency accounts to the required financial statements.

8. Adjustment and Closure of Accounts

After preparation of the financial statements, two types of entries should be made: adjusting entries and closing entries.

a. Adjusting entries are part of the accrual accounting system. Because of the matching concept used in accrual accounting, the agency wants to match revenue with expenses incurred during any par-

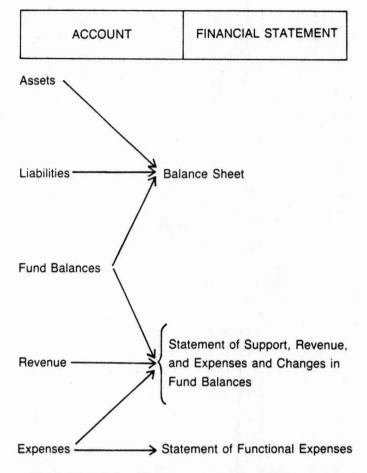

Figure 9-4: Relationship of Accounts to Financial Statements

ticular fiscal period. However, because of the fact that revenue and expenses may not always fall exactly within a fiscal period, it is necessary to make adjusting entries. Also, certain activities that may take place during a period will not be recorded in the books and have to be taken care of by means of adjusting entries. Some items that may be included in adjusting entries are: depreciation of buildings and equipment and uncollectible accounts and pledges (United Way, 1974:66).

Adjusting entries may be done on the same work sheet that is used for the trial balance and the preparation of interim financial statements.

b. Closing entries are usually only done at the end of the fiscal year. Closing entries "close" or reduce the balance of all revenue and expense accounts and transfer them to an Income Summary (or Revenue Summary) Account. The purpose of this is to be able to start the new fiscal period with zero balances so that the agency can accurately "match" expenses and revenues during the new period. Remember, these entries will not be done at the end of a quarter or a month, they are usually done at the end of the fiscal year.

9. Preparation of Post-Closing Trial Balance

The purpose of the post-closing trial balance is to see if the ledger account debits equal account credits. As in any trial balance, just the fact that debits and credits balance does not mean that there are no errors in the records, but if they do not balance it is an obvious indication of error.

One important aspect of the accounting cycle to remember is that while the processing of transactions does have a logical flow, many of the activities discussed occur continuously and simultaneously. For example, even though journalizing must take place before posting to the ledger, they both may occur on the same day. Other activities, such as the preparation of financial statements, will occur much less frequently—once a month, once a quarter, or once a year. The concern is that you, as a human service professional, have an overall picture of the accounting process as it may take place in the human service agency.

We will now look at the accounting cycle in an agency that has multiple funds. For the sake of simplicity, the focus will be on journalizing, posting to the ledger, trial balances, work sheets and preparation of financial statements.

The Accounting Cycle in a Human Service Agency: The Case of the Metropolitan Family Services Center, Inc.

Metropolitan Family Services, Inc., is an agency that was set up as the result of work by a coalition of concerned citizens, business people, and social workers. They perceived a need for an agency in their community that would provide counseling services to individuals and families regardless of income. Some of the coalition members became the nucleus of the Board of Directors that was formed. It secured a nonprofit corporation charter from the State, secured seed money in the amount of $50,000 from the local United Way, and hired an Executive Director to recruit and hire other staff. One of the members of the Board of Directors was an accountant who volunteered his time to help the new Director to set up the accounts of the agency and secure a bookkeeper who was somewhat familiar with nonprofit bookkeeping.

Since one of the goals of the agency was to provide services to all regardless of income, the agency set a sliding scale fee schedule that started at $1 and went up to $50 based on income. As it is a new agency, it has only two functional areas at the present time: program services (counseling) and support services. The director, a professional social worker, has split her time as follows: 50% program services, 50% support (25% fund-raising, 25% administration). The full-time counselor's salary is 100% program services. The secretary-receptionist's time is split the same as the director's. Other expenses are allocated 75% to program services, 15% to fundraising, and 10% to management and general.

At present the agency is using the following funds: Current Unrestricted, Current Restricted, and Land, Building, and Equipment Fund. Since the agency is very small at the present time, it has a very simple accounting system with only a general journal and general ledger for each fund.

We will assume that the agency's fiscal year began January 1st and ended December 31st. During the first year the following transactions took place at the agency. After a description of each transaction, the appropriate journal entry is recorded. Following accounting convention, accounts to be debited are flush with the left margin, and accounts to be credited are indented. The relevant funds in each transaction are underlined.

(a.) Received $50,000 allocation from the local United Way.

This allocation increased the asset cash and increased the revenue account public support. The appropriate journal entries are:

Current Fund—Unrestricted

Cash	$50,000	
Public Support		$50,000

(b.) Fees from services during the year amounted to $40,000. Of this amount, $5,000 was billed but not received by the end of the fiscal year.

Revenue differs from public support in that public support comes to the agency from allocations, grants, and contributions while revenue comes to the agency as a result of it providing a service or product. In this case, the provision of services resulted in an increase in the assets cash and accounts receivable and an increase in the revenue account.

Current Fund—Unrestricted

Cash	$35,000	
Accounts Receivable	5,000	
Revenue		$40,000

(c.) Received pledges in the amount of $92,000 as a result of agency's fund-raising. $10,000 of this was restricted for a needs assessment to determine the need for a special teen program. $15,000 was restricted to renovations in the office the agency was in, $5,000 was restricted for the acquisition of a computer system.

Receiving these pledges increases the asset pledges receivable as well as increasing fund balances. Remember that because of the accounting equation, both sides must be equal or balance. So, an entry on one side of the equation must be balanced by an entry on the other side. The account called deferred support is used because the agency has not received the money, and it does not know if it will, therefore, it cannot be counted as public support yet. When the money is received it will be transferred to the cash account and to the public support account.

Current Funds—Unrestricted

Pledges Receivable	$62,000	
Deferred Support		$62,000

Current Funds—Restricted

Pledges Receivable	$10,000	
Deferred Support		$10,000

Land, Building, and Equipment Fund

Pledges Receivable	$20,000	
Deferred Support		$20,000

(d.) Received $90,000 of monies pledged.

When an agency receives pledges, it can never be quite sure how much of the money pledged will actually be received. In this case, the agency received all of the money pledged for the needs assessment, $10,000 as well as the money for the renovation, $20,000. But it only received $60,000 of the rest of the money pledged.

Current Fund—Unrestricted

Cash	$60,000	
Pledges Receivable		$60,000
Deferred Support	$60,000	
Public Support		$60,000

Current Fund—Restricted

Cash	$10,000	
Pledges Receivable		$10,000
Deferred Support	$10,000	
Public Support		$10,000

Land, Building, and Equipment Fund

Cash	$20,000	
Pledges Receivable		$20,000
Deferred Support	$20,000	
Public Support		$20,000

As you can see, in each fund entries have been recorded to reflect that the money pledged has actually been received. The $2,000 in pledges not yet received will stay in the Pledges Receivable account for another quarter or longer, if cash is not received by that time the agency will write off the pledges as uncollectible.

(e.) Salaries paid out during the year were as follows: Director = $25,000; Social Worker = $20,000; Secretary-Receptionist = $15,000. In actuality, in addition to salary the agency would have expenses for employee benefits, payroll taxes and so forth. These other expenses would each have their own account. For the sake of simplicity all these expenses related to salaries have been lumped together into one account, called Salary Expense.

Current Fund—Unrestricted

Salary Expense	$72,000	
Cash		$72,000

As you can see, the salary account is decreased, or debited, and the cash account is also decreased, or credited.

(f.) The agency had overhead expenses for rent, utilities (gas, water, electricity) and telephone of $12,600. Of this amount, $6,000 was for rent, $3800 was for utilities and $2800 was for telephone.

Current Fund—Unrestricted

Rent Expense	$6,000	
Utilities Expense	3,800	
Telephone Expense	2,800	
Cash		$12,600

As you can see, the expense accounts have been debited or decreased, and the asset cash has also been decreased or credited.

(g.) The agency purchased a computer system, including a micro-computer, monitor, modem, printer, and software for $4,800.

Land, Building, and Equipment Fund

Equipment	$4,800	
Cash		$4,800

The buying of equipment increases the asset account, equipment, but decreases the asset account, cash.

(h.) Program expenses incurred during the year amounted to $9,800. This included Travel = $2,200; printing and postage = $3,200; It also rented a copier for $3,200 for one year with an option to buy, and it bought a service contract for the office machines, including the computer system, for $1,200. Total for rental and maintenance of office equipment = $4,400.

Current Fund—Unrestricted

Travel Expense	$2,200	
Printing and Postage Expense	3,200	
Cash		$5,400

Land, Building, and Equipment Fund

Rental and Maintenance-Office eqmt	4,400	
Cash		$4,400

(i.) The agency bought office furnishings and typewriters for $5,000. It paid $1,000 cash and charged the rest.

Land, Building, and Equipment Fund

Office Furnishings	$5,000	
Cash		$1,000
Accounts Payable		$4,000

(j.) Office supplies purchased during the year amounted to $3,800. Of this, $2,000 was paid in cash and the balance, $1,800 was charged. So the agency not only acquired an asset called office supplies, it also incurred a liability (account payable) with these purchases.

Current Fund—Unrestricted

Office Supplies	$3,800	
Cash		$2,000
Accounts Payable		$1,800

(k.) The agency director had written a grant proposal to start a new program aimed at unwed parents. Before the end of the year, she received notice that a foundation would fund $5,000 for program.

Current Fund—Restricted

Grant Receivable $5,000
    Public support $5,000

This is entered as a grant receivable because the agency has not yet received the money, only notification of funding.

Table 9-3 lists the ledger entries that were posted from the general journal.

Table 9-4 shows the work sheet prepared from the ledger, along with the adjusting entries and trial balances. There are two adjusting entries on the work sheet. The first one is to record supplies consumed. Office supplies are an asset, but they are consumed by the agency in the process of its daily activities. In order to accurately reflect the amount of office

Table 9-3

LEDGER ENTRIES

CURRENT FUND – UNRESTRICTED

CASH		Dr	Cr	ACCOUNTS PAYABLE		Dr	Cr
a)		$50,000.00		j)			$1,800.00
b)		$35,000.00					
d)		$60,000.00					
e)			$72,000.00	PUBLIC SUPPORT			
f)			$12,600.00	a)			$50,000.00
h)			$5,400.00	b)			$60,000.00
j)			$2,000.00		Bal.		$110,000.00
	Bal.	$53,000.00					
ACCOUNTS RECEIVABLE				REVENUE			
b)		$5,000.00		b)			$40,000.00
PLEDGES RECEIVABLE							
c)		$62,000.00		DEFERRED SUPPORT			
d)			$60,000.00	c)			$62,000.00
	Bal.	$2,000.00		d)		$60,000.00	
OFFICE SUPPLIES					Bal.		$62,000.00
j)		$3,800.00					
SALARY EXPENSE							
e)		$72,000.00					
OTHER EXPENSE							
f)		$12,600.00					
h)		$5,400.00					
	Bal.	$18,000.00					

Table 9-3
(**continued**)

CURRENT FUND – RESTRICTED

CASH				PUBLIC SUPPORT		
d)	$10,000.00			d)		$10,000.00
				k)		$5,000.00
PLEDGES RECEIVABLE					Bal.	$15,000.00
c)	$10,000.00					
d)			$10,000.00			
	Bal.	$0.00		DEFERRED SUPPORT		
				c)		$10,000.00
GRANTS RECEIVABLE				d)	$10,000.00	
k)	$5,000.00				Bal.	$0.00

LAND, BUILDING, EQUIPMENT FUND

CASH				ACCOUNTS PAYABLE		
d)	$20,000.00			i)		$4,000.00
g)		$4,800.00				
h)		$4,400.00				
i)		$1,000.00		PUBLIC SUPPORT		
	Bal.	$9,800.00		d)		$20,000.00
PLEDGES RECEIVABLE				DEFERRED SUPPORT		
c)	$20,000.00			c)		$20,000.00
d)		$20,000.00		d)	$20,000.00	
	Bal.	$0.00			Bal.	$0.00
OFFICE FURNISHINGS						
i)	$5,000.00					
OFFICE EQUIPMENT						
g)	$4,800.00					
RENT & MAINT. EXP.						
h)	$4,400.00					

supplies remaining on hand at the end of the year, the office supplies account has to be reduced by the amount used. So an expense account called "office supplies expense" would be used to record this amount, and the office supplies account reduced by $2,300 to show that $1,700 worth of supplies were on hand at the end of the year.

1) Office Supplies used $2,300.

Current Fund—Unrestricted

Office Supplies Expense	$2,300	
Office Supplies		$2,300

The second adjusting entry is to record depreciation. Depreciation is an accounting technique that distributes the cost of a tangible physical asset over its estimated useful life. That is, physical assets may wear out and need to be replaced, they do not last forever. The cost of the physical assets acquired by the agency is part of agency expenses for the period of time the assets are used. These assets are periodically "depreciated," that is their value is decreased by recording a depreciation expense in each year the asset is used. The accumulated depreciation account shows the total amount of decrease in the original value of an asset.

2) Depreciation on typewriters and computer system = $500.

Land, Building and Equipment Fund

Depreciation Expense	$500	
Accumulated Depreciation		$500

Table 9-4

WORKSHEET

LEDGER ACCOUNTS	TRIAL BALANCE		ADJUSTMENTS		ADJUSTED TRIAL BALANCE		SR&E& CFB		BALANCE SHEET	
	Dr	Cr	Dr	Cr	Dr	Cr	Dr	Cr	Dr	Cr
Current Funds-Unrestricted										
Cash	$53,000				$53,000				$53,000	
Accounts Rec.	$5,000				$5,000				$5,000	
Pledges Rec.	$2,000				$2,000				$2,000	
Office Supplies	$3,800			$2,300	$1,500				$1,500	
Accounts Payable		$1,800				$1,800				$1,800
Fund Balance										$59,700
Public Support		$110,000				$110,000		$110,000		
Revenue		$40,000				$40,000		$40,000		
Deferred Support		$2,000				$2,000		$2,000		
Salary Expense	$72,000				$72,000		$72,000			
Rent Expense	$6,000				$6,000		$6,000			
Utilities Expense	$3,800				$3,800		$3,800			
Telephone Expense	$2,800				$2,800		$2,800			
Supplies Expense	$0		$2,300		$2,300		$2,300			
Travel Expense	$2,200				$2,200		$2,200			
Print. & Post. Exp.	$3,200				$3,200		$3,200			
Excess/Deficiency							$59,700			
Total	$153,800	$153,800	$2,300	$2,300	$153,800	$153,800	$152,000	$152,000	$61,500	$61,500

Table 9-5 shows the interim balance sheet prepared from the work sheet.

Table 9-6 shows the interim Statement of Support, Revenue, and Expenses, and Changes in Fund Balances prepared from the work sheet.

Table 9-4
(continued)

WORKSHEET

LEDGER ACCOUNTS	TRIAL BALANCE		ADJUSTMENTS		ADJUSTED TRIAL BALANCE		SR&E& CFB		BALANCE SHEET	
Current Funds-Restricted										
Cash	$10,000				$10,000				$10,000	
Pledgs Rec.										
Grants Rec.	$5,000				$5,000				$5,000	
Fund Balance										$15,000
Public Support		$15,000				$15,000		$15,000		
Deferred Support										
Excess/Def.							$15,000			
Total	$15,000	$15,000			$15,000	$15,000	$15,000	$15,000	$15,000	$15,000
Land, Building, Equipment Fund										
Cash	$9,800				$9,800				$9,800	
Pledges Rec.	$0									
Equipment	$4,800				$4,800				$4,800	
Accum. Dep.-Eqpt				$500			$500			
Office Furnishings	$5,000				$5,000				$5,000	
Accounts Payable		$4,000				$4,000				$4,000
Fund Balance										$15,100
Public Support		$20,000				$20,000		$20,000		
Deferred Support										
Maint. Expense	$4,400				$4,400		$4,400			
Depreciation Exp.			$500		$500		$500			
Excess/Def.							$15,100			
Total	$24,000	$24,000	$500	$500	$24,000	$24,000	$20,000	$20,000	$19,100	$19,100

Chapter 9
Questions and Topics for Discussion

1. What is fund accounting? Why is it used in the human services?
2. What are the appropriate funds for the nonprofit human service agency?
3. What is the fundamental accounting equation as it relates to non-profits? How does it differ from the accounting equation used in for-profit accounting?
4. What are the steps in the accounting cycle?
5. What are journals and ledgers? Debits and credits?
6. What accounts are increased by a debit entry? Decreased by a debit entry?
7. How are the financial statements related to the accounts?
8. What is the importance of the worksheet?
10. Where can you find more information on nonprofit accounting?

Table 9-5

INTERIM BALANCE SHEET

METROPOLITAN FAMILY SERVICES
Year Ended 198X

Current Fund — Unrestricted

Assets		Liabilities	
Cash	$53,000		
Accounts Rec.	$5,000	Accounts Payable	$1,800
Pledges Rec.	$2,000		
Office Supplies	$1,500	Fund Balance	$59,700
Total	$61,500	Total	$61,500

Current Fund — Restricted

Assets		Liabilities	$0
Cash	$10,000		
Grants Receivable	$5,000	Fund Balance	$15,000
Total	$15,000	Total	$15,000

Land, Building, Equipment Fund

Assets		Liabilities	
Cash	$9,800		
Office Equipment		Accounts Payable	$4,000
less $500 accum. depr.	$4,300		
Office Furnishings	$5,000	Fund Balance	$15,100
Total	$19,100	Total	$19,100

Date

1/1	Public support received: $44,000.
1/4	Contributions pledged: $20,000.
1/4	Purchased equipment for $500 cash deposit and $1500 credit.
1/5	Paid rent for storefront office: $400.
1/7	Bought $300 worth of office supplies on credit.
1/9	Paid $250 cash for sign painting.
1/15	Paid $50 for newspaper ads and announcements.
1/15	Cash received from pledges: $5,000.
1/29	Paid telephone and utility expenses of $150.
1/30	Paid salary of social worker/director: $1800.
1/30	Paid salary of receptionist: $1200.

REQUIRED: a. Prepare journal entries for the month.
b. Post journal entries to ledger accounts.
c. Prepare a trial balance for January 30.

Table 9-6

INTERIM STATEMENT OF SUPPORT, REVENUE AND EXPENSES
AND CHANGES IN FUND BALANCES

METROPOLITAN FAMILY SERVICES

Year Ended 198X

| | Current Funds | | Land, Building, | Total |
	Unrestricted	Restricted	Equipment Fund	All Funds
Public Support and Revenue				
Public Support	$110,000	$15,000	$20,000	$145,000
Revenue	$40,000			$40,000
Deferred Support	$2,000			$2,000
Total Public Supp. and Rev.	$152,000	$15,000	$20,000	$187,000
Expenses				
Program Services				
Counseling	$69,225	$0	$3,675	$72,900
Support Services				
Management and General	$9,230	$0	$490	$9,720
Fundraising	$13,845	$0	$735	$14,580
Total Expenses	$92,300	$0	$4,900	$97,200
Excess of Public Support and Revenue over Expenses	$59,700	$15,000	$15,100	$89,800
Fund Balances, beg. of year	$0	$0	$0	$0
Fund Balances, end of year	$59,700	$15,000	$15,100	$89,800

Exercise 9-1: The Metro County I and R Service

The Metro County Information and Referral Service has only been open one month. During that time it completed the following economic transactions:

Exercise 9-2: The Family Counseling Center, Inc.

Shown below are a record of transactions completed by the Family Counseling Center, Inc. during its first year of operation. The agency has only one fund at present, the Current Unrestricted-Fund. It uses a general journal and a general ledger. Its transactions were as follows:

1. United Way allocation received: $50,000.
2. Contributions pledged: $35,000.
3. Office equipment purchased: $1500 cash and $3500 credit.
4. Office rental paid: $7200.
5. Office supplies purchased: $2400.
6. Printing and postage: $1250.
7. Cash received from pledges: $30,000.
8. Telephone and utility expenses: $1800.
9. Billed clients: $15,000; amount received: $12,000, amount owed: $2,000.
10. Salaries paid (including fringes): $40,000.

Agency accounts used:

Account:	What it includes:
Asset Accounts	
Cash	Cash
Receivables	Accounts receivable, pledges receivable
Other assets	Office equipment, office supplies
Liability Accounts	
Accounts payable	Accounts payable
Fund Balances	
Current Unrestricted	
Revenue Accounts	Contributions, fees, allocations
Expense Accounts	Office supplies, salaries, rent, utilities

REQUIRED: a. Prepare appropriate journal entries.
   b. Post them to the appropriate ledger account.
   c. Complete a worksheet.
   d. Prepare a balance sheet for December 31st.

Case 9-1: Accounting and the Small NonProfit Organization ... •

This study was designed to provide baseline data on the accounting practices of small Chicago area nonprofit organizations to assess their need for an accounting assistance program. The study focused on four issues:

1. How well nonprofit organizations managed fiscal matters.
2. What specific organizational accounting and reporting problems they had.
3. What accounting-related assistance they had received.
4. What accounting-related assistance they needed.

Efforts were made to obtain a representative sample of social service, neighborhood or community based, or public interest organizations, generally with budgets under $300,000. . . . 31 organizations which appeared to meet the criteria regarding size and type were selected. Eleven additional agencies were obtained by personal contacts. While the resulting sample is not representative in a statistical sense, a strong effort was made to include as many appropriate organizations as possible, while maintaining a mix of types of organizations and limitations on budget size. . . . this report was based on these 39 interviews.

Description of the Sample

Most of the organizations in this study are community-based or public-interest groups with annual budgets under $300,000. Six of the 39 organizations had budgets over $300,000. . . . The nonprofit organizations represented different funding profiles, revenue levels, and years of experience.

At the time of the study, the most common major funding source was the government. This was especially true for neighborhood and community organizations. Over 80% of these groups had from 51 to 100 percent government funding. Three ethnic organizations had from 66.7 to 99 percent government funding. About 15 percent of the organizations relied either upon foundations or corporations for 55 to 91 percent of their funding. Another 15 percent (15.8%) of the organizations relied on fees and subscriptions.

The organizations also varied in the size of their staffs. They had an

---

average (median) of four full-time, two part-time, and three volunteer staff members. They ranged from eight organizations with no full-time staff to one with 15 staff members. Seven organizations each had no part-time or volunteer staff. Eleven organizations had 10 or more volunteers; two of these had 98 volunteers each.

FINDINGS

The 39 interviews illustrated how a diverse sample of nonprofit organizations managed their fiscal matters, experienced organizational problems related to accounting, tried to solve these problems, and indicated the kinds of accounting assistance they needed.

Fiscal Management

Internal Management

... Over 90 percent of nonprofit organizations in the survey accomplished the basics of cash receipts and cash disbursements journals; marking paid bills as paid; budgeting by functional and program areas; and bank reconciliation. On the other hand, almost 40 percent... did not require written approval of bills for payment and... over 60 percent did not prepare monthly reports on functional expenses..., budget comparisons..., or cash flow... Over 60 percent... did not transfer excess money to savings accounts.

External Reporting Practices

Organizational representatives were asked to indicate their compliance with various federal and state reporting requirements.... Over 90 percent of the organizations complied with federal payroll tax reporting requirements, and almost that percentage (86.1%) did so with state payroll tax reporting. However, beyond these tax reports, there was much less unanimity among the sample regarding external reporting requirements. For example, even in the tax area, nearly 70%... of the organizations had, at least once, been assessed a penalty for late deposit of taxes. Of the 36 organizations in the study with federal tax exempt status, four failed to file their required annual report (Form 990) to the Internal Revenue Service.

Almost one-fifth (17.9%) to almost two-fifths (40%) of the organizations failed to file certain required reports with the State of Illinois. For example, the Illinois Solicitation Act of 1963, as amended, requires that charitable organizations receiving over $25,000 in contributions during the fiscal or calendar year (exclusive of bequests, community chest or governmental funding) must file a report with the Illinois Attorney General. The report must be "accompanied by an opinion signed by an independent certified public accountant that the financial statement therein fairly represents the financial operations of the organization in sufficient detail to permit public evaluation of its operations." (This signed opinion, with an accompanying financial report, is commonly referred to as an audit.) Although over 60 percent (64.1%, n = 25) of the organizations had been audited at least once by an independent certified public accountant, 40 percent (n = 10) of the 25 organizations required by the Illinois Solicitation Act to have an audit had not been audited for their most recent fiscal year. Thus, the 10 organizations that had not had audits were not fulfilling one of their principal external reporting requirements.

What is especially significant about this finding is that failure to pay taxes on time, or to file state and federal annual reports, could, in the extreme, threaten the very existence of an organization. The consequences of such failures range from no action to a firm reminder letter to assessment of late penalties or severe monetary penalties, revocation of tax exempt status or dissolution of an organization.

In summary, this survey of the fiscal management practices of a sample of Chicago nonprofit organizations indicates that:

1. Most complied with the most basic internal practices such as recording cash receipts and disbursements, bank reconciliations, and budgeting by functional and program areas.

2. Fewer complied with more sophisticated accounting practices which provide greater internal control over fiscal matters, such as preparation of monthly balance sheets, revenue and expense reports, budget comparisons, and segregation of duties involving the receipt and depositing of cash and the preparation of bank reconciliations and posting of the general ledger.

3. Just over half did not have major items of budgetary information readily available in either one or two or more of their financial records.

4. Although most organizations met various governmental reporting

requirements, the approximately three percent...to 40 percent which did not meet particular requirements risked serious consequences.

5. Of the organizations for which an audit was required, 40 percent failed to obtain an audit in the last complete fiscal year before the study.

6. Over half (60.9%) of the audit reports reviewed contained all the elements for a complete audit report as prescribed by GAAP.

Problems Experienced by NonProfit Organizations

The interviews show that more key staff members experienced problems with internal than with external accounting matters. These findings were compatible with the preceding description of the elementary nature of most organization's internal accounting practices and their relatively greater compliance with external requirements than with internal accounting practices.

Internal Management

...Over half of the organizations in the sample experienced problems with the quality and quantity of staffing for accounting and reporting. In addition, 32.4 percent indicated problems with turnover of accounting staff. These results are not surprising given the fact that in almost half (44%) of the organizations, the person in charge of accounting functions had no prior accounting experience. No organization had a CPA in this position and only three had persons with accounting or business management majors.

The staffing problems were revealed in comments made to interviewers. A representative of a performing arts group said, "Everybody is overworked and underpaid. There's not enough time to do it right the first time." Showing how difficult it is to manage, a staff member of a neighborhood group said,

> Our part-time bookkeeper is hard to get in touch with. The executive director has no knowledge of accounting or bookkeeping. As such, the numerous accounting problems tend to go unanswered.

This problem was echoed in the words of several people who were interviewed. As the director of a small public interest organization said, "The biggest problem is there is no money to get an accountant."

Although the problem of staff unknowledgeable about accounting was found in organizations of all sizes in terms of total revenue, it was a much greater problem in the smaller organizations in the sample. All organizations with total revenue of $50,000 and less experienced unknowledgeable staff as a problem. . . . Only 30 percent of organizations with revenue of $200,000 and over experienced this problem.

Organizational representatives identified two other problems. Conflicting terms used by different funding sources was a problem to over one-third of the groups, and petty cash fund maintenance was a problem to just under one-third of the sample. Staff time billing sheets presented a problem to about 15 percent of the sample.

Internal accounting problems also could be linked to the lack of written guidelines for accounting tasks. Over 60 percent (61.5%, n = 24) of the 39 organizations did not have written guidelines for operating their accounting systems. Most organizations did not have serious problems preparing financial reports for funding sources. However, the following problems were experienced by some organizations: number of reports required, documentation required, relationship with funding agency staff members, confusing report formats, and the volume of information required.

Over 90 percent of the organizations had made efforts to solve accounting-related problems. Over 80 percent had sought expert advice, over 60 percent used staff training, and over one-third changed their accounting systems.

One-fifth or more, and sometimes over 40 percent, of the organizations experienced as serious or very serious the following problems with obtaining accounting assistance: the dollar cost of getting information, not knowing what to ask for, not knowing where to go, not available when needed, time cost of getting information, understanding the information, finding reliable sources, and being ineligible for free assistance. Each of these problems was experienced by a higher proportion of organizations with the lowest total revenue than with the total sample.

Case 9-1 Questions:

1. What, in your opinion, are the major accounting problems found among small nonprofit organizations in this survey?
2. What recommendations for change would you make to the community coalition which carried out this survey?

Reading 9-1: Evaluating Accounting Firms by John T. Schiffman*

Top management depends on audit reports prepared by outside accountants for a complete and accurate financial picture of a company. But evaluating a CPA firm is too often based on some vague evaluation of a firm's reputation or image. Now, peer review reports offer top management an important tool for evaluating the qualifications and capabilities of an accounting firm.

In the past, accounting professionals usually practiced as individuals; today, most operate as a firm. Therefore, it is the capabilities of an entire firm that must be evaluated.

The American Institute of Certified Public Accountants has addressed this problem. In 1977, the Institute formed a voluntary CPA quality control program known as the "Division for CPA Firms."

The Division promotes CPA excellence through an effective peer review and continuing education program. The program calls for an accounting firm to be reviewed once every three years by qualified CPAs familiar with that firm's practice. The peer review carefully scrutinizes a firm's auditing and accounting procedures. The review further requires that each accountant receive a minimum of 120 hours of continuing professional education every three years.

Auditing the Auditors

The Division for CPA Firms consists of two sections: the Private Companies Practice Section and the SEC Practice Section. Membership is voluntary and firms may join either or both sections. Quality control standards, however, are identical for both.

A peer review in either section concludes with a public report. The report clearly states a clean, modified, or adverse opinion of the firm's practices and methods. Suggestions for improvements are also made in the peer review.

Since the beginning of the program, most reviewed firms have rated a clean report. Even clean reports, however, are accompanied by improvement recommendations about 90 percent of the time. Moreover, firms must respond in writing to these improvement suggestions.

A minority — 12 percent — of the reports reveal serious deficiencies in

---

*Reprinted by permission, *Small Business Report,* Copyright September 1985.

quality control methods or procedures. In these cases corrective action is taken. The corrective actions taken in such circumstances are described in the publicly available peer review file.

Nine Checkpoints

The peer review looks at nine major areas in evaluating a CPA firm's quality control system.

- Independence from financial, family, business, or other relationships contrary to the profession's code of ethics.
- Assignment of personnel with the technical expertise required by the particular task.
- Consultation with the appropriate authorities to resolve accounting or auditing issues.
- Supervision that ensures accounting services are delivered efficiently and to professional standards.
- Hiring of competent, motivated people.
- Continuing professional education.
- Advancement of capable personnel.
- Client selection and retention of companies committed to management integrity.
- Internal reviews of quality control systems.

Peer Review Benefits

Peer reviews benefit both CPA firms and their clients. The CPA firm immediately benefits from the information generated to improve professional services. Clients—both current and potential—benefit from the information revealed by peer reviews. Companies can engage CPA firms based on facts, not secondhand reports or intangible reputations. A peer review also keeps businesses informed about quality standards in their current CPA firm.

Peer reviews examine one-person practitioners to the largest national firms. Reciprocal reviews between firms are not permitted and review teams must have a working knowledge of the type of practice that is going to be reviewed. Peer review reports are publicly available from the Division of CPA Firms, American Institute of Certified Public Accountants, New York, N.Y. A directory is available from the division and any company seeking a CPA firm can determine if the firm is a member, and, if so, how that firm fared under review.

Reading 9-1 Questions:

1. How has the AICPA addressed the question of quality control and evaluation of accounting firms?
2. What are the nine areas reviewed in evaluating a CPA firm?
3. What is the outcome of the review process?
4. How do peer reviews benefit clients of CPA firms?

Chapter Ten

FINANCIAL REPORTING AND ANALYSIS

After reading this chapter you should be able to:

1. Understand the purposes and uses of financial statements.
2. Understand how financial statements are prepared.
3. Read financial statements.
4. Use ratios and other techniques to analyze financial statements.
5. Understand the audit function.

INTRODUCTION

Until recently, financial reporting by human service agencies was of very little interest to most people, including the accounting profession. An attitude of laissez-faire permeated public thinking about these agencies and was even perpetuated by the agencies themselves. The idea was that these agencies did "good works" that were unquantifiable. This, along with the tendency of human service administrators to be poorly prepared in the financial aspects of agency management, led to a situation in which financial statements of nonprofits were often incomplete and misleading. So prevalent was this attitude that even the accounting profession took very little leadership in the setting of standards and guidelines for nonprofit agencies (Racek, 1980:6-3). Recently, this attitude has changed for a variety of reasons: increased pressure from the public, funding agencies, and the federal government for greater accountability of public spending; competition from the private sector; and the need for greater efficiency due to cutbacks in funding for social services. As was discussed previously, there are now general guidelines for agencies to follow.

As you will recall, in the accounting cycle financial reports are an output of the financial management subsystem of the agency. As such they are or should be, a mirror to the outside world, a reflection of the agency's activities expressed in monetary terms. What are the purposes served by such reports? Who are the target audiences or interested receivers of this information? What are the guidelines one should be familiar with in preparing financial reports? What type of information can one glean from them? This chapter will address these questions.

PURPOSES OF FINANCIAL REPORTS

Financial statements are reports that describe financial activities at different points in the financial management subsystem process. Some of the purposes of financial statements are the following:

To Describe Inputs

Financial statements describe the importation of resources into the organization, for example, revenues. As historical documents, financial statements show the types of support and revenue received by the agency during an accounting period. They explain to the reader where resources were obtained and for how much. By looking at these reports, major funding sources can be spotted easily.

To Describe Throughputs

There are two types of processes that take place within the agency that can be reflected in financial statements: accounting processes and management processes. In addition to reflecting management processes, financial statements as end products of the accounting cycle, are also used by management to facilitate its activities.

Accounting Processes:

Accounting processes are those activities that take place in the human service agency that involve monetary transactions. Some of the activities that can be seen in perusing the agency's financial statements are:

- the allocation of resources by the organization among its various components, for example, the allocation of revenues to various funds and programs. Because of the fund accounting used in many human service agencies, it is important for users of financial statements to be able to quickly discern how resources have been used by the agency for its various programs.
- the consumption of assets by the organization, for example, expenses

for office supplies, and materials. The expense statement format used for nonprofits shows not only expenses, but further breaks them down by program area so that the reader can see how much was spent by each program.

- the acquisition of new assets by the organization during the period being reported in the statement, for example, new office equipment.
- the division of operating expenses among the various programs. By allocating costs to each of the agency's programs, the comparison of program expenses is facilitated.

Management Processes:

In addition to accounting processes, there are many other activities going on in the human service agency. Besides the major function of providing services, there are a myriad of management tasks that need to take place to ensure the continual operation of the agency and to provide support to the service delivery staff. One important management process reflected in the human service financial statements is:

- The operationalization of the agency's goals and objectives during a specific period of time. Many small human service organizations do not have written goals and objectives, strange as it might seem. It is assumed by the people who work in the organization that there is an implicit consensus among staff, board members, and even clients as to what the goals of the agency might be. But often the perceptions of management, staff, and the board are very different. Whether the organization's goals are written or not, its financial statements are a reflection of these goals.

In addition, financial statements are an important tool in human service management decisionmaking and planning. Some of the uses of these statements that help facilitate the management process are:

- To provide information to be used by the agency and its officers for planning purposes. The financial statements of the agency are crucial to budgeting and other planning that takes place in the organization. The information can also be used for marketing purposes, that is, parts of the agency's financial statements may be printed in a brochure that is distributed to the public and other funding sources.
- To provide a basis of comparison from one fiscal period to the next. By looking at past performance over time and taking into account any environmental factors such as changes in level or source of

funding, state of the economy, changes in function or goals of the agency, changes in the demography of the client population, and so forth, one can discern trends in the organization's allocation of resources.

- To have data available that can be used in evaluating the effectiveness and efficiency of the agency's programs. Measuring efficiency (maximum use of resources) and effectiveness (reaching stated goals) are important functions that can be measured in an agency. By looking at measures such as ratios and fund mixes one can evaluate efficiency, economic stability, and stewardship. Measuring effectiveness, on the other hand is a much more difficult evaluative process. One thing that can be gleaned from the financial reports though, is whether the agency's stated priorities are reflected in the allocation of resources and costs.

To Describe Outputs

Financial statements provide a quantitative record of the agency's activities during a specific period of time, usually one year. One can get a more accurate picture of the agency's activities by taking these "snapshots" that show the agency's financial picture at any one moment in time. Sometimes the statements are broken up into smaller units of time, as in quarterly reports. This documentation can be presented to funding sources as a basis for current and future funding decisions. Funding sources need some information on which to base decisions about the agency's performance, whether or not it is meeting its stated goals, and providing the services for which it was initially funded. In addition, "doing good works" is no longer enough; in an era of scarce resources funders are also concerned about efficient use and looking to management to provide some evaluative indicators of effectiveness as well.

USERS OF FINANCIAL REPORTS

Among the potential audiences of an agency's financial statements are interested groups such as the following (FASB, 1980:15–18):

Resource Providers

Resource providers are those who are directly compensated for providing resources such as creditors, suppliers, and employees, as well as those who are not directly compensated such as members, contributors and taxpayers. Resource providers may contribute directly in the form of grants, loans, credit, or contributions. They may also contribute indirectly in the form of taxes.

Resource providers, such as contributors, are interested in agency financial statements because this information can help them make decisions regarding continued financial or material support on the basis of how efficiently the agency has met or tried to meet its goals. Other resource providers, such as creditors, are interested in whether or not the agency has the ability to meet its financial obligations to them as well as the ability to generate sufficient cash flow for present and future operating expenses.

Constituents

Constituents are those who are served by the organization, such as members, clients, and potential clients. There may be members who pay dues to belong to a voluntary organization, tax payers whose taxes may help support the organization, and clients who may pay on a sliding fee scale for services. Thus, in the last analysis, the organization's constituency is made up of the community itself. There is, or may be, an overlap between resource providers and constituents. But as a constituent one's concerns may be different. The resource provider wants to know whether the agency is using its resources to meet organizational goals and financial obligations. The constituent may be interested in another set of issues however, that is, are resources being allocated in such a manner as to attempt to meet the social and material needs of the community? This has been a particular sore spot for some groups, such as ethnic minorities, who have pressured agencies for change because of a perceived lack of sensitivity to the needs of the constituent community.

Governing and Oversight Bodies

Governing and oversight bodies include accrediting agencies, regulatory agencies, taxing agencies, other units of government, federated fund raising and allocation agencies, legislatures, and boards of trustees. These bodies are responsible for setting policies, administrative rules, and laws that regulate human service agencies. They are also responsible for overseeing, reviewing, and sometimes evaluating top management performance as well as agency conformance and compliance with the various laws and regulations that govern the agency. These groups therefore use financial statements to help them carry out their oversight/ evaluative mission and perhaps to suggest changes in goals, policies, or programs when necessary. These suggestions can provide important feedback to an agency.

Managers

Managers of human service organizations have the responsibility of implementing policy formulated by the board of directors and other governing bodies, as well as overseeing day-to-day operations. Managers include agency heads, program directors, supervisors, and directors of fund-raising activities. They, along with the governing board, may be considered internal users of financial reports.

Managers use information garnered from financial statements along with accounting information for purposes of planning and control, as was discussed earlier. The information may be needed for decisionmaking related to asset acquisition, or capital projects. The information may also be needed in order for the manager to carry out his or her stewardship function regarding proper use of resources, whether restricted or not. The manager also needs information from the statements to oversee and demonstrate compliance with established funder guidelines.

In summary, the human service agency has a responsibility to provide useful information to its users of financial statements to help them:

- in making resource allocation decisions;
- in assessing services and ability to provide services;
- in assessing management stewardship and performance;
- in being aware of economic resources, obligations, net resources, and any changes that have occurred in them;
- in evaluating organizational performance during the period;
- in understanding service efforts and accomplishments of the agency (FASB, 1980:18–27).

QUALITATIVE ASPECTS OF FINANCIAL STATEMENTS

The information reflected in financial reports is affected by many factors because human service agencies do not operate in a vacuum, but in a highly charged social-political economic environment. Changing social values, social policies, and economic conditions affect the financial condition of the agency. Along with environmental factors that effect the agency's financial statements are constraints due to the nature of the reports themselves. That is, the information in the financial statements is quantitative and expressed in monetary terms. Thus, money is the common denominator that depicts economic things and events in the statements. The problem with this is that accounting is an art, not a science, and even though it is surrounded by an aura of preciseness due to its numerical format, it is subject to an enormous amount of judgements, estimates, classifications, and summarizations. Therefore, often what appears to be unequivocal are "approximations which may be based on rules and conventions rather than exact amounts" (FASB, 1980:13).

What are largely reflected in financial statements are historical data, events and transactions that have occurred in the past. These statements may be contrasted with budgets, which reflect future goals and plans. Even so, this historical information can be extremely useful to many groups, as been previously pointed out. It is important to remember that the information from financial statements needs to be used in conjunction with other social, political, and economic information about an agency.

Social information answers questions such as: what is the demographic profile of the clients served by the agency? Are clients served representative of a cross-section of the community and/or target population? Do minorities use the agency in proportion to their numbers in the population? Is the agency trying to be responsive to the needs of the community?

Political information answers questions such as: what are the background and makeup of the board and agency administrators? What political interests are represented on the board? Is the composition of the board representative of the client group? What community issues is the board concerned with? What political factors facilitate or hinder the delivery of services? Have political views regarding the client group or the services offered affected funding?

Economic information not shown on financial statements answers such questions as: what is the economic level of the clients being served? Does the agency serve indigent clients as well as those able to pay or that have third-party payers? Are the outcomes of the program producing a positive result in relation to the material and human costs incurred?

Other types of nonmonetary information can be found in the notes accompanying financial statements or from budget information on number of clients served, and so forth. Nonmonetary information may be needed to understand and evaluate the significance of information contained in financial statements. Thus, financial reports are only one type of information about an agency that is needed by interested parties; there are other types of information that has to be taken into account. In trying to assess financial reports it must be kept in mind that "financial reporting by nonbusiness organizations—is limited to its ability to provide direct measures of the quality of goods and services provided in the absence of market-determined exchange prices or the degree to which they satisfy the need of service beneficiaries and consumers" (FASB, 1980:13).

REQUIRED FINANCIAL STATEMENTS

Interested users of an agency's financial statements obviously want to know the sources and disposition of an agency's funds. Two of the statements used by the nonprofit agency, known as operating statements, are 1) the Statement of Support, Revenue, and Expenses and Changes in Fund Balances (SRECFB), and 2) the Statement of Functional Expenses. Another required report is known as the Balance Sheet, and you will recall that in a previous chapter its relationship to accounting was illustrated. Agencies may be required to prepare other types of special reports for internal use or for funders, and the format of these other reports will vary depending on the needs of the users. But the format of the financial statements is pretty much standard, although not all agencies will use all of the categories listed in the sample statements shown in this book. The *STANDARDS* and the *AUDIT GUIDE* both use the same format. An agency should also check with its state's civil codes regulating nonprofit corporations to find out the reporting requirements for the agency. Most states follow the AICPA audit guidelines.

As you may remember from the last chapter, financial statements are prepared from information gathered from the accounting records. The information needed for the Statement of Support, Revenue, and Expenses and Changes in Fund Balances comes from the Fund Balance Ledgers, The Revenue Ledgers, and the Expense Ledgers.

Statement of Support, Revenue and Expenses and Changes in Fund Balances

The Statement of Support, Revenue, and Expenses and Changes in Fund Balances is "simply an all-inclusive, multi-column statement"

(*STANDARDS*, 1974:33). As you can see from Table 10-1, this statement has a functional format in that support, revenue, and expenses are allocated to the various programs that the agency has. The SRECFB statement is divided into a number of sections. The first section is called **public support,** and it is subdivided into two areas: support received directly and support received indirectly. **Direct public support** includes charitable giving by the public to an agency in the form of cash donations and pledges, restricted gifts, endowments, as well as donated goods and services.

Indirect Public Support: includes funds received from a federated fundraising and allocation agency such as a United Way. Thus the difference between direct and indirect public support is that direct support is received by an agency as a result of its own fundraising efforts, while indirect support is received through another organization. One reason for this separation on the statement is so that readers can associate fundraising costs with funds raised in the same period.

Government Fees and Grants: are another section in the statement. As the government has become an increasingly important third-party payer of social services through fees, and contracts, as well as grants, it is necessary to highlight this source of funds separately.

Other Revenue: is the next section in the statement. Revenue is distinct from support in that support is money received from the general public for philanthropic purposes, while revenue is income earned by an agency for services rendered, goods sold, investments, or other income producing efforts. Thus revenue includes fees, sales, dues, interest, and so forth.

The next section of the statement covers expenses, and it is designed to reflect all of the expenses of an agency in three main categories: program services, supporting services, and payments to affiliated organizations. **Program service expenses** are those amounts "spent by an agency in providing the services for which it has been organized and exists" (*STANDARDS*, 1974:36). **Supporting services,** on the other hand, refer to those expenses "an agency incurs to provide the administrative and fund-raising services that support and make possible its service programs" (*STANDARDS*:36). Included here are both administrative and fundraising expenses. The third section, **payments to affiliated organizations,** is usually a fee that local agencies pay to their state or national chapters for affiliation and to help cover costs of the parent organization for services provided to the local affiliates.

The Statement of Support, Revenue, and Expenses and Changes in

Table 10-1
STATEMENT OF SUPPORT, REVENUE AND EXPENSES AND CHANGES IN FUND BALANCES
Family Service Agency of Utopia, Inc.

Year Ended December 31, 19X2
With Comparative Totals for 19X1

	Current Funds Unrestricted	Restricted	Equipment Fund	Land, Bldg and Endowment Fund	Total All Funds 19X2	19X1
Public Support and Revenue						
Public Support						
Contributions	$70,925	$16,200	$7,200	$200	$94,525	$91,500
Special Events	26,455	---	---	---	26,455	21,250
Legacies and Bequest	9,200	---	---	400	9,600	12,000
Allocated by United Way	286,000	---	---	---	286,000	259,000
Total Public Support	$392,580	$16,200	$7,200	$600	$416,580	$383,750
Fees and grants from govt. agencies	---	9,300	---	---	9,300	8,000
Other Revenue:						
Membership dues	500	---	---	---	500	400
Program service fees	41,000	700	---	---	51,000	47,400
Investment income	1,500	---	---	6,300	8,500	9,100
Gain (or loss) on investment transaction	---	---	---	2,500	2,500	1,500
Miscellaneous	1,800	---	---	---	2,800	3,600
Total Other Revenue	$ 44,800	$ 700	---	---	$ 65,300	$ 62,000
Total Public Support and Revenue	$437,380	$26,200	$7,200	$3,100	$491,180	$453,750

Table 10-1
(continued)

Expenses:						
Program Services						
Counseling	$158,829	$24,500	$1,630	---	$184,959	$174,836
Adoption	65,998	---	620	---	66,618	75,260
Foster home care	147,225	---	1,410	---	148,635	124,206
Total Program Services	$372,052	$24,500	$ 3,660	---	$400,212	$374,302
Supporting Services:						
Management and general	50,120	---	420	---	50,540	45,069
Fundraising	11,843	---	120	---	11,963	12,198
Total Support Services	61,963	---	540	---	62,503	57,267
Total Expenses	$434,015	$24,500	$4,200	---	$462,715	$431,569
Excess of Public Support and Revenue Over Expenses	$3,365	$1,700	$3,000	$3,100		
Other Changes in Fund Balances:						
Property and equipment acquisition from unrestricted funds	($1,700)	---	$1,700	---		
Transfer of realized endowment fund appreciation	$2,500	---	---	($2,500)		
Fund Balances, beginning of year	80,280	2,300	64,900	62,300		
Fund Balances, end of year	$84,445	$4,000	$69,600	$61,000		

(See accompanying notes to financial statements)

Adapted from: Standards of Accounting and Financial Reporting for Voluntary Health and Welfare Organizations, 1974.

Fund Balances reports all income and expenses in reference to the various fund categories that an agency may have. The statement also compares the totals for the current year with the previous year's totals. Finally, it shows the fund balances for each fund at the beginning and end of the year. While the Balance Sheet reflects the financial position of the agency at one point in time, the SRECFB reflects the activity of the agency between two points in time. In other words, the financial position of the organization at the end of the year is explained by financial transactions that occurred since the beginning of the year. This is illustrated by the following equation:

$$R - E = \triangle \, FB$$

Revenue Less Expenses Equals Changes in Fund Balances

This equation says that the changes in the fund balances of the agency between two points in time is the difference between the resources that enter the agency (revenues) and the resources that are consumed by the agency (expenses). These changes are shown in the SRECFB statement.

The other operating statement, the Statement of Functional Expenses, gives a more detailed breakdown of the expenses listed in the SRECFB statement. The information needed to prepare the Statement of Functional Expenses is obtained from the various Expense Ledgers.

Statement of Functional Expenses

"The Statement of Functional Expenses is a summary statement which presents an analysis of the organization's OBJECT expenses by program function and support function" (United Way, 1974:42). Object expense categories represent specific classifications for objects such as salaries, telephone, travel, etc. Obviously, the number of program service categories and object expense classifications will depend on the size and nature of the reporting agency. Table 10-2 shows a representative Statement with the main types of expenses included.

Besides the usual object expense categories such as salaries, employee benefits, payroll taxes, equipment, supplies, travel, telephone, etc., you will note the following categories that may need some explanation:

Professional Fees: are for those outside consultants such as doctors, lawyers, accountants, and auditors, who may have a contract for services with the agency.

Table 10-2
STATEMENT OF FUNCTIONAL EXPENSES
Family Service Agency of Utopia, Inc.

Year Ended December 31, 19X2
With Comparative Totals for 19X1

	Program Services				Supporting Services			Total Program and Supporting Services Expenses	
	Counseling	Adoption	Foster-home Care	Total	Management and General	Fund-Raising	Total	19X2	19X1
Salaries	$86,068	$33,776	$77,306	$197,150	$32,517	$7,503	$40,020	$237,170	$223,086
Employee benefits	16,625	6,846	15,453	38,924	6,591	1,520	8,111	47,035	44,360
Payroll taxes, etc.	4,283	1,657	3,497	9,437	1,595	368	1,963	11,400	10,768
Total salaries and related expenses	$106,976	$42,279	$96,256	$245,511	$40,703	$9,391	$50,094	$295,605	$278,213
Professional fees	29,105	9,905	12,090	51,100	3,500	—	3,500	54,600	50,459
Supplies	3,391	1,281	2,864	7,536	758	206	964	8,500	8,006
Telephone	3,965	1,498	3,349	8,812	565	233	798	9,610	9,065
Postage and shipping	2,701	1,020	2,282	6,003	583	164	747	6,750	6,090
Occupancy	9,658	3,649	8,155	21,462	2,540	598	3,138	24,600	23,092
Rental and maintenance of equip.	3,937	1,488	3,325	8,750	—	—	—	8,750	7,127
Printing and publications	2,563	1,245	1,291	5,099	850	1,251	2,101	7,200	6,043
Travel	11,301	2,015	10,504	23,820	180	—	180	24,000	22,460
Conferences, conventions, meetings	7,447	755	5,178	13,380	320	—	320	13,700	12,430
Miscellaneous	2,285	863	1,931	5,079	121	—	121	5,200	4,823
Total before depreciation	$183,329	$65,998	$147,225	$396,552	$50,120	$11,843	$61,963	$458,515	$428,169
Depreciation of buildings and equip.	1,630	620	1,410	3,660	420	120	540	4,200	3,400
Total Expenses	$184,959	$66,618	$148,635	$400,212	$50,540	$11,963	$62,503	$462,715	$431,569

(See accompanying notes to financial statements)

Adapted from: Standards of Accounting and Financial Reporting
for Voluntary Health and Welfare Organizations, 1974.

Table 10-3
BALANCE SHEET
Family Service Agency of Utopia, Inc.
December 31, 19X1

Current Funds
UNRESTRICTED

Assets	19X2	19X1
Cash	$45,747	$52,667
Short-term investments	20,000	10,000
Accounts receivable	2,165	3,087
Pledges receivable	4,968	3,724
Supplies	22,875	14,925
Prepaid expenses	3,516	3,769
Board-designated long-term investments (Note 2)	15,000	15,000
	$114,271	$103,172

Liabilities and Fund Balances	19X2	19X1
Accounts payable	$24,611	$18,702
Deferred Revenue	5,215	4,190
Total liabilities and deferred revenue	$29,826	$22,892
Fund balances:		
Designated by the governing board for—		
Long-term investments	15,000	15,000
Purchases new equipment	8,300	10,000
Special Outreach Project (Note 3)	25,000	—
Undesignated, available for general activities	36,145	55,280
Total fund balances	$84,445	$80,280
	$114,271	$103,172

Table 10-3
(continued)

RESTRICTED

Assets			Fund balance:		
Cash	$4,000	$2,300	Professional education	$4,000	2,300

LAND BUILDING AND EQUIPMENT FUND

Assets			Liabilities and fund balance		
Cash	$1,123	$700	8-¼% mortgage payable, due 19Z5	$52,370	$54,194
Short-term investments	15,000	—	Fund balances:		
Pledges receivable	11,203	21,250	Expended	42,274	42,950
Land building, and equipment	94,644	97,144	Unexpended-restricted	27,326	21,950
	$121,970	$119,094	Total fund balance	69,600	64,900

ENDOWMENT FUND

Assets			Fund balance:		
Cash	$300	$700		$62,300	$61,700
Investments (Note 2)	62,000	61,000		$62,300	$61,700
	$62,300	$61,700			

(See accompanying notes to financial statements)

*Adapted from: Standards of Accounting and Financial Reporting
for Voluntary Health and Welfare Organizations, 1974.*

Occupancy: includes rental, utilities, mortgage and any other costs associated in using a building and land for the agency's purposes. It does not include depreciation because this is covered elsewhere in the statement.

Awards and Grants: are monies paid by the agency to support research, scholarships, or other welfare programs. For example, some organizations provide seed money to community groups to start new projects, while other organizations provide money to encourage research in a specific problem area such as alcohol abuse, teenage pregnancy, child abuse, and so forth.

Depreciation or Amortization: allocates the cost of an asset over its useful life. Its useful life is the time that it benefits the agency. Some types of assets that may be depreciated are equipment, buildings, and automobiles.

The method of classifying expenses by object categories across programs requires that those expenses falling into more than one program area be coded at the time they are entered into the books. This will facilitate the preparation of the statement. But, sometimes agencies find it difficult to ascertain what proportion of an expense falls under two or more programs. This uncertainty may be minimized by instituting some procedures to allocate costs such as those discussed in Chapter Six, and certainly the agency should consult with its accountant regarding the procedures. The accountant must determine whether the methods used are reasonable and a somewhat accurate reflection of agency activities so as to be able to render an unqualified opinion in the notes accompanying the statements. While some methods for allocating costs have bee previously discussed, it must be remembered that accounting is an art and therefore "it may be impossible, even with the most meticulous accounting, completely to isolate and precisely report ALL of an agency's expenses for any single function, whether fundraising, management and general, or a particular program service" (United Way, 1974:93).

Balance Sheet

The financial statements of the agency would be incomplete if only the operating statements were used. The public has a right to know the extent of assets owned by the agency as well as the liabilities it owes. It also has a right to some assurance that the agency has made a distinction among Funds that must be separately accounted for. Thus, the Balance

Sheet presents further evidence of the stewardship and accountability of the agency.

As you will recall, the Balance Sheet is a representation of the accounting equation, assets = liabilities + fund balances. That is, it presents the assets and liabilities of the agency along with the residual, or difference between the two, the fund balances. As you will note in Table 10-3, the Balance Sheet has divided the assets and liabilities of the agency among its various Funds—Current Unrestricted, Current Restricted, Land, Building and Equipment Fund, and Endowment Fund. A Balance Sheet may also compare the previous year's totals with the current year's totals.

The reason for the separation of assets and liabilities by Fund grouping is so that the reader will be able to ascertain the extent to which the agency has adhered to restrictions associated with gifts from donors.

After the agency has prepared its financial statements, it is required by law in many states to have a periodic check or "audit" of its records by an accountant. In many cases, the accountant must be a Certified Public Accountant (CPA) who will examine agency records and render an opinion as whether the agency's financial statements fairly represent its financial position.

AUDITS

"The primary purpose of an audit is to enable an independent auditor to express an opinion on the fairness of the financial statements, their compliance with generally accepted accounting principles and the consistency of their application" (United Way, 1974:45). In an audit, the auditor does not examine every recorded transaction in the books; rather he or she selectively tests transactions and internal controls to form an opinion as to the fairness of the representation of the financial statements. The auditor looks at a random representative sample of the transactions, but there are two tests the auditor cannot omit (Gross and Warshauer, 1979:373):

- confirmation of accounts receivable: this involves contacting those owing money and asking them to confirm that they do. This is especially important if the agency shows a large amount of pledges receivable.
- observation of physical inventories: this involves checking the existence of the inventory to make sure that assets are not overstated.

And even though to some the audit may appear to be a nuisance, there are some benefits to be gained from it. Some of these benefits are (Gross, in United Way:45):

- The audit lends credibility to the financial statements of the agency.
- The auditor can provide assistance in the preparation of statements so that they meaningfully reflect the monetary transactions of the agency.
- The auditor can provide advice on developing internal controls.
- The auditor can help the agency meet its legal requirements for compliance as well as in tax reporting.

Types of Audit Opinions

After the auditor has examined the agency's books, he or she will write an audit opinion. Depending on the individual circumstances of the agency, there are five types of formal opinions that the auditor may write (United Way, 1974:46):

Unqualified Opinion

An unqualified opinion is given if the auditor thinks that the financial statements were prepared in accordance with generally accepted accounting principles and accurately reflect the financial position of the agency, its operations and changes in fund balances. (See the notes accompanying the financial statements in this chapter for an example of an unqualified opinion.)

Qualified Opinion

A qualified opinion is given in those cases in which the auditor thinks that there are certain aspects of the financial statements that vary from generally accepted accounting principles, yet are not material enough to require an adverse opinion.

Disclaimer of Opinion

A disclaimer of opinion may be given when the auditor is not satisfied with the statements. This may occur for a number of reasons, for example, the auditor was not able to examine sufficient documentary evidence, or not able to contact donors to verify pledges receivable, and so forth.

Table 10–4
NOTES TO FINANCIAL STATEMENTS
Family Service Agency of Utopia, Inc.
December 31, 19X2

1. Summary of Significant Accounting Policies: The Agency follows the practice of capitalizing all expenses for land, buildings and equipment in excess of $150; the fair value of donated fixed assets is similarly capitalized. Depreciation is provided over the estimated useful lives of the assets. Investments are stated at cost. All contributions are considered available for unrestricted use, unless specifically restricted by the donor. Pledges for contributions are recorded as received, and allowances are provided for amounts estimated as uncollectible. Policies concerning donated material and services are described in Note 5.

2. Investments: All investments are in marketable common stock and bonds. Market values and unrealized appreciation (depreciation) at December 31, 19X2 and 19X1 are summarized as follows:

	December 31, 19X2		December 31, 19X1	
	Quoted Market Value	Unrealized Appreciation	Quoted Market Value	Unrealized Appreciation (Depreciation)
Current Unrestricted Fund. Board-designated investments:	$15,165	$ 165	$14,720	$ (280)
Endowment Funds:				
Common stocks	$32,822	$1,426	$30,737	$(244)
Corporate bonds:	31,534	930	29,531	(488)
	$64,356	$2,356	$60,268	(732)

Table 10–4
(continued)

3. Special Outreach Project: At December 31, 19X2, $25,000 had been designated by the governing board from prior year's un-designated fund balance for a "Special Outreach Project" to be conducted on an experimental basis during 19X3.

4. Land, Building and Equipment and Depreciation: Depreciation of buildings and equipment is provided on a stright-line basis over the estimated useful lives of the assets (2% per year for buildings, 5% for furniture and equipment, and 30% for automobile).

At December 31, 19X2 and 19X1, the costs of such assets were:

	19X2	19X1
Land	$15,500	$15,500
Buildings	42,500	52,500
Furniture and Equipment	36,309	34,609
Automobile	2,900	2,900
Total	107,209	105,509
Less — accumulated Depreciaiton	12,565	8,365
	$94,644	$97,144

5. Donated Materials and Services: Donated materials and equipment are reflected as "Contributions" in the accompanying statements at their estimated values at date of receipt. No amounts have been reflected in the statements for donated servies since no objective basis is available to meaure the value of such services. Nevertheless, a substantial number of volunteers donated significant amounts of their time in the organization's program servies and its fund-raising campaigns.

Adapted from: Standards of Accounting and Financial Reporting for Voluntary Health & Welfare Organizations, 1974

Adverse Opinion

An adverse opinion is given when the auditor thinks that the agency's financial statements are not a fair reflection of its financial position and were not prepared in accordance with generally accepted accounting principles.

Special Report Opinion

A special report opinion is given when the financial statements are not meant to be a reflection of financial position and results of operations. In these cases, the auditor must then decide what they do reflect and on what basis they were prepared, and tell this to the reader.

In the end, the responsibility for accurate records prepared in accordance with generally accepted accounting principles rests with the agency, its administrator and board of directors. As officers of the agency, the board may be legally liable for any mishandling of funds. Therefore, it is in the best interest of everyone concerned — board, administration, staff, and clients — that an annual audit be conducted by a CPA knowledgeable in nonprofit accounting whether required or not by the state.

In addition to knowing which financial statements are required by state, federal and other funding authorities, to achieve maximum usefulness from the statements one must have an idea of how to interpret them according to one's own needs. In the next section, methods of analyzing financial statements will be discussed.

ANALYSIS OF FINANCIAL STATEMENTS

Financial statements provide neutral information, that is, in and of itself, the information is neither good nor bad. Thus, it is only within the context of the agency, and the analyses applied to the statements that value inferences may be made. Users of financial statements have a need for financial information that can be classified into four main categories: questions regarding 1) fiscal compliance; 2) stewardship; 3) financial strength; and 4) operating efficiency (Ramanathan, 1982:50–51). In this section, discussion will center on how interested users can meet their information needs, but the focus will be on quantitative methods of analyses, especially regarding financial strength and operating efficiency.

Fiscal Compliance

Fiscal compliance refers to whether or not the agency is complying with the regulations, laws, guidelines, and rules of its funding sources as well as governmental bodies. Questions regarding compliance address issues that are somewhat straight-forward, for example, has the agency filed required reports and statements in a timely manner, in a format prescribed by the regulatory agency, and with the required information?

Stewardship

An agency can stick to the letter of the law and its funding guidelines and not benefit a single client. Stewardship, an important category, refers to whether or not the agency is really spending its money for its stated goals, and whether it is doing this in a way that is really benefiting its constituency. It is not a question here of costs/benefits, or even compliance. Rather, its a question of stated goals/priorities vs. actual spending/priorities.

One method that the user of financial reports can use to measure spending priorities vs. stated goals is to examine the Statement of Functional Expenses (SFE). In looking at the SFE, one can get an idea of the percentage of costs allocated for each program by turning the money spent for each program into a percentage of the total expenses (see Table 10-5).

Table 10-5

PERCENT OF COSTS ALLOCATED

Formula	Source of Data
Program Expense	Statement of Functional Expenses
Total Program Expenses	

This examination of the allocation of expenses should be compared with the agency's mission statement or statement of goals in its annual report. If it reveals that the agency is pursuing goals unstated, perhaps even unrelated to its main mission and original purpose, then it needs to clarify its goals, or re-write its mission statement and goals to reflect its new reality. Otherwise, this contradictory evidence may be misleading to funders, clients, and other interested readers of the financial statements. Thus, stewardship is a managerial as well as a fiduciary function.

Financial Strength

Financial strength refers to whether the agency has adequate resources to carry out its mandated objectives, and whether its resources help it to maintain viability and flexibility of operations. Whether the agency has financial strength depends to some extent on the composition of its resources, for example, the liquidity of its assets, the extent to which funds are restricted, how dependent the agency is on one funding source, and so forth. Some measures used to determine financial strength are the following:

Working Capital

As users of financial statements, creditors are interested in whether the agency has the ability to pay its bills on time. The ability to pay bills promptly is increased if the agency's cash and near-to-cash assets are high in comparison to current liabilities. Remember that current assets are cash, or liquid assets that can be converted to cash rather quickly such as stocks, bonds, mutual funds, CD's, and so forth. Current liabilities, on the other hand, are those monies owed by the agency that are due within one year or less. Thus, working capital is found by subtracting current liabilities from current assets (see Table 10-6).

Table 10-6

WORKING CAPITAL

Formula	Source of Data
Current Assets - Current Liabilities	Balance Sheet

A high working capital figure is indicative of financial solvency, that is, the ability of the agency to pay its bills in a timely manner. However, a very high amount of working capital may be an indication that there are idle current assets that could either be put into existing programs, fixed assets, or income-producing investments.

Current Ratio

The current ratio is used in business frequently by credit and financial analysts to ascertain the risk of insolvency or bankruptcy. This ratio shows the ability of the agency to pay its bills from current funds. Traditionally, a ratio of 2 to 1 is considered adequate. An appropriate ratio is one adequate to meet current expenses, but a large surplus would be questionable. It may be the result of some unexpected large contribution, or grant. But a very high ratio would not necessarily be good, as with the working capital ratio, it may be reflective of idle assets that could be used for investment or programs. To find the current ratio, divide current unrestricted assets by current unrestricted liabilities (see Table 10-7).

Table 10-7

CURRENT RATIO

Formula	Source of Data
Current Unrestricted Assets	
Current Unrestricted Liabilities	Balance Sheet

Before a final conclusion from the analyses can be made, these figures should be compared with agency trends over time. Data from other agencies providing similar types of services would be useful as a way of comparing whether the figures are too high or too low. Working capital and the current ratio should only be interpreted after taking into account any restrictions on the use of current assets.

Unrestricted Fund Balance

It is desirable, although not always possible, for human service agencies to have an excess of revenues over expenses at the end of the fiscal year. If the agency does have an excess, it could be used to cover unanticipated expenses, revenue short-falls, or anticipated increases in variable costs such as travel, utilities, telephone, etc. Unfortunately, some funders have policies that do not allow carryover of funds from one fiscal period to the next. These types of policies encourage inefficient use of funds, such as the common practice of expending all unused funds in the last quarter in order to avoid a decrease in funding in the next year. On the other hand, agencies that have a large fund balance in their operating fund should be examined closely. Agencies with large accumulations of fund reserves (up to 20% of their annual budget) may tend to engage in another type of inefficiency, that is, the expansion or initiation of unneeded or duplicative services (Hall, 1982:30). An important trend to watch for is whether the agency's unrestricted fund balance shows a decline over a period of time. This may indicate that the agency will have a difficult time if it is subject to budget cutbacks by funding sources. To determine unrestricted fund balance, divide current unrestricted fund balance by net operating revenue (see Table 10-8).

Table 10-8

UNRESTRICTED FUND BALANCE

Formula | Source of Data

Current Unrestricted Fund Balance | Balance Sheet

Net Operating Revenue | Statement of Support,

Revenue and Expenses and

Changes in Fund Balances

Percent of Revenue/Public Support from Various Sources

In a time of declining availability of funds for human service agencies and programs, agencies that are dependent on only one or two funding sources are in a precarious financial position. Funding instability may result from dependency on too few funding sources. In addition, agencies with large amounts of restricted funds are in the situation of being less able to respond to necessary programmatic changes or client needs.

Many agencies are seeking to diversify their funding bases in order to avoid or minimize fiscal dependence. The degree of diversification of an agency can be measured by calculating the percentage each funding source represents of the total funding base. For example, what percentage of total revenue/public support is from government sources? From membership fees and contributions? From client fees? (see Table 10-9).

These percentages will tell the reader to what extent the agency is being funded from any one source, and how potentially unstable its funding base may be. For example, if 50 percent or more of revenue from

Table 10-9

PERCENT OF REVENUES FROM VARIOUS SOURCES

Formula	Source of Data
Revenues from all Government Sources	Statement of Support,
Total Public Support/Revenue	Revenue, and Expenses,
	and Changes in Fund Balances
Membership Dues	
Total Public Support/Revenue	Same
Contributions	
Total Public Support/Revenue	Same
Revenues from Client Fees	
Total Public Support/Revenue	Same

client fees is from clients who are on Medicaid, this could be a warning signal. If over 80 percent of revenue comes from government sources, this should also be a sign that the agency is in a potentially vulnerable position (Hall, 1982:31). The agency must then take steps and develop strategies to expand its funding base.

Operating Efficiency

Operating efficiency refers to how much unrestricted money was obtained by the agency during the report period, how successful the agency has been in diversifying its funding base, the proportion of costs allocated to programs as opposed to administrative or other support costs, how reasonable the costs of operations are, personnel costs per client, and other sorts of similar measures. Some tests to measure operating efficiency are the following:

Support Test

As you know, the main purpose of human service agencies is to provide services. It is important to be able to measure the efficiency of these services. One way to do this is to compare the percentage of resources used for agency programs to the percentage used for administrative and fundraising, or support services. The resulting ratio is called the support test (see Table 10-10). There is no set ratio that is considered good or bad; generally, the higher the percentage used for programs the more efficient the agency. In some cases, a funding source may have a guideline that they use in evaluationg agencies, for example it may expect no more than 15–20% of expenses to be for support services. But the support figure must be viewed in terms of past agency performance, that is, what do the trends show? It must also be viewed in relation to the ratios of other agencies that provide similar services.

Table 10-10

SUPPORT TEST

Formula	Source of Data
$\dfrac{\text{Total Support Service Expenses}}{\text{Total Expenses}}$	Statement of Functional Expenses
or	
$\dfrac{\text{Total Program Service Expenses}}{\text{Total Expenses}}$	Same

Personnel Costs Per Client Served

Personnel costs are the largest expense in the human service agency budget; in fact, some have estimated the percentage to be as high as 80 percent (Hall, 1982:32). Just as in the health field, rising costs of providing human services may be partly attributed to rising labor costs. In looking at personnel costs in relation to clients served, one can get an indication of an agency's pattern of growth as well as its efficiency in use of personnel. If the number of employees is rising in relation to clients served, there are some questions that need to be addressed such as: Why is the ratio of personnel to clients increasing? Are the personnel program or support staff? What activities are taking place in the agency to account for the change? Has the ratio of program personnel to support personnel changed as well? These questions need to be answered in order to evaluate management practices and organizational efficiency. Of course, they need to be addressed within the context of the long-term plans and goals of the agency as well as current events. To measure personnel costs per client served, divide total personnel expenses by the unduplicated count of clients served (see Table 10-11).

Table 10-11

PERSONNEL COSTS PER CLIENT SERVED

Formula	Source of Data
Total Personnel Expenses	Statement of Functional Expenses
Unduplicated Count of	
Clients Served	Budget

Fund Mix

An important financial objective is to be able to maintain or increase flexibility in financial operations, to have sufficient current operating funds to move where needed quickly. To be able to do this, an agency needs current unrestricted funds as a large proportion of total net assets. This is called fund mix. To measure fund mix, divide current unrestricted funds by total fund balances (see Table 10-12). A high percentage of current unrestricted funds, for example over 65 percent, would show that the agency has adequate financial flexibility. However, any fund mix

Table 10-12

FUND MIX

Formula	Source of Data
Current Unrestricted Funds	Balance Sheet
Total Fund Balances	

figure must be viewed in relation to past trends within the agency, figures of other agencies offering similar services, as well as current events.

Drtina (1982) has said that quantitative indicators do serve some purposes for interested users, but they must be used sparingly in a careful manner. First of all, not all human service agencies use the same accounting format. This creates problems in trying to compare agencies on some of the measures discussed above. Secondly, it must be reiterated that these indicators do not measure quality or effectiveness of services. Quality and effectiveness measures are part of program evaluation and cannot be gathered from reviewing financial statements. However, financial information is important for planning and decision making. Some of the measures used here can help users evaluate whether or not an agency has the ability to maintain or increase services at a given level, adapt to a changing funding environment, and creatively adjust to changing socio-economic and political conditions in its environment by being able to modify its patterns of resource acquisition, allocation, investment, reporting, and service provision.

Chapter 10
Questions and Topics for Discussion

1. What are the purposes of financial statements?
2. What are some functions of financial statements?
3. What financial statements are required by the AICPA Audit Guide?
4. Who are the principal users of financial statements?
5. Where is information for preparing the statements obtained?
6. What information is reflected in each of the statements?
7. What are the legal requirements in your state regarding the financial statements of nonprofit human service agencies?
8. What types of opinions may an auditor write about an agency's financial statements?
9. What are the kinds of questions that need to be answered by users of human service agency financial statements?
10. What other data should be gathered to make maximum use of financial reports?

Exercise 10-1: Financial Statement Analysis

Using the financial statements shown in Tables 10-1, 10-2, 10-3 in this chapter, please calculate the following and explain what each means:

1. Support test
2. Current ratio

3. Working capital
4. Fund mix
5. Percentage of costs allocated.

Analyze the results of your calculations; what do they tell you about this agency? What would you say the goals of this agency are?

Case 10-1: Suite Charity by Larry Williams and Clifford Teutsch*

The mother of the Muscular Dystrophy Association's national poster child was explaining during the Labor Day telethon how the charity spends its money:

"The important thing to remember is that 75 cents of each dollar is used for program services to allow each patient the best medical care today and hope for tomorrow through research," said Dorie Rush, mother of 7-year-old Christopher Rush. The other 25 cents is kept to run MDA and to raise more money.

The 75-25 split came straight out of MDA's annual report, but information from MDA employees, state regulators and private watchdog agencies suggests that programs to benefit people such as Christopher get no more than 67 cents of the dollar—a difference of $6 million last year.

To professional charity-watchers, MDA is the most disturbing example of a trend among the nation's most prominent charities. They are using, the critics say, self-serving accounting practices to make themselves look leaner and more efficient.

"The one who shows the best figures may just have the biggest creative accountants," says Larry W. Campbell, registrar of charitable trusts in California and president of the National Association of State Charity Officials.

The charities, backed by their auditors, defend their practices as fairer and more sophisticated, not manipulative—although they admit they are looser.

Campbell and other charity watchdogs are not questioning the integrity of the charities or diminishing their accomplishments. They acknowledge that the sums involved so far may seem relatively small, but they insist that the public is being misled nonetheless.

They predict manipulative practices will snowball as competition continues to increase for the $60 billion Americans give annually to charities.

"As money gets tight, as more people are scrambling for the dollar, it's

---

*Reprinted by permission of the *Hartford Courant* © 1983.

going to get worse," said M.C. Van de Workeen, the executive director of the National Information Bureau, one of the country's leading charity-rating services.

The most hotly contested accounting practice involves reporting some of the costs of a fund-raising effort, such as a mailing or a telethon, as "public education." The charities consider public education as part of their charitable program, in the same category as medical research or helping patients.

This shifting of fund-raising costs to education is done even though a strict standard that the charities developed in 1964 prohibits it, and even though, in the case of mailings, the "educational" message is being sent to a computerized list of individuals screened, at great expense, for their potential as donors.

The educational message on a mailing can be somewhat skimpy. It is difficult to appeal for funds without saying where the money will go, and this information often passes for education.

For example, one March of Dimes mailing includes a four-page brochure consisting mostly of color pictures of two children wearing leg braces. The back page says they are two of 15 million children who live with birth defects. Another 60,000 children die of birth defects each year, it says.

The mailing includes a computer-addressed sheet asking for money. On the back of that, a message says that a newborn baby may be in danger from birth defects caused by a genetic abnormality, pollution, chemicals, drugs, or malnutrition. It concludes, "You can help" by supporting the March of Dimes.

Although the mailing is a fund-raising effort, sent only to previous contributors, March of Dimes treats it as 40 percent education and 60 percent fund-raising.

Last year, that split let the charity, which took in $83.2 million, subtract $891,000 in postage, printing and other mailing costs from fund-raising expenses and count it as public education.

Other charities, including the American Lung Association, United Cerebral Palsy Associations and Leukemia Society of America, have begun similar accounting.

They say it is proper to report some of the expenses of a fund-raising mailing as education costs.

"We know that there's an educational benefit that accrues to individuals that receive this message who either don't give or give," said Matthew G. McCrossen, the financial vice president of the March of Dimes.

Critics scoff at such assessments, contending the "educational" messages are strictly part of the pitch.

"They're just asking for money," remarked Robert J. Cozzens, a senior accountant in the New York state Office of Charities Registration, referring to a March of Dimes mailing.

To the regulators, the charities' argument is like saying a billboard that reads, "Milk is good for you. Buy Mallory's milk," is only part advertising.

To the charities, the regulators seem bent on imposing rules that are easy to enforce but unfair.

"Let's face it, the most effective form of government is tyranny," said Edward H. Van Ness, the executive vice president of the National Health Council, a group of 19 health charities.

"I know politicians. It's always easy to have one little criterion or rule of thumb," Van Ness said. "However, that doesn't say that's the most equitable way of dealing with it."

To image-conscious charities, much hinges on how efficient they look in their financial reports.

About 20 states limit what charities can spend on fund-raising efforts or management. Two influential charity-rating services, the National Information Bureau and the national Council of Better Business Bureaus, look at these figures in deciding whether to endorse a charity. The rating bureaus influence donors ranging from large corporations to $5 givers.

And the $100 million-a-year Combined Federal Campaign, the federal government's employee-giving drive, also looks at the figures in deciding whether to include a charity.

"The whole measure of success in the nonprofit world is to show that you're cutting down on administrative costs and increasing your program expenses," said Elizabeth Doherty, assistant director of the CBBB's Philanthropic Advisory Service.

Van de Workeen and others say the new accounting practices are so subjective that they have drained much of the meaning from charities' financial reports. This threatens their usefulness for comparing charities. The reports are filed for public inspection at state charity registration offices throughout the nation.

In five years, Van de Workeen said, "There won't be two figures you can bump together that will make sense."

A task force set up to resolve the conflict two years ago by the Financial

Accounting Standards Board, the accounting profession's rule-making body, is sharply divided and has achieved little.

While the regulators have criticized many major charities, they have gone farthest in challenging the Muscular Dystrophy Association.

Besides questioning an MDA shift of $2 million in mailing costs, similar to what the March of Dimes did, New York state says the charity is underreporting the time its employees spend on fund-raising and management.

MDA paid salaries of $16 million last year, of which only $2 million was listed as going to fund-raising and management. Joseph G. Shea, who heads New York's charities registration office, said another figure, conservatively put at $4 million, should be reported as fund-raising and management. MDA's total budget was $76 million.

MDA said its total expenses for fund-raising and management last year were $19 million, but New York officials believe the figure is at least $25 million.

If that is the case, the ratio of MDA's fund-raising and management costs to its overall budget, portrayed as among the lowest of the major health charities, actually is among the highest.

The heart of the issue is how workers spend their time in MDA's 160 offices. In each local office, MDA has a patient coordinator, whose time is spent helping patients. The charity maintains that the other employees also spend much of their time on patient services, and little, if any, time on fund-raising and management.

MDA reports that these employees, including office directors, average only about 40 minutes a day on fund-raising and management.

The watchdogs believe those time allocations are unrealistically low. Information from MDA's office directors in Connecticut supports the critics' assertions.

Daniel Marquis, the director of the South Windsor MDA office, which covers the northern half of the state, said he spends seven hours of an eight-hour day on fund-raising and management duties. His program coordinator spends all his time on fund-raising.

Paul Barry, the director of the Fairfield office, which serves the rest of the state, said he spends about 55 percent of his time on fund-raising and management around telethon time and about half as much time during the rest of the year.

He said his program coordinator spends half his time on fundraising and the other half on public relations and other activities to support fund-raising endeavors.

The only other employees in either office are a secretary and a part-time clerk.

Shea has asked MDA to make a "significant shift in amounts of salaries allocated to program and supporting services."

MDA has refused to budge.

Like Shea, the National Information Bureau doubts that as much time is spent on patient care as MDA claims.

"NIB believes that a significant portion of the expenses . . . should more properly be allocated to fund-raising and management," an October 1982 report said.

MDA vigorously defends its figures, but, when asked for time sheets or other material to back up its claims, it refused, calling such information confidential.

Gerald C. Weinberg, the national director of field organization, says the watchdogs don't understand how MDA works.

MDA, he said, keeps management costs low by being more centralized than other big health charities and by relying more heavily on volunteers.

Weinberg said his staff spends more time on patient and community services than either the information bureau or New York's Shea appreciates.

"If he would visit a home, accompany a family, be involved in a clinic, and the total personal problems that those people (muscular dystrophy victims) have, he couldn't question those figures, nor could you," he said.

Shea has ordered the MDA, the March of Dimes and the Lung Association to abandon their new accounting methods for fund-raising mailings and, in their New York reports, to return to the standard they adopted in 1964.

That standard was part of an accounting guide, known as the "black book," published by the Health Council and the National Assembly, another group of major charities. It was reissued in 1974 with the added blessing of the United Way of America.

The rule said that if the primary purpose of an activity was fundraising, all expenses had to be charged to fund-raising, even if a charity might argue that some other purpose, such as education, also was served. The sole exception was the cost of developing and printing a separate educational message enclosed with a fund appeal.

The black book conceded that the line between fund-raising activities and education could sometimes be a fuzzy one, and thus a simple and uniform standard was essential if organizations were to be compared. The tightening was designed to eliminate abuses that led to some charity fund-raising scandals in the early 1960s.

It particularly irritates the regulators that the prestigious charities that set this standard are now retreating from it.

They obeyed the rule until the mid-1970s, when they were buffeted by soaring expenses—especially for postage—and by competition from a new breed of advocacy and political pressure groups never bound by the old rules.

"Other agencies were at an advantage in terms of presenting their picture to the public. It's as simple as that," Van Ness said.

In April, 1976, the black book's sponsors issued a memo that effectively nullified the rule.

Timothy J. Racek, a leading authority in the field and a partner in Arthur Andersen & Co., the prominent accounting firm, said he had always believed the rule exaggerated fund-raising expenses.

In 1964, when fund-raising costs were lower and few states had ceilings on them, the exaggeration was harmless, he said. The new pressures, Racek said, made deciding what rule to use "no longer just an accounting nicety, but a matter of life or death."

The American Cancer Society and the American Health Association, both so successful that their wealth has become a touchy subject, have adopted a technique that reduces that wealth on paper.

They recently began deducting the total cost of future research grants— some extending 25 years—from current assets. The charities are thus subtracting from their current wealth money they will not pay out for years.

Last year, the Heart Association reduced its reported liquid assets— essentially its readily available money—from $149 million to $109 million by using this technique. The Cancer Society's fell from $228.8 million to 206.5 million.

Shea said the new practice is a gimmick to make the charities look needier. He has added a note to their New York reports to alert the public to the unusual accounting.

Robert J. Makarski, the Heart Association's vice president for finance, defended the practice. "That is spent money," he said. "It would be fiscally imprudent to respend that money."

Several charities resent the attention their fund-raising ratios get, saying it obscures the good work they do.

"Their just seems to be an effort to evaluate organizations not on how much they do or accomplish, or whether they have integrity," said the Lung Association's managing director, James A. Swomley, "but on whether or not they meet some mythical or magical formula in terms of fund-raising cost."

But any meaningful evaluation of charities depends on their filing accurate financial reports to the states, said David E. Ormstedt, assistant attorney general in Connecticut.

"If you can't rely on the figures," he said, "there's no point in having them filed at all."

Case 10-1 Questions:

1. Define the problem in this case.
2. What stance do the two sides take to defend their points of view?
3. Which position do you support and why?
4. As a human service agency administrator, how would you deal with the issue of allocation of fund-raising costs in your agency's financial statements?

Reading 10-1: "Checklist for Charitable Nonprofit Organizations"* by Gary N. Scrivner

For many nonprofit organizations the maintaining of a tax-exempt and public charity status is critical to survival. This is particularly true for charitable organizations because the loss of this status might severely impair fund-raising efforts through contributions, gifts, grants and bequests. For this as well as other reasons, it is all but imperative that a tax professional be assigned to review the audit workpapers and activities of each nonprofit audit client. Unfortunately, little guidance is provided in auditing literature about how the auditor or tax specialist might approach such an assignment.

One useful approach is the development of a checklist for charitable organizations designed to provide the auditor with an idea of the information the tax specialist needs to express an opinion on the continued maintenance of exempt and public charity status and to determine the liability for income taxes on the organization's unrelated business activi-

---

*Reprinted with permission from the *Journal of Accountancy*, July 1981, pp. 42–47. Copyright 1981 by the American Institute of Certified Public Accountants, Inc.

ties for the year(s) audited. Such a checklist might also allow for identification of problem areas or planning ideas for discussion with the client.

The checklist is divided into two parts. Part 1, dealing primarily with the client's status and activities for the year, is to be completed by the audit senior and reviewed by the audit manager or partner and the tax specialist. Part 2, dealing primarily with the procedures for completing the review, is to be prepared by the tax specialist and reviewed by a tax manager or partner.

A special checklist might also be adapted for use on noncharitable, nonprofit organizations such as exempt cooperatives, social clubs, trade associations, employee benefit organizations or business leagues. It might also be useful for compilation and review engagements and for preparation of a private foundation's annual report (form 990AR).

A typical checklist might include the items listed below.

Checklist for Charitable Organizations

Part 1—to be completed by an audit senior or an in-charge accountant. Each item should be reviewed by the client, and a response should appear opposite each item, signifying completion.

Review of Exempt Status Documentation

1. Review the determination letter from the Internal Revenue Service awarding exempt status and all subsequent IRS correspondence, particularly with respect to advance or final determination of nonprivate foundation status. Briefly describe any possible modifications in status not previously identified.

2. Review any IRS correspondence closing the most recent revenue agent's examinations. Consider the effects of your findings on the current review.

3. Review and discuss with tax specialist any special tax status, such as operating foundation or "pass through" foundation status, which appears to be in effect based on correspondence, tax returns, or other information.

4. Verify whether the exemption letter specifies whether and to what extent contributions received by the organization are deductible from the taxable income of the donor.

5. Review board of directors' minutes and any other source for changes in character, purpose, or method of operation. Are these changes evidenced by changes to the articles of incorporation, bylaws, or other

governing instruments? Have all significant changes been communicated to the IRS?

6. Describe to what extent, if any, the organization has participated either directly or indirectly in any political campaign or voter registration drive. Describe the activities and expenditures made for lobbying or similar purposes.

7. Does it appear the organization may have allowed its assets to be used, or made disbursements to or for the benefit of any individual or entity, for other than charitable purposes that are not in furtherance of the organization's exempt purpose? If so, describe fully.

8. Obtain for the files (if prepared by the client) and review a copy of the organization's most recent annual information return. Discuss any questions or problems with the tax specialist. Was the return filed on time?

9. Review all states in which the organization is active to determine state filing requirements for registration and tax purposes.

Unrelated Business Taxable Activity

1. Does every activity of the organization contribute importantly to the accomplishment of the organization's exempt purpose (other than by the mere production of income and regardless of the use to which such income is put)?

2. Has every significant program or activity, the amount of time devoted to it and the income derived from it been reported to the IRS either in the original application for exemption or through separate correspondence?

3. Obtain all significant documentation with respect to the recognition of revenue from the following sources:
   a. Rental of real or personal property.
   b. Advertising.
   c. Research.
   d. Income-producing property of any type acquired or improved with borrowed funds.
   e. Partnership investments.
   f. Operation of any frequent fund-raising event or any other activity conducted on a regular basis.
   g. Sales of timber or coal.
   h. Working interest (as opposed to royalty) in oil, gas, or other mineral property.

i. Income from trade show, exposition, agricultural, or similar activities.

j. Income from a controlled corporation.

k. Sale of membership lists.

4. An activity may still be an unrelated trade or business even if conducted within a larger aggregate of similar activities. Activities of this type include further processing of an exempt product, dual use of exempt facilities or exploitation of an exempt function, trademark, or reputation. Review and describe activities that could fall within this category such as sales of advertising in a trade journal or regular sales of real estate.

5. There are a number of exceptions to the unrelated business income requirements. Identify whether the organization conducts activities

    a. Substantially all of which are performed by volunteer workers.

    b. Primarily for the convenience of its members, students, patients, officers, or employees.

    c. By selling merchandise, substantially all of which has been donated to the organization.

Other activities and documentation

1. Has the organization filed form SS-15 waiving exemption from Social Security taxes?* Does the organization have sufficient documentation to support witholding and remittance of income and other payroll taxes on a timely basis?

2. Obtain information as to pension, annuity or other benefit plans maintained by the organization.

3. Has the organization sold, exchanged, or leased its property; lent money; furnished other goods, services, or facilities; paid excessive compensation or reimbursed expenses; or transferred any income or assets or their use or enjoyment either directly or indirectly to any individual?

Describe all such transactions in detail.

Completed by_____

                                     Auditor in-charge

Reviewed by_____

---

*Note: Nonprofit agencies are now required to pay social security taxes.

Audit partner or manager

_____

Tax specialist_____

Date

Tax Specialist

Part 2—to be completed by the assigned tax specialist.

Preaudit Procedures

1. Review current year's correspondence for particular tax problems, attend the preaudit planning conference and provide a status report of the client's current tax position. Report any pertinent law changes. Discuss the need for any required additional audit work so that it may be scheduled and performed on a timely basis.

2. Ensure that any special research or assembly of necessary data is completed on a timely basis.

3. Coordinate timing of the final tax review with the audit senior and manager to ensure that all necessary audit work (including completion of part 1 of this checklist, a draft copy of the audit report with footnotes and manager review) is ready for final tax review.

Review Procedures

1. On notification from the audit senior that the work is completed, review the audit tax accrual, if any, and tax footnotes to the financial statements, including a review of the appropriate audit working papers, permanent files, board of directors' minutes, responses to questions in part 1 and such other information as may be necessary to conclude on the continued tax-exempt and public charity status and liability for federal and state taxes on unrelated business taxable income, if any.

2. When agreement is obtained on whether the lack of a tax provision is appropriate, the tax specialist should sign part 1 and prepare a tax memorandum to the audit partner indicating he has reviewed the tax provision, or lack thereof, and is satisfied with the adequacy of the work performed.

3. Review those areas of the management letter that discuss tax matters or have tax consequences.

4. If necessary, ascertain that all information required to prepare or

review the client's tax return is available in the audit workpapers or special tax workpapers.

Post-audit Procedures

1. Assist, when required, the assigned audit personnel in the preparation of necessary tax returns, including any special tax working papers.

2. Review in detail the prepared tax returns and follow up to ensure delivery to the client on a timely basis.

3. Discuss with audit manager any unusual items that occurred during the review that may affect future reviews. Discuss in detail procedures to facilitate improved review next year.

4. Review items of tax significance that warrant further research and followup.

Completed by_____

Tax specialist

Reviewed by_____

Tax partner or manager

_____

Date

Reading 10-1 Questions:

1. Why would the auditor or in-charge accountant be concerned about whether the agency's character, purpose, or method of operation had changed?
2. Why does the auditor want to know whether every activity of the organization contributes to the accomplishment of the organization's exempt purpose?
3. With whom in the agency should this checklist be discussed?
4. At what point in time should this checklist be discussed?

Chapter Eleven

COMPUTERIZED FINANCIAL INFORMATION SYSTEMS

After reading this chapter, you should be able to:

1. Understand what a computer system in a human service agency can do;
2. Understand the process of converting from a manual to an automated financial information system;
3. Make decisions regarding the acquisition of a system for an agency;
4. Develop the criteria for acquiring a system.

INFORMATION SYSTEMS

Computerized information systems are part of the formal information system of an agency. They are a comparatively recent phenomenon in small human service agencies, spurred by the proliferation of microcomputers. With the cost of new systems constantly decreasing due to rapidly changing technology and intense competition in the microcomputer market, the price of a computerized system is within the reach of almost any human service agency. The computerization of client information systems is still underdeveloped in the human services and fraught with much more controversy than any other functional areas in the organization. This may be due to the perceived threat to client confidentiality and other issues related to computerization. There are many functions that a computer system can perform, but the easiest and simplest are in the area of financial management.

The necessity of mechanizing financial applications such as payroll, inventory, and bookkeeping was often the primary reason that computers were acquired by business organizations and these functions were among the first to be computerized. The desire to automate the financial information system in an agency, including bookkeeping, financial reporting, fundraising, and data base management, is the main reason that computers are sought by human service agencies.

287

The kinds of information that a financial management system is concerned with deal with all aspects of the agency's activities that can be expressed in monetary terms. "The basis of the financial information system is the flow of dollars throughout the organization ..." (Joel E. Ross, 1976: 131). Although most of the data used in a financial information system (FIS) are historical and internal in nature, a good computer package should be able to provide future projections and simulations if so desired by the agency. The difficulty in converting from a manual to an automated system is to be able to design and/or use the types of sophisticated programs that will make the computer system a real management tool for planning, operation, and development rather than just a rapid data processor and record keeper. The two main functions of a financial information system for a nonprofit human service agency are:

- Internal: to provide quantitative measures of the agency's performance for purposes of planning, evaluating, and controlling of the resources used by the organization.
- External: to provide information of a financial nature to outside funding sources and the public at large for purposes of fund raising and accountability.

In this chapter, an overview of financial information systems will be presented as they apply to the nonprofit human service agency. The point of view presented in this chapter will be that of the professional manager and staff. Therefore, there will be very little discussion of the technical aspects of computers, that information may be found elsewhere. Rather, this chapter tries to focus on helping professionals make decisions based on some rational criteria, the two most obvious being cost and product, that is, how much will this cost my agency and what types of products can I expect from a system? Other topics in this chapter include choosing computer consultants and packages. The type of computer system to be discussed revolves around the microcomputer, rather than a mini or a mainframe computer. Minis and mainframes are too big and expensive to be even considered by most nonprofit human service agencies, and microcomputers have been developed that have the speed and storage capacity needed by most agencies. Again, the aim is not to make you a computer expert, rather it is to make you an informed user. In order to facilitate the discussion that follows, a brief overview of computer systems will be presented.

COMPUTER SYSTEMS

Computers are machines that can be programmed to perform routine tasks, especially calculations, at very high rates of speed. A computer system consists of input devices, such as keyboards, throughput devices, called central processing units (CPU's) or motherboards on microcomputers; and output devices such as printers or monitors (see Figure 11-1).

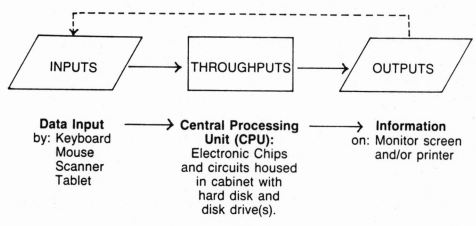

Figure 11-1: Computer System

The machinery or equipment including the box that houses that electronic circuitry of the computer, and the keyboard, are called hardware. Peripherals are hardware items such as printers, modems (machines that hook up the computer to other computers via telephone), and assorted other equipment used with the computer. The computer program(s) that tell the computer what to do and how to do it are called software. Usually the programs are on floppy disks (5 and ¼" or 3 and ½") that are inserted into a disk drive in the computer. There are also hard disks that can store vast amounts of information and are usually installed internally in the computer. This reduces the need for floppy disks and the constant changing of disks when working on the computer.

ADVANTAGES AND DISADVANTAGES
OF COMPUTERIZED SYSTEMS

Computerizing the agency's financial information system is not an answer to any of the agency's management or financial problems. There are many things a computer system can do, but one of the things it cannot do is improve an inefficient system. If the agency's financial and accounting system is not very good in its manual form, it will be no better computerized except that it will do it what it is programmed to do faster. There is an expression in the computer field: GIGO (garbage in, garbage out), this means that if the data entered into the computer is not good, incomplete, or inaccurate, it will come out the same way. Everyone has heard of all kinds of errors blamed on the computer, but the truth of the matter is that the computer just processes what it is given by humans to do. Agencies should bear this in mind in contemplating the move to a computer system, and should be prepared to do the necessary thinking and planning to make it work effectively. There are advantages as well as disadvantages of acquiring a computerized system that have to be taken into account by the agency in making its final decision. All variables should be discussed by the Executive Director with board members and staff before making a decision. Some of these advantages and disadvantages are (DeJacimo, et al, 1985: 89–90; Silver, 1981: 768–772; Schoech, 1985: 339–342):

Advantages

The Speed of Processing

Computers can process large amounts of data and make millions of calculations much more quickly than clerks doing the same chores manually or even with electronic calculators and bookkeeping machines. In addition, the turnaround time for important financial information may be reduced substantially, so that the agency may receive reports in days instead of weeks.

The Accuracy of the Equipment

Computer systems are extremely accurate from both a hardware and a software perspective. That is, microcomputers are made with silicon chips and sophisticated electronic technology that have high rates of accuracy. In addition, computer software is (or should be) "de-bugged" (have errors eliminated) before the agency uses it. While the computer equipment itself may be extremely accurate, the same cannot be said for the humans who enter the data. For a variety of reasons, such as fatigue, stress, distractions, etc., errors in data entry may be made (and then blamed on the computer!). But many computer programs try to take this (human) error factor into account by having an editing function and/or numerous spots where entries can be re-checked and verified.

Elimination of Repetitive Data Entry and Greater Processing Control

Being able to store data that can be easily retrieved as well as manipulated in a variety of ways helps eliminate the need to repeatedly enter the same data. This also is helpful in eliminating errors that may occur in continually having to transpose data from one record or report to another.

Consistency of Processing

Once a computer is programmed to follow a certain rule in every case, for example, to reject every travel voucher over one hundred dollars, it will make no exceptions. Computers cannot make decisions, they do as they are programmed, however, in routine clerical decisions, the computer can be programmed so that the agency will be assured of consistent application of procedural rules.

Smaller Physical Storage Requirements

A microcomputer and printer take up much less room than some older sorts of bookkeeping systems, for example, punched card systems. They can also store much more data on a hard disk in a small space than the old ledger books and journals. However, having a computer does not eliminate the need for paper backups of all transactions recorded, thus paper files are still necessary.

Operating Costs

Computerized systems may be less expensive for processing large amounts of data compared to manual systems. Economies of scale result from larger amounts of data to be processed, that is, the more work processed, the cheaper each transaction becomes. In addition, there are other cost savings. For example, the elimination of need to hire additional staff to maintain a manual system for bookkeeping and reporting functions. Also, if purchased, a computer system could be depreciated over a fixed period of time.

Disadvantages

Long Planning and Implementation Period

An agency cannot go out and buy a computer, its associated peripherals and software, plug it in and be up and running. The planning and implementation of a computerized information system, of which the financial system may be only a part, is a long, time-consuming process that involves almost everyone in the organization if it is to be successful. The successful implementation of a new system involves commitment of top management to supply the necessary resources, as well as hard thinking on the part of the organization regarding needs, goals, and so forth. Even after an analysis of alternative types of systems, and the acquisition of a system, there is still much work to be done. For a period of time, the old system and the new system have to be run simultaneously to "de-bug" the system. This may entail extra work for staff and they have to be prepared for this. Thus, there may be a long lag time between decision to acquire a computer system, and the actual and final total conversion to the new system.

High Start-Up Costs

During the planning and initial implementation stages of conversion to a computerized system, there will be costs associated with these stages that will not be recouped by the agency for quite a while. In addition, staff and board may not see benefits of the system since it may not be operational during the initial periods. The agency must be prepared for these initial start-up costs which include such things as the hardware and software for the system, consultant fees, staff training, and so forth.

Greater Need for Controls

While most computer programs have built-in controls for certain kinds of errors, there is always the element of human error in the entry of data to be processed. Therefore, there is a need to establish controls at each stage of the processing to recognize and correct errors. This holds more true for computerized systems because of the speed of processing, as well as the fact that fewer staff will have access to files and therefore, there may be less chance for detection of some types of errors. For example, in a manual accounting system, the general ledger accounts may be readily available to administrators to view, but in a computerized system, they may have to wait for someone to log on to a computer, and print out information.

Centralization of Processing

In any organization, when more than one person is involved in a job or task, the burden of work is spread among workers and helps insure that someone can take over if something happens to one worker. In the human service agency that is computerized, all of the processing activities may be centralized in that one computer system. Thus, if the machine breaks down (a rare occurrence), the hard disk crashes (a not so rare occurrence), or there is a power failure of some sort, it becomes a problem for the agency. All of us have tried to get information from some organization only to be told "the computer is down." In an agency with only one microcomputer, this is one of the disadvantages.

Organizational Implementation Problems

Major changes in organizations are not only a slow process, but they may entail changes in the way work is structured, in power relationships, in responsibilities, and even who has access to certain kinds of information. Humans are often resistant to change and this is why the support of all staff, not just top management and board is so important.

Flexibility

Computerized systems can bring many advantages to an organization, but in some ways they are not as flexible as manual systems. Some programs may be very difficult to change, and may entail the expense of a programmer. This is very different than teaching a clerk or other staff a new procedure. This is one of the reasons that agencies need to look for as much flexibility as possible in the software they purchase.

Fixed Cost of Operation

In some ways a computer system is similar to any other office equipment or machines that the agency may possess. That is, whether they are being used or not, they still cost money. The computer system has both fixed and variable costs attached to it, but these costs do not start at zero. Therefore, increased volume will bring cost savings in some areas (e.g., average cost per transaction may decrease), but other costs will increase (e.g., more use means more wear and tear, more electricity, more disks or other backups). "Rather than expect cost reductions, it is better to expect more accountable and improved service delivery and the ability to hold down future costs. The chance of future cost reductions can be increased by dove-tailing several applications . . . " (Schoech, 1985: 341).

Rapid Obsolesence of Hardware and Software

The computer field is undergoing such rapid change that any system bought today, no matter how technologically advanced, will be obsolete in ten years or less. This is not to say that the system will not retain some usefulness for the agency, but new improvements and changes will mean that something even better will be available to be used by the agency. Twenty years ago, massive mainframe systems that took up whole rooms did not have the capacity or power of some microcomputers of today. Prototypes of the systems of tomorrow are already being tested, for example, the use of compact discs (CD's) and other new media will make the floppy disk a thing of the past. This is not to discourage the agency from acquiring a computer system, rather it is to alert all to the fact that this is a rapidly changing field, there is no best time to buy except when the agency is ready to do so with the full knowledge that the computer system will eventually have to be discarded and replaced.

In summary, computer systems are superior in the areas of processing speed, accuracy, information retrieval, consistency of processing, ability to handle complex processing problems (if programmed correctly), and ability to handle workload changes (within the limits of the computer system). But they are not as good as manual systems in terms of flexibility, learning ability (machines can't think), and the time and trouble required to install a new system.

COMPUTER ACQUISITION DECISIONS

Agencies want to acquire a computer system for a variety of reasons. Sometimes there is the need to have a computer because it seems the thing to do. In other cases people want to acquire computer systems because they somehow believe that it will solve some of their organizational problems and make work more efficient. The decision to acquire a computer system in the human service agency involves some initial analysis, study, and planning before the agency even decides whether it should buy, rent, or lease a computer. It must first decide whether it should acquire one at all. Some steps in the acquisition process include: 1) setting up a computer committee; 2) agency selfstudy; 3) feasibility study; 4) choosing a consultant; 5) systems study; 6) choosing a vendor; 7) conversion to new computer system.

Setting Up Computer Committee

The setting up of a computer committee is a crucial first step of acquiring the computerized system for the agency. The committee should be made up of board members, administrative staff, and line staff as well. It is important for staff to be involved all along in the decisions involved in the computer system acquisition. If staff have no input, they will very likely be resistant to using it, or resistant to filling out the necessary forms that need to be entered in order to be able to generate reports for management decision makers and funders.

The role of the computer committee may be an advisory one, in other cases the committee may be authorized to make major decisions regarding the acquisition and installation of a new computerized system. The committee will represent the agency throughout the process, and in order for it to be effective, staff workloads need to be adjusted so that time is available for the necessary work to be done in the process (Schoech et al, 1981:17).

Agency Self-Study

The agency needs to do some self-analysis in order to determine whether in fact it really needs to computerize its current manual information system. How does it know it needs computerization of its present system? For example, are there problems in the processing of data now? Does it take too long for routine records and reports to be processed and received by decision-makers? Is the agency growing faster than its ability to process transactions taking place, so that staff are getting further behind? Does the agency have long-term goals and objectives that include expansion of services, necessitating computerization?

Why does the agency need a computer system? In thinking about the acquisition of a computer system, the agency must be clear about what it wants a computer for and what it wants the computer to do. Knowing what the computer is to do for the agency is a crucial question to be answered. It is imperative to remember that the computer does not solve agency problems of efficiency, rather computers perform functions. Some functions that computers may perform are simple ones such as mathematical and statistical calculations; other functions of a more intermediate nature include such things as word processing, spread sheet applications, and data processing of bookkeeping functions; More complex functions would involve interactive, or simulation-type programs.

Acquiring a computer is not a solution, rather a computer is a tool to be used by agency staff to solve problems. Often, agencies think a computer is like a typewriter or television that can be simply plugged in and will perform all sorts of wonderous feats. To be effective, the software that runs the computer system must be able to handle the types of data processing and report generating that the agency can use. Acquiring a system entails hard thinking and planning on the part of the agency.

What are the information needs of the agency? Is there enough paper work generated to warrant the acquisition of the computer system? Knowing the current and future information needs of the agency is an important question that needs to be answered. That is, considering the flow of information in the agency at present, could a computer system enhance the processing of data/information or make it more efficient? What could a computer system bring to increase efficiency, processing, productivity? What will be the information system needs of the agency five years from now?

The agency must review its willingness and ability to plan for a system, as well as train staff in using it. The implementation of a new system can be quite time consuming, does the agency have the time to give for staff training on the new system? Who will manage the new system?

Feasibility Study

While the agency self-study is concerned with questions regarding the agency's need for a computerized system, the feasibility study is concerned with issues regarding the agency's ability to plan for, design, pay for, and implement a new system. Thus questions of feasibility ask whether a new system is practical, cost-effective, affordable, and capable of being implemented successfully at the present time.

In the area of economic feasibility, the agency is concerned with a number of cost issues. There are equipment, personnel, development, and operating costs that will accrue to the agency as a result of the acquisition of a computerized system. Can the agency afford the initial upfront cost as well as long-term costs? Does the agency have the financial capability to pay for the computer system as well as the capability to pay for the ongoing maintenance of the system? If it does not have the funds to pay for whatever arrangement is agreed upon (purchase, rental, lease), how will it pay for the system? If the system will be donated, can the agency afford the maintenance and training costs?

Another factor to be considered in the feasibility study is whether the agency has the space and personnel to use the computer system. If there are no staff who know how to use the system, can the agency afford to retrain available staff or hire additional staff to use it? The final question is: is this the right time for the agency to embark on this project, knowing the time and expense involved? If the answer is yes, the agency should proceed to the next step.

Choosing a Consultant

Since it is unlikely that an agency will have a staff or board member with the necessary expertise in designing and installing a computer system, the agency may have to hire a consultant. One of the problems in choosing a consultant is that most of them are not familiar with the peculiar needs of the human service agency. And while they may have the technical expertise, consultants do not always have the ability to speak clearly, and non-technically to computer novices. The danger in this is that there may be problems in communication between the agency and the consultant and the agency may end up with less than the optimal product. Often, the consultant may also be a vendor whose aim is not so much to design a system tailored to the agency's needs, but rather to sell computer systems. So there are a number of questions that must be asked in choosing a consultant:

- What is reputation/experience of this person? The reputation of a consultant can be checked in several ways. One is by checking with the Better Business Bureau to see if there are any unresolved complaints filed against this person or company. This also should be done when screening vendors. Another way to screen a consultant is to check references. Even though references in and of themselves are not always meaningful, but should be checked out in addition to other sources. A third source of information would be other human service agencies.
- Have they worked with other nonprofit agencies that you know of? Are the agencies satisfied with the resulting system and the consultant's work? Ask for the names of consultants who have provided satisfactory service in the planning and installation of a computer system.

After choosing a consultant, the agency should sign a short-term contract, and be specific about what the consultant will do in that time period. The contract should specify outcomes or results. Usually what the agency should expect from the consultant is a systems study, a systems design, and some recommendations about hardware and software. The consultant may or may not be involved in the actual purchasing of the equipment, but may help with systems installation. On the other hand, if the consultant is not also a vendor, he or she may not be involved in the actual installation of the system. This is because most vendors will not want to guarantee a system if it is not installed by the vendor.

Systems Study

In the systems analysis phase of the conversion process to a computerized system, the consultant must answer a number of questions in order to be able to design a system tailored to the specific needs of the human service agency. Some of the questions that need to be answered in the systems study include: What are the information needs of the organization? What documents are generated by the information system now? What documents does the agency need to be generated by the new system? What current users get information from the system? What other users need information from the system? What is the easiest way to capture data that will be able to be used by more than one department for more than one application? What applications would it be used for? What is the volume of processing? How much storage space (disk, tape) does the organization need? What types of expansion capabilities are needed from the computer system based on the agency's long-range plans?

Based on the consultant's findings to these and other questions regarding the present and future information needs of the agency, the consultant will submit a report detailing:

- major assumptions used by the consultant in analyzing the agency's system
- major organizational/information problems identified
- performance requirements for the system (what the agency wants it to be able to do)
- any recommendations regarding the system, including whether the project to convert to a computerized system should proceed.

- projected costs and resources required to install the new system (Burch et al, 1979: 258).

The consultant, in doing the systems study or analysis, will also conduct another type of feasibility study. For the consultant will look at feasibility from a somewhat different view than the agency. That is, besides economic feasibility, the consultant will also be interested in technical and operational feasibility. The final result of the systems study will be a recommendation to proceed with the process, wait, or stop. If the agency decides to proceed, the next step is the design of the system.

Designing the System

Designing the system involves choosing a microcomputer configuration to meet the current information needs of the agency with capabilities for future expansion as needed. The design of the system should be modular, flexible, simple, and involve all potential users in its preparation. Modular design means that one component of a system is implemented with success before other components are tried. There are a number of factors to take into account in the design of the system. Some of these factors involve the hardware and software of the system.

Buying Hardware: Many people advise that a user should first decide what software he/she wants to run, and then buy the hardware that will run it. Buying hardware and software is more complex than that, for there are a number of features that make up the systems:

- compatibility: compatibility refers to the type of operating system used by the computer and whether it will be compatible with the industry standard IBM operating system, or only with its own products such as the Apple. In general, it is better to have a system that is compatible with a wide range of software products so that some software packages may be used "off the shelf", for example, a word-processing or maillist program.
- capacity of system: when microcomputers were first marketed for small-business and home use, they had very little storage capacity, i.e., 64K (kilobytes) or less. Nowadays, capacity is discussed in megabyte terms. The first microcomputers had no hard disks, now there are hard disks with 40 megabyte capacity and even more. There are also computers with removable hard disks so that the

capacity of the system may be almost infinite. The agency should try to acquire a system with more capacity than it needs at present.

- printer: The agency will most certainly need a printer. Until recently, the choice was between a dot matrix printer, which had a printhead of nine or more pins that printed impressions that formed words on a page, and a letter quality printer that used a daisy wheel similar to a typewriter's wheel. The choice has been widened considerably now with the advent of dot-matrix printers that print "near letter-quality" print, as well as the development of laser printers. The choice should be based on two criteria: cost and use. That is, how much can the agency afford to spend and what will it use the printer for? If the agency can only spend under $600, then there are some excellent 24-pin letter quality printers available. If the agency can afford to spend up to $2000, and plans to use the printer for a wide range of functions such as reports, newsletters, brochures, and so forth, then a laser printer is the best bet. Daisy wheel printers are becoming obsolete, due to the decreasing price of laser printers which have much more capability, on the one hand, and the improved technology of dot matrix printers, which has brought improved print at even lower cost.
- modem: A modem connects one computer to another via telephone lines. A modem may be necessary if the agency wants to use its computer for networking or to access a mainframe or a bulletin board.

Buying Software: A fund accounting package is a software program specifically designed to perform the types of accounting tasks unique to the nonprofit organization, that is, separate revenues, public support, and expenses by funds. In addition, it should be able to generate the special kinds of financial statements required for nonprofit human service agencies: the Statement of Support, Revenue and Expenses, and Changes in Fund Balances; the Statement of Functional Expenses; and the Balance Sheet.

The problem for human service agencies is not in acquiring hardware, or the machines themselves, it is in acquiring software, or the programs to run the machines. This is because there are very few software accounting packages that are written to fit the unique requirements of the nonprofit human service agency. This leaves the agency with only a few options: 1) buy one of the few available programs written for the nonprofit agency; 2) have someone write a program specifically for the agency; or 3) try to modify an existing general accounting package.

If the agency has someone write a program specifically for the agency, it could be very costly, and may not meet the agency's expectations. To successfully write such a program, the programmer(s) would have to be knowledgeable about not just programming, but nonprofit accounting. How well the job is done depends on finding this unique person as well as being able to communicate agency needs to him or her (See Case 11-1 for an example of an agency that took this approach).

If the agency tries to modify an existing general accounting package, its success depends on whether it has anyone on staff with the expertise to do it, or whether it has to hire someone. If it has to hire someone, the agency will have some of the same problems mentioned above in dealing with a programmer.

There are some fund accounting packages available for nonprofit agencies. If an agency were to buy an existing fund accounting package, there are a number of features that it would want to look for in trying to determine whether it would be an appropriate accounting package for a human service agency. Here are some guidelines to use in choosing a package (Pescow, 1981:1308–1309):

- tutorial provided: there should be a tutorial on disk with an accompanying tutorial in the manual to help the novice learn the program with a minimum of outside assistance (see Table 11-1).
- clear manuals: manuals accompanying the package should be clearly written for an ordinary mortal to understand. That is, they should be written in simple English and not "computerese". They should assume minimal knowledge on the part of the reader. The illustrations should be clearly marked and related well to the text. There should be a complete index and table of contents, with sections easy to find.
- understandable menus: menus are those parts of a program that let you choose what actions you want to do next. They should be understandable enough so that a novice can understand and use them.
- interactive program: an interactive program is one which responds to an inquiry or answer or converses with the user in some way (Hicks and Leininger, 1981:559). Thus an interactive program should have easy to understand prompts and menus and a help key that lets

Table 11-1

COMPARISON LIST FOR FUND ACCOUNTING/FIS PACKAGES

Package Name

Features	_____	_____	_____
1. tutorial provided			
2. clear manuals	_____	_____	_____
3. understandable menus	_____	_____	_____
4. interactive program	_____	_____	_____
5. flexible chart of accounts	_____	_____	_____
6. easy to modify data	_____	_____	_____
7. easy to correct mistakes	_____	_____	_____
8. fund accounting based on United Way Chart of Accounts as well as agency's	_____	_____	_____
9. appropriate financial statements	_____	_____	_____
10. calculates financial ratios, other statistics	_____	_____	_____
11. agency can design format	_____	_____	_____
12. summarizes data	_____	_____	_____
13. integrative package	_____	_____	_____
14. quarterly reports	_____	_____	_____
15. variance budgeting	_____	_____	_____
16. funder accounting	_____	_____	_____

the user ask for assistance form the program itself. It should tell the user when he or she has made a mistake or neglected to do something, and it should have explanations for every action to be taken.

• flexible chart of accounts: the program should make it easy to change the chart of accounts and report parameters.

- easy to modify data: it should be easy for the user to go backward and forward during data entry to correct and modify data and descriptions.
- easy to correct mistakes: it should be simple for the user to do this.
- fund accounting based on United Way Chart of Accounts as well as agency's: the program should have a chart of accounts based on the United Way's, and in addition, let the agency devise its own if needed.
- prepares financial statements: the program should be able to prepare the necessary financial statements: a balance sheet, statement of support, revenue, expenses, and changes in fund balances, and a statement of functional expenses. Watch for programs that purport to be fund accounting programs, yet do not prepare the proper financial statements. When a fund accounting program prepares an income statement, the user can assume that the program was written by someone who did not really understand the needs of nonprofits.
- calculates financial ratios, other statistics: it is helpful if the program can calculate financial ratios as well as unit costs, cost per client, and so forth.
- agency can design own format for reports: the agency may have a need to design different formats for some of its reports, either for internal uses, or for funding sources.
- summarizes data: the program should be able to summarize data on financial statements and print individually selected schedules and analyses, as needed.
- integrative package: it should be able to be used with other available programs such as payroll, accounts receivable, accounts payable, and others that may be offered.
- generates quarterly reports: the program should generate reports on quarterly basis or for any other period needed by the agency, for example, monthly reports (see Table 11-2 for a sample report).
- can be set up for variance budgeting: variance budgeting can be an important control mechanism. The software package should have the ability to do budgeting as well as variance budgeting.
- funder accounting: the program should give the agency the ability to set up accounts by funding source, if so desired, and merge these accounts with others in the financial reports.

Table 11-2

SAMPLE COMPUTER OUTPUT

PAGE NO. - 1
REPORT RUN DATE - 02/04/87
REPORT RUN TIME - 12:12

AUDIT TRAIL LISTING OF WORKING JOURNAL FILE

LINE ITEM	R/U	DESCRIPTION	DATE	DEBIT	CREDIT	CURRENT	YTD	AUDIT	TYPE
1008	000	CASH OPERATING/CORPORATE	01/30/87		7101.71	1132.50	1132.50		AP3
1009	000	MUTUAL FUND-CKS/CORPORATE	01/09/87	2001.87		28006.87	28006.87	CF 001	DEP
1009	000	MUTUAL FUND-CKS/CORPORATE	01/16/87	2301.48		30308.35	30308.35	CF 001	DEP
2010	000	ACCTS. PAYABLE/CORPORATE	01/16/87		13830.66	13830.66	13830.66		AP2
2010	000	ACCTS. PAYABLE/CORPORATE	01/30/87	7101.71		6728.95	6728.95		AP4
4005	001	CLIENT FEES/OUTPATIENT	01/09/87		2001.87	2001.87	2001.87	CF 001	CR
4005	001	CLIENT FEES/OUTPATIENT	01/16/87		2301.48	4303.35	4303.35	CF 001	CR
6005	001	RENT/OUTPATIENT	01/01/87	606.62		606.62	606.62		AP1
6005	002	RENT/VOCATIONAL	01/01/87	433.30		433.30	433.30		AP1
6005	011	RENT/OUTPAT FUND 1	01/01/87	1343.23		1343.23	1343.23		AP1
6005	012	RENT/VOCA FUND 1	01/01/87	996.59		996.59	996.59		AP1
6005	013	RENT/ADMIN FUND 1	01/01/87	953.26		953.26	953.26		AP1
6021	001	HEALTH INSUR./OUTPATIENT	01/01/87	555.66		555.66	555.66		AP1
6021	002	HEALTH INSUR./VOCATIONAL	01/01/87	351.54		351.54	351.54		AP1
6021	003	HEALTH INSUR./ADMINISTRATIVE	01/01/87	226.80		226.80	226.80		AP1
6260	003	LEGAL FEES/ADMINISTRATIVE	01/13/87	1470.71		1470.71	1470.71		AP1
6260	013	LEGAL FEES/ADMIN FUND 1	01/13/87	876.05		876.05	876.05		AP1
6430	011	HEAT COSTS/OUTPAT FUND 1	01/20/87	304.73		304.73	304.73		AP1
6430	012	HEAT COSTS/VOCA FUND 1	01/20/87	275.00		275.00	275.00		AP1
6430	013	HEAT COSTS/ADMIN FUND 1	01/20/87	163.52		163.52	163.52		AP1
6441	011	ELECTRICITY/OUTPAT FUND 1	01/07/87	970.03		970.03	970.03		AP1
6441	012	ELECTRICITY/VOCA FUND 1	01/07/87	875.40		875.40	875.40		AP1
6441	013	ELECTRICITY/ADMIN FUND 1	01/07/87	520.52		520.52	520.52		AP1
6510	001	OFFICE SUPPLIES/OUTPATIENT	01/13/87	35.67		35.67	35.67		AP1
6510	001	OFFICE SUPPLIES/OUTPATIENT	01/28/87	26.98		62.65	62.65		AP1
6510	002	OFFICE SUPPLIES/VOCATIONAL	01/28/87	32.58		32.58	32.58		AP1
6510	003	OFFICE SUPPLIES/ADMINISTRATIVE	01/13/87	8.09		8.09	8.09		AP1
6510	003	OFFICE SUPPLIES/ADMINISTRATIVE	01/28/87	6.42		14.51	14.51		AP1
7200	001	TELEPHONE/OUTPATIENT	01/29/87	74.99		74.99	74.99		AP1
7200	002	TELEPHONE/VOCATIONAL	01/29/87	134.99		134.99	134.99		AP1
7200	003	TELEPHONE/ADMINISTRATIVE	01/29/87	165.00		165.00	165.00		AP1
7400	011	TRANSPORTATION/OUTPAT FUND 1	01/15/87	147.56		147.56	147.56		AP1
7400	012	TRANSPORTATION/VOCA FUND 1	01/15/87	211.42		211.42	211.42		AP1
7400	012	TRANSPORTATION/VOCA FUND 1	01/09/87	54.00		265.42	265.42		AP1
7510	001	CLIENT SERVICES/OUTPATIENT	01/21/87	55.00		55.00	55.00		AP1
7510	002	CLIENT SERVICES/VOCATIONAL	01/21/87	55.00		55.00	55.00		AP1
7511	001	MEDICATION/OUTPATIENT	01/19/87	1900.00		1900.00	1900.00		AP1
		TOTALS:		25235.72	25235.72				

Courtesy: Echo Consulting Services, Inc.

Selecting Vendors (Osborne and Cook, 1981):

With the price of microcomputers so low, it does not make much sense for an agency to rent or lease this equipment. Therefore, the most viable option is to buy a system at the most reasonable price. Remember that nonprofit organizations usually do not pay sales taxes, and that many retailers extend discounts to nonprofits. The vendor may even be willing to make a tax-deductible contribution of all or part of the system itself (it never hurts to try!).

The consultant you have chosen may be a supplier of hardware and/or software. Hopefully, this person will have a wide range of products that may be suitable for your agency. In other cases, the consultant may not sell any computer product but will try to help the agency make the most appropriate acquisitions.

In choosing a vendor, remember it is not just a matter of buying/ leasing/or renting some equipment. Acquiring computer equipment, and the necessary staff time involved in setting up and running a system is expensive for an agency. These resources have to be used wisely.

There are some advantages of using a vendor with staff who have experience in both computer technology and human services, but they are not always easy to find. One resource might be to contact a School of Social Work in the area, or other human service agencies for references. Some advantages in using such a vendor are (DeJacimo et al, 1985:90–91):

- personnel familiar with the human services field do not need to spend as much time learning the operations of a human service agency;
- personnel familiar with the needs of nonprofit human service agencies in the areas of accounting and financial management will know what type of software will be appropriate;
- personnel will be available who have the capability of designing a system to meet the individual needs of the human service agency.

Often, human service agencies are unable to find vendors with this dual background in computers and human services. If the vendor has not dealt with human service agencies before, there are some guidelines that the agency should follow in selecting a vendor (Pescow, 1981:1307–1308):

- Deal only with a reputable dealer who is established in your community. Check with the Better Business Bureau for complaints.

Find out how long the company has been in business. Inquire as to whether this is part of a national chain of stores, a franchise operation, or a one-site company.

- Ask for references of other agencies using the dealer's services.
- Make sure staff have the necessary expertise in programming, systems, and equipment servicing to be able to provide adequate backup support.
- Check to make sure an adequate network of other dealers handling this product are available in your area in case your dealer goes out of business.
- Make sure the dealer is responsive to the needs of your agency and willing to help you install the system.
- Find out if the dealer will let you trade in your equipment or help you dispose of it as it becomes obsolete, or you want to upgrade your equipment.
- Ask if the supplier will provide temporary replacement equipment if your equipment needs to be in the shop for an extended period of time.
- Determine how much hands-on training the dealer will provide to agency staff. Inquire as to whether the training is included in the package price or if the agency must pay extra for it.
- Inquire as to what protection the agency has against sudden discontinuance of the line you are interested in.
- Ask if the brand sold by the dealer is backed by a well-known national manufacturer that provides user support if the company goes out of business.

Once the agency has contracted with the vendor, it will now be ready to install the new computer system.

Installing the Microcomputer System

Installing the new computerized system involves conversion of record-keeping and files from one system to another. This conversion process entails three aspects: equipment conversion, data processing method conversion, and procedural conversion (Burch et al, 1978:435). Equipment conversion is changing from handwritten or bookkeeping machine to the computer. Data processing method conversion means that the person in charge of the accounts will now enter transactions directly into the computer to be processed. And procedural conversion means that new procedures have to be instituted to accommodate the new system. In the conversion stage, the manual system must be run side-by-side with the new computerized system for testing purposes and to check for errors. One segment of the system should be converted at a time before another segment is introduced.

After the new system is totally installed, there should be ongoing evaluation in the operation and maintenance of the system. Modifications should be made, as necessary, in the program that has been acquired by the agency and well as upgrades made to both hardware and software as new technological changes occur.

Conclusion

This chapter has attempted to point to some of the crucial ingredients in the acquisition of a computerized financial information system. The successful conversion from a manual to a computerized information system entails a number of components. Some of these important components are (Bowers, and Bowers, 1977: 38–54; DeJacimo et al, 1986:92–93; Ross, 1976:15–30):

- **Commitment of a "Key Person":** The success of a system is highly influenced by the presence of a key person. The commitment of the Executive Director is critical, since he/she will oversee implementation of the computer system. If the Executive Director is not the project officer, a staff person should be designated responsibility for the overall project and its successful completion. It is important to have representatives of the board involved in the project since the board will make final decisions regarding the new system. It is useful to have a board member with computer knowledge/expertise or access to it.
- **Involvement of Staff:** Acceptance of the system by staff will be facilitated by involving staff at every stage in the process, especially the design and development stages, and keeping all staff informed of the progress of the implementation as well as the benefits of the system. If staff are not involved in the whole process, it will be very difficult to generate staff acceptance after the computers have been installed.
- **Long-Term Planning:** Even though the majority of computer applications are for clerical work and not managerial decisionmaking,

the opportunity should not be lost by the agency to take a hard look at its information needs and ways in which its information system can become a real management information system. This entails an analysis of agency goals and operations, and present and future information needs of the agency. If the current management system is inadequate and the current information system is weak, these problems need to be corrected before the implementation of the computerized system. If the inadequacies are not rectified, they will be incorporated into the new system.

- **Documentation:** Perhaps the most apparent weakness in human service information systems is the absence of proper documentation or documentation at all. It is helpful to the agency to incorporate some feedback mechanisms in the agency's annual planning cycle to include review and evaluation of the computer system. Documentation at all stages of the process is very important, especially documentation of system specifications and procedures. All documentation should be kept on hand at the agency for training and reference purposes.

- **Relationship with Consultant:** The agency must always remember that it is, or should be, in command, not the consultant. Users should not let themselves be dazzled by the expertise of the consultant. Two of the biggest implementation problems for agencies are overreliance on the consultant (thinking he/she knows best) and poor communication between the consultant and user (because of the technical jargon of the consultant). The agency should not settle for anything less than the type of system that will best meet its financial information needs within its financial constraints.

- **Relationship with Vendor:** It is highly recommended that the vendor have staff with experience in human service organizations or experience in installing systems in other human service organizations. Some have suggested selecting a vendor through an RFP, that is, the specifications for the system and other requirements are written up in a Request for Proposal, including timetables for completion of each step (see Case 11-1 for an example of this). A formal RFP may not be necessary, but it certainly is important to shop around for the best prices and service.

- **Evaluation:** periodic reviews and evaluations, even modifications if need be, should be done to make sure that the system is meeting the information needs of the agency.

- **Training:** Adequate training and orientation for staff in system utilization should be planned for and implemented early in the development process. A discussion of staff training may be found in Reading 11-1.

A computerized financial information system can be an asset to the human service agency, helping it perform needed and important functions more quickly and accurately than ever before. It may also help give needed information that will be useful in the whole planning process. But before an agency embarks on the long task of converting to a computerized system, it must be prepared to take the time and make the commitment to make it work as an effective tool in the furtherance of its goals.

Chapter 11
Questions for Review and Discussion

1. What is meant by the terms hardware and software?
2. What are some advantages of computerized information systems?
3. What are some disadvantages of computerized information systems?
4. What are some steps in the computer acquisition process?
5. Why is it important for staff to be involved in the computer acquisition and conversion process?
6. What factors could help an agency determine whether it needs a computerized information system or not?
7. What should an agency expect from the consultant it retains to help in the acquisition and conversion process?
8. What are important considerations in purchase of hardware and software?
9. What should an agency look for in choosing a vendor?
10. What are the most important components in successful conversion to computerized systems in human service agencies?

Exercise 11-1: Analyzing and Choosing a System

As a staff member knowledgeable about information systems, you may occasionally be called upon for your opinion regarding the acquisition of new machines used to process, record, and/or store data and information. The buy/sell/lease decisions may involve upgrading an existing system, or converting from a manual to a computerized system. Thus, you must have some familiarity with issues involved in such a major, expensive decision. In this assignment, you have been appointed to a staff committee to look into the feasibility of acquiring a computer system.

You and your advisory committee have decided that it is feasible to convert your present manual system to a microcomputer system. You hire a consultant to come in to design a system to fit the needs of your agency. He/she will also advise on purchase of hardware and software. But you want to be an informed user, so you decide to look into factors that should be taken into account in deciding on a system. Please make a list, for comparative purposes, of these important factors and give your rationale for each one.

Case 11-1: Nonprofit Accounting: The Search for a Solution*
by Arnold B. Simonse

Nonprofit organizations have special bookkeeping needs which traditional accounting systems simply do not address. As the executive director of an nonprofit organization (the Prevention of Blindness Society of Metropolitan Washington), I have long been frustrated by the problems of nonprofit bookkeeping. This article will document my search for a solution, a search which ultimately resulted in a new accounting system of potential value to all nonprofits.

In our nonprofit organization, typical of many, bookkeeping services were provided by an outside bookkeeper. But this independent bookkeeping service had two main drawbacks. First, it was outside the office and entailed a mail correspondence or delivery of check requests and the like. Secondly, and more importantly, this bookkeeping service could not provide functional accounting except at a far greater cost than we could afford. And functional accounting was what we needed in order to parcel out each expense and income item to the specific function or program for which it was spent or acquired—a necessity for most nonprofits.

As a result, I found myself doing the functional accounting—a process which entailed keeping a "double" set of books. Each expense item and income item was assigned a line item number and, also, was allocated according to the program(s) or function(s) to which it was related. Thus, I created a breakdown in matrix format of all functional costs. It was done entirely by hand with all the concomitant problems that manual computation involves. Accuracy was the last of my worries. In fact, I

---

*Reprinted with permission from the *Nonprofit World Report*, 3(1):23–24, 30, 1985.

always came close, or at least close enough. The problem was not accuracy but, rather, time and efficiency. It just didn't seem right that I had to do all this extra work in order to come up with functional figures. There had to be an easier way. But what?

The Search Begins: Our Own Computer

It was 1980, the beginning of the microcomputer boom. Wouldn't it be possible to find a microcomputer that carried out functional accounting as needed by a nonprofit? The answer, I discovered after much talk and false promises, was no. First of all, most computer retailers didn't understand what I was talking about. They reassured me that their computer did exactly the sort of accounting I needed. But when pressed about a functional accounting system, their eyes glazed over with that unmistakable look of misunderstanding.

Our organization's first microcomputer came with some accounting software. One of the reasons for purchasing this computer was the promised ability to do in-house accounting. It's true that the accounting package was there, but who could use it? Designed for small business, it offered none of the functional accounting which we, as nonprofit organization, needed. Besides, it took a programmer to use the programs. Despite many fine and valuable features, our microcomputer simply could not answer our nonprofit accounting needs.

The Search Continues: Our Own Program

I then began the search for a nonprofit functional accounting program. I presumed that this would be a short task with the only problem being to ferret out the right software supplier. Surprise! No one had the accounting package that every nonprofit needs. Yes, many claimed such a program, but when I talked with salespeople, it became clear that they did not fully grasp what I needed nor have a program that did the job. I began to think that maybe I was operating in a world by myself. Hadn't anyone asked for such a program before? If every nonprofit organization needed a functional accounting program, why didn't such a program exist?

My next step was rather obvious. If no program existed, I would commission to have one done. Such is the folly of the uninformed! The first, but by no means the least, problem was to try to explain to a programmer what kind of bookkeeping setup I wanted. Simply stated, I wanted an accounting system that would use the line item numbers and titles established by the National Standards of Accounting and Financial Reporting as published by the American Institute of Certified Public Accountants. Furthermore, I wanted line items subdivided according to a functional breakdown. For instance, I wanted the line item for the telephone bill spread out in 12 columns, giving me a functional breakdown of where that telephone bill was spent. Was the telephone bill to be charged to management, to fundraising, or to a government grant, or was it to be spread out evenly among all our services and programs?

I began to lose a few programmers at this point. I also wanted the program to run on a microcomputer. "Impossible!" was the answer I first received. And that was before I made a further request. I wanted to make only one insertion of the information and let the computer do everything else. This meant that if I wished to enter the check request for that pesky telephone bill, I would type in the name of the payee, the number of the check, the check amount, the date, and the allocation of that expense across the different programs of our organization. I wanted the computer to do the rest, including giving me a printout of the check requests for a given period, a printout of all the expenses by line item, and a matrix printout which would show not only line items but all the expenses allocated according to different functions with functional totals.

With the wisdom brought on by lack of understanding, I kept reassuring programmers that this did not seem like too much to ask. Not everyone turned me down. Some programmers were quite supportive, and I felt encouraged until I heard their cost estimate for the program. Maybe $10,000, with no guaranteed, said one.

Success at Last: The Program is Born

As most things happen, it was a fluke that helped me find an answer. I was having lunch with an old friend, a mathematician who was an original IBM programmer back in the days of vacuum tubes and rooms full of computer equipment. I mentioned how I had been searching and had come up against a blank wall or, at best, a very small hole in the wall with a very large price tag. Intrigued by my needs, he offered to give it a try. And so the job began.

The program needed to have the following characteristics. It had to be completely "user friendly." I wanted a program that I could run—

otherwise, why bother? It had to run on a small computer such as the Apple or IBM PC. (The Apple would be preferable since it is much less expensive). This would ensure keeping the cost of the system within the range of a small nonprofit organization. And finally, of course, the program had to do the job. It had to produce a large printout of the functional expense report matrix using an inexpensive printer with standard 8" × 11" paper.

The programmer took the above requirements as an Olympic challenge, but little did either of us realize what high goals we had set. Major problems arose. First, there was the storage capacity of the microcomputer floppy diskette. We wanted to get the entire program onto one diskette; otherwise, we would defeat our "simple to use" criterion. We also had to be able to get enough expense records onto one data diskette to make it feasible.

Secondly, we had to worry about the limited memory capacity of the microcomputer. The solution was to chop the program up into many segments. Thirdly, there was concern about the speed of the microcomputer as it related to the execution time of a large program. The program code had to be very efficient so that we wouldn't have to wait all day for a set of reports to be produced.

I knew, and still know, nothing about the technical solutions to these challenges. Thus, at this point, my role changed from player to coach and counselor, offering encouragement and sympathy when the project seemed to be proving impossible. My administrative assistant and I met with the programmer every two weeks to check his progress and make suggestions. As the project progressed and the program grew in size and complexity, the task of finding and eliminating "bugs"—the sinister gremlins that exist in every big new program—caused us delay and great frustration.

Five weary months later, the call finally came from our programmer, "It's finished. Whew."

The Program Comes to Life: The First Trial Run

Like anxious parents of a debutante, we hovered around our administrative assistant as she put our first quarter's financial information into the computer. The thought that it wouldn't work was simply too dreadful to imagine after all the time, effort, and lunches that went into producing this program.

The first step involved initializing the data diskettes to prepare them for use. Our administrative assistant breezed through that task successfully. All the program commands led her simply and easily through the process. If a mistake was made, the program would recognize the error and prompt her to try again until the correct entry was made.

The next step involved defining the program centers (functional categories showing the names of our agency programs) and cost centers (line item names and numbers). Once these definitions were completed and stored on a data diskette, it was time to begin entering actual expense data.

The expenses of our organization for the first three months of the current year, represented by 187 check requests, were entered into the machine. This involved following the directions from the program and entering the following information: date, cost code (line item number), check number, amount of check, number of allocations for the expense, type of allocation (percentages or actual dollar amounts), description of the expense, specific programs to which the expense should be allocated, and amount of total expense to allocate to each particular program.

Through all this, the computer program did the work for us. It asked us, at each step, to fill in the needed information. All the user had to be able to do was to read simple English (no computerese allowed in this program) and follow directions. We couldn't have asked for more "user friendliness."

Now it was time for the final test. After all the months of working on all the pieces and overcoming all the minor disasters, it was time to see if the program did the job it was intended to do. Would it produce the final product—a matrix printout of all the expense and income items according to cost center (line item) and program center (function)? Confidence was high—but so was the confidence level on the Titanic.

As you can well imagine, I would not be chronicling this saga if the program was a bust. Yes, our functional accounting program for nonprofits worked like the proverbial charm.

Space doesn't allow me to lay out a sample of all the program's output, but I can tell you that we worked that little old Apple to its core. The first thing that we printed out was a listing of all the expense records (check requests) with the identifying information detailed above. This gave us a hard copy printout of those expense items to serve as a visual record backup to the data stored on the floppy diskette.

Next came the printout of the itemized allocations for each expense item grouped by cost center. This included the descriptive information about each expense record along with a listing of all the program allocations for the record. This offered us an "audit trail" so that we could go back and see exactly how the different expense records contributed to the total costs of each program function—necessary information when one is trying to determine, for example, why those fundraising costs have skyrocketed.

Then came the final printout. The program generated the matrix type functional expense report. This included a listing of the cost centers—the major ones, as well as their subdivisions—along with the the functional expenses listed according to program area. The master sheet, as it were, included everything we'd ever want to know about our expenses. And all of this information was retrieved from the information put into the computer the first time around. From that single entry of information came all those generated reports. It worked!

Epilogue

Our organization bought a simple Apple IIc computer for $1,500. This, combined with the program, gives us the opportunity of doing all our bookkeeping in-house. The short time that our administrative assistant takes to enter new expense records into this automated bookkeeping process is now all the work that has to be done. No more mailing information back and forth. No more waiting for financial reports to arrive in time for the upcoming board meeting. No more sitting down and figuring out all the functional expenses for the various financial reports. And no bookkeeper cost of several hundred dollars per month. At this rate, after one year I not only will have a better hold on the financial picture, I will have saved money and have a computer to show for it!

If it sounds as though I'm waxing a bit eloquent on the glories of this bookkeeping program, I am. It's been a great help in keeping financial records—and it's done that at a savings to our organization. I can't imagine doing it any other way.

Reading 11-1: Learning to Compute: "No Train, No Gain"?*
by Emmanuel Rosales

Beware the myth of instant computer productivity. The standard computer ad makes computer learning sound easy; even relatively complex tasks such as creating a budget analysis or computerizing your accounting are billed as effortless.

Although there are computer programs that require less learning time—for example, Volkswriter Deluxe for word processing, PC-talk for telecommunications, and Apple's MacIntosh for a complete system—most computer applications and systems require systematic, expert training (and/or lots of independent effort) to develop and maintain productive skills. This is particularly true if you are creating sophisticated financial or database applications.

One more important point: there may be another myth obscuring the value of formal training—the notion that trial and error is "the only effective way to learn." In reality, trial and error is helpful only if it gives you enough success to make you want to proceed.

Anything you can do to improve on raw trial and error is a boost toward imminent, if not instant, productivity. As Peter Drucker might have put it, you don't really learn from your failures, you learn from your successes. Appropriate training definitely structures successes into the computer learning experience.

Computer Training: Who Needs It?

What kind and how much training is necessary depends on the computer system, the applications (word processing, accounting, etc.), and who needs the training. Training can take place on site or off, in groups or one on one, at beginning or advanced levels.

Perhaps the first consideration is just who in the organization needs what kind of training. Here is a quick rundown of potential computer users and their training needs:

- Decision makers or managers, who have little interest and less time to learn the technicalities of the computer system, yet have to know the system well enough to do word processing and budget projections and quickly get information from existing databases.

---

*Reprinted by permission of *Nonprofit World*, 5(2):10,12, 1987.

- Technical users (such as the system administrator), who are actually responsible for implementing, maintaining, and managing the computer system. They need to be knowledgeable enough to trouble-shoot hardware and software, as well as to anticipate future system requirements.
- Clerical users, who are primarily responsible for entering information into the computer system. Their knowledge of the system is usually restricted to a program or application.

On Site or Off?

If you have the option of "our place or theirs," consider the following:

- On-site training, though usually more convenient, may not be the most beneficial, especially if the training session is allowed to be interrupted by phone calls and work-related questions. Often, there are insufficient computers for the number of users who need to be trained.
- Consider having the lead user or supervisor formally trained, then having that person train the rest of your staff on site. This is excellent way to stretch training dollars.

It is typical for the vendor who sells you your computer to provide one to four hours of free introductory training—and perhaps discounts on additional sessions. However, most of that training involves only the basics of how to enter and exit the system, back up disks, access files, and the like. It is also usually limited to one to four people. Extra time and extra people usually mean extra money.

Some vendors will provide between two and four hours of training for each software package you buy. This training is usually enough to begin using the software, and often more than enough to confuse you. You may need more training unless you have a knowledgeable computer user on staff.

Evaluating Training Vendors

The following questions should help you evaluate vendors of computer training:

- How long have they been in the training business?

- What is the cost per hour per student for their training? (A typical hourly, per student rate is $25).
- How many students can they handle at one time? What do they consider as optimum number of students? How many students will be at your session?
- What materials do they provide along with the training? Good reference material can be more valuable than the newly acquired skills themselves.
- At what level is instruction really given. One source's advanced class may be another source's intermediate class. Try to get an outline of the class to find out whether it matches the level of instruction you need.
- Can they schedule their classes to suit you, or must you (perhaps inconveniently) follow their schedule?
- How many machines do they provide per student? (One machine per two students is typical; one per student may be best but loses the "buddy" system advantage).
- Other than computers, what kind of equipment (overhead projectors, giant screen monitors, videotape, etc.) do they use for training?

Shopping Tips

When you decide who needs to be trained, where to do it, consider the following when shopping for computer trainers:

- It is possible to price shop for training. Computer retailers and training companies often list only a sampling of their training class and class cost in their ads. Expect to receive a group or organizational discount.
- It is sometimes advisable to hire consultants who specialize in installing and providing training for specific packages. Many accounting software companies, such as State of the Art, have manufacturer certified consultants who can help you.
- Training for widely used programs, such as dBase-III, WordStar, and LOTUS 1-2-3, is available not only from the manufacturers, computer retailers, training companies, and consultants, but also from user groups, university and community college extension classes, and city recreation departments. Costs for the latter sources are often lower than the others.

In Conclusion

Appropriate computer training is a crucial part of the entire automation experience. If you budget and plan carefully for training, your whole experience will be much more satisfying.

V. BIBLIOGRAPHY

Abels, Paul and Murphy, Michael J.: *Human Services Administration: A Normative Systems Approach.* Englewood Cliffs, Prentice-Hall, 1981.

Agranoff, Robert (Ed.): *Human Services on a Limited Budget.* Washington, D.C., International City Management Association, 1983.

American Institute of Certified Public Accountants: *Audits of Voluntary Health and Welfare Organizations.* New York, 1974.

Amling, Frederick: *Investments, An Introduction to Analysis and Management (5th Edition).* Englewood Cliffs, Prentice-Hall, 1984.

Andreasen, Alan R.: Nonprofits: check your attention to customers. *Harvard Business Review, 60*(3): 105–110, 1982.

Annual Register of Grant Support (*21st Edition*). Wilmette, National Register Publishing Co., 1987.

Anthony, Robert N.: *Essentials of Accounting, 2nd ed.* Reading, Addison-Wesley, 1978.

——————: Making sense of nonbusiness accounting. *Harvard Business Review, 58*(3): 83–93, 1980.

Anthony, Robert N. and Herzlinger, Regina E.: *Management Control in Nonprofit Organizations.* Homewood, Richard D. Irwin, 1980.

Anthony, Robert N. and Reece, James S.: *Management Accounting: Text and Cases.* Homewood, Richard D. Irwin, 1975.

A private group whose word is law. *Nation's Business,* December, 1982.

Berg, William E. and Wright, Roosevelt: Program funding as an organizational dilemma: goal displacement in social work programs. *Administration in Social Work, 4*(4):29–39, 1980.

Beck, Henry J. and Parrish, Roy James Jr.: *Computerized Accounting.* Columbus, Charles E. Merrill, 1977.

Blodgett, Terrell: Implementing ZBB: steps to success with zero-base budgeting systems, pp. 187–200 in Murray Gruber (Ed.): *Management Systems in the Human Services.* Philadelphia, Temple University Press, 1981.

Blumenthal, Susan: *Understanding and Buying a Small-Business Computer.* Indianapolis, Howard W. Sams, 1982.

Bodnar, George H.: *Accounting Information Systems.* Boston, Allyn and Bacon, 1980.

Bowsher, C.A.: Sound financial Management: a federal manager's perspective. *Public Administration Review, 45*(1):176–184, 1985.

Bradley, Joseph H.: *Administrative Financial Management (3rd. Edition).* Hinsdale, The Dryden Press, 1974.

321

Braswell, Ronald, Fortin, Karen, Osteryoung, Jerome S.: *Financial Management for Not-For-Profit Organizations.* New York: John Wiley, 1984.

Bresnick, David A.: *Managing the Human Services in Hard Times.* New York, Human Services Press, 1983.

Buckley, John W. and Lightner, Kevin M.: *Accounting: An Information Systems Approach.* Encino, Dickensen, 1973.

Burch, John G. Jr., Strater, Felix R. and Grudnitski, Gary: *Information Systems: Theory and Practice (2nd Edition).* New York, John Wiley, 1979.

Butler, Stuart M.: *Philanthropy in America: The Need for Action.* Washington, D.C., The Heritage Foundation, 1980.

Carver, John: Profitability: useful fiction for nonprofit enterprise. *Administration in Mental Health,* 7(1):3–20, 1979.

Cheek, Logan M.: *Zero-Base Budgeting Comes of Age.* New York, AMACOM, 1977.

Christy, George A. and Clendenin, John C.: *An Introduction to Investments.* New York, McGraw-Hill, 1978.

Collins, Frank: Managerial accounting systems and organizational control: a role perspective. *Accounting, Organizations and Society,* 7:107–122, 1982.

Congressional Quarterly, Inc.: *Budgeting for America.* Washington, D.C., 1982.

Connors, Tracy D. (Ed.): *The Nonprofit Organization Handbook.* New York, McGraw-Hill, 1980.

Connors, Tracy D. and Callaghan, Christopher T. (Eds.): *Financial Management for Nonprofit Organizations.* New York, AMACOM, 1982.

Consumer Reports, 49(1), January 1984.

Consumer Reports, 51(1), January 1986.

Cross, Edward M.: *How to Buy a Business Computer and Get it Right the First Time.* Reston, Reston Publishing, 1983.

D'Ambrosio, Charles A.: *Principles of Modern Investments.* Chicago, Science Research Associates, 1976.

DeJacimo, Sandy, Kropp, David, and Zefran, Joseph: Success is possible: one agency's experience with a vendor. *Computers in Human Services,* 1(2): 85–95, 1985.

de Oliveira, Fred H.: Management accounting techniques for not-for-profit enterprises. *Management Accounting,* 62(5):30–34, 1980.

Department of Health and Human Services: *Rate Setting in the Human Services: A Guide for Administrators.* by Richardson, David A. Project Share, Human Services Monograph Series, No. 24. Washington, D.C.: U.S. Government Printing Office, 1981.

Department of Health, Education and Welfare: *The Elusive Unit of Service.* by Bowers, Gary E. and Bowers, Margaret R. Project Share, Human Services Monograph Series, No. 1, Washington, D.C.: U.S. Government Printing Office, 1976.

——————: *Cultivating Client Information Systems.* by Bowers, Gary E. and Bowers, Margaret R. Project Share, Human Services Monograph Series, No. 5, Washington, D.C., U.S. Government Printing Office, 1977.

DiGiulio, Joan Ferry: Marketing social services. *Social Casework,* 65(4):227–234, 1984.

Dixon, Robert L.: *The Executive's Accounting Primer.* New York, McGraw-Hill, 1982.

Drtina, Ralph E.: Financial indicators as a measure of nonprofit human service organization performance: the underlying issues. *New England Journal of Human Services, 2*(3):35–41, 1982.

Ehlers, Walter H., Austin, Micheal J., and Prothero, Jon C.: *Administration for the Human Services: An Introductory Programmed Text.* New York, Harper & Row, 1976.

Enockson, Paul G.: *A Guide for Selecting Computers and Software for Small Businesses.* Reston, Reston Publishing, 1983.

Federal Register, Part V, Department of Health and Human Services, Office of Human Development Services, FY 1984, Coordinated Discretionary Funds Program, October 18, 1983.

Fess, Philip E. and Niswonger, C. Rollin: *Accounting Principles, (13th Ed.)* Cincinatti, South-Western Publishing, 1981.

Federal Emergency Management Agency: *Basic Skills in Creative Financing. Student Manual.* EMI Professional Development Series. National Emergency Training Center. Emergency Management Institute. Emmitsburg, Maryland, 1983.

Financial Accounting Standards Board: *Objectives of Financial Reporting by Nonbusiness Organizations.* Statement of Financial Reporting Concepts No. 4. Stamford, 1980.

Financial Reporting for Non-Profit Organizations. Toronto, The Canadian Institute of Chartered Accountants, 1980.

Financial World, August 31, 1983.

Fischer, Donald E. and Jordan, Ronald J.: *Security Analysis and Portfolio Management, 2nd Edition.* Englewood Cliffs, Prentice-Hall, 1979.

Fort Worth Star-Telegram. January 24, 1984.

Foundation Directory (*11th Edition*). New York, The Foundation Center, 1987.

Francis, D. Pitt: *The Foundations of Financial Management.* London, Pitman, 1973.

Freyd, William: Methods for successful fund raising, pp. 4–19 to 4–28 in Tracy D. Connors (Ed.), *The Nonprofit Organization Handbook.* New York, McGraw-Hill, 1980.

Fulmer, Vincent A.: Cost/benefit analysis in fund raising. *Harvard Business Review, 51:*103–110, 1973.

Gaby, Patricia V. and Gaby, Daniel M.: *Nonprofit Organization Handbook: A Guide to Fund Raising, Grants, Lobbying, Membership Building, Publicity and Public Relations.* Englewood Cliffs, Prentice-Hall, 1979.

Gaedeke, Ralph M.: *Marketing in Private and Public Nonprofit Organizations.* Santa Monica, Goodyear, 1977.

Gaertner, James: Revenue budgets, pp. 28–34 in Tracy D. Connor and Christopher T. Callaghan (Eds.). *Financial Management for Nonprofit Organizations.* New York, AMACOM, 1982.

Gambino, Anthony J. and Reardon, Thomas J.: *Financial Planning and Evaluation for the Nonprofit Organization.* New York, National Association of Accountants, 1981.

Genkins, Mary: Strategic planning for social work marketing. *Administration in Social Work, 9*(1):35–46, 1985.

Gitman, Lawrence J. and Joehnk, Michael D.: *Fundamentals of Investing.* New York, Harper & Row, 1981.

Goodman, Sam R.: *Financial Manager's Manual and Guide.* Englewood Cliffs, Prentice-Hall, 1973.

Gross, Arnold M.: Appropriate cost reporting: an indispensable link to accountability. *Administration in Social Work, 4*(3):31–41, Fall 1980.

Gross, Malvern J. Jr. and Warshauer, William Jr.: *Financial and Accounting Guide for Nonprofit Organizations, Revised 3rd Ed.* New York, John Wiley, 1983.

Gruber, Murray L. (Ed.): *Management Systems in the Human Services.* Philadelphia, Temple University Press, 1981.

Gurin, Maurice G.: *What Volunteers Should Know About Successful Fund Raising.* New York, Stein and Day, 1981.

Haakenson, John: Firm cited for violating permit: fund raising practices reported. *Arlington Citizen-Journal,* December 21–22, 1983.

Hairston, Creasie Finney: Financial accountability: new challenges for voluntary boards of directors. *Social Casework, 63:*370–373, 1982.

_____: Financial management in social work education. *Journal of Education for Social Work, 17:*113–118, 1981.

_____: Improving cash management in nonprofit organizations. *Administration in Social Work,* 5(2):29–36, 1981.

Hall, Mary: *Developing Skills in Proposal Writing.* Portland, Continuing Education Publications, 1971.

Hall, Mary D.: Financial condition: a measure of human service organizational performance. *New England Journal of Human Services,* 2(1):25–34, 1982.

Hartogs, Nelly and Weber, Joseph: *Impact of Government Funding on the Management of Voluntary Agencies.* New York, Greater New York Fund/United Way, 1978.

Hasenfeld, Yeheskel: People processing organizations: an exchange approach. pp. 60–71 in Yeheskel Hasenfeld and Richard A. English (Eds.). *Human Service Organizations.* Ann Arbor: The University of Michigan Press, 1974.

Henderson, Scott and Peirson, Graham: *An Introduction to Financial Accounting Theory.* Melbourne, Longman Cheshire Pty, 1977.

Henke, Emerson O.: *Introduction to Nonprofit Organization Accounting.* Boston, Kent Publishing, 1980.

Herzlinger, Regina E. and Sherman, H. David: Advantages of fund accounting in "nonprofits." *Harvard Business Review, 58*(3):94–105, May–June, 1980.

Heyel, Carl (ed.): *The VNR Concise Guide to Accounting and Control (2nd ed.),* New York, Van Nostrand Reinhold, 1979.

Hicks, James O. Jr. and Leininger, Wayne E.: *Accounting Information Systems.* St. Paul, West, 1981.

Hofstede, Geert: Management control of public and not-for-profit activities. *Accounting, Organizations and Society, 6:*193–211, 1981.

Holmes, Jan and Riecken, Glen: Using business marketing concepts to view the private, non-profit, social service agency. *Administration in Social Work, 4*(3):43–52, 1980.

Huang, Stanley S.C.: *Investment Analysis and Management.* Cambridge, Winthrop, 1981.

Impact. Texas Department of Mental Health and Mental Retardation, September/October 1984.

Jick, Todd D. and Murray, Victor V.: The management of hard times: budget cutbacks in public sector organizations. *Organization Studies,* 3:141–169, 1982.

Johnson, Eugene M.: Marketing planning for nonprofit organizations. *Nonprofit World,* 4(3):20–21+, 1986.

Kamerman, Sheila B.: The new mixed economy of welfare: public and private. *Social Work,* 28(1):5–10, 1983.

Katz, Daniel and Kahn, Robert L.: *The Social Psychology of Organizations (2nd Edition).* New York, John Wiley, 1978.

Khoury, Sarkis J.: *Investment Management: Theory and Application.* New York, McGraw-Hill, 1983.

Koontz, Harold, O'Donnell, Cyril, Weihrich, Heinz: *Essentials of Management (3rd Edition).* New York, McGraw-Hill, 1982.

Kotler, Philip: *Marketing for Nonprofit Organizations.* Englewood Cliffs, Prentice-Hall, 1982.

——————: Strategies for introducing marketing into non-profit organizations. *Journal of Marketing,* 43:37–44, 1979.

Kugajevsky, Victor: Zero-base budgeting, pp. 177–186 in Murray L. Gruber (Ed.). *Management Systems in the Human Services.* Philadelphia, Temple University Press, 1981.

Kurzig, Carol M.: *Foundation Fundamentals: A Guide for Grantseekers.* New York, Foundation Center, 1980.

LaMendola, Walter: Feasibility as a consideration in small computer selection. *Administration in Social Work,* 5(3/4):43–56, 1981.

Lauffer, Armand: *Grantsmanship.* Beverly Hills, Sage, 1977.

——————: *Strategic Marketing for Not-for-Profit Organizations.* New York, Free Press, 1984.

Leduc, Robert and Callaghan, Christopher T.: Accounting procedures for the nonprofit organization. pp. 6–63 to 6–81 in Tracy D. Connors (Ed.). *The Nonprofit Organization Handbook.* New York, McGraw-Hill, 1980.

Lee, Robert D. Jr. and Johnson, Ronald W.: *Public Budgeting Systems (2nd Edition).* Baltimore, University Park Press, 1977.

Leitch, Robert A. and Davis, K. Roscoe: *Accounting Information Systems.* Englewood Cliffs, Prentice-Hall, 1983.

Letzkus, William C.: Zero base budgeting and planning-programming-budgeting: what are the conceptual differences? pp. 17–25 in Vargo, R.J. and Dierks, P.A.: *Readings and Cases in Governmental and Nonprofit Accounting.* Houston: Dame Publications, 1982.

Levin, Henry M.: *Cost-Effectiveness: A Primer.* Beverly Hills, Sage, 1983.

Lewis, Judith A. and Lewis, Michael D.: *Management of Human Service Programs.* Monterey, Brooks/Cole, 1983.

Lindholm, Kathryn J., Marin, Gerardo, and Lopez, Richard E.: *Proposal Writing*

Strategies. Monograph Number 9. Los Angeles, Spanish Speaking Mental Health Research Center, UCLA, 1982.

Listro, John P.: *Accounting for Nonprofit Organizations.* Dubuque, Kendall/Hunt, 1983.

Lohman, Roger A.: Break-even analysis: a tool for budget planning. *Social Work, 21:*300–307, 1976.

_____: *Breaking Even.* Philadelphia, Temple University Press, 1980.

Lucas, Charlotte-Ann: Accountability: Dallas regulators fear they may not detect creative accounting. *Dallas Times Herald,* October 16, 1983.

Lynn, Edward S. and Freeman, Robert J.: *Fund Accounting: Theory and Practice (2nd Edition).* Englewood Cliffs, Prentice-Hall, 1983.

Mauldin, Elaine G.: How not-for-profit organizations should value investments. *Management Accounting, 62*(5):35–38, November 1980.

Meigs, Walter B. and Meigs, Robert F.: *Accounting: The Basis for Business Decisions.* New York, McGraw-Hill, 1981.

Meyer, Daniel R., and Sherraden, Michael W.: Toward improved financial planning: further applications of break-even analysis in not-for-profit organizations. *Administration in Social Work, 9*(3):57–68, 1985.

Mikesell, John L.: *Fiscal Administration.* Homewood, Dorsey Press, 1982.

Milani, Ken: Overview of the budgeting process, pp. 10–13 in Tracy D. Connors and Christopher T. Callaghan (Eds.). *Financial Management for Nonprofit Organizations.* New York, AMACOM, 1982.

Miringoff, Marc L.: *Management in Human Service Organizations.* New York, Macmillan, 1980.

Mittra, Sid with Gassen, Chris: *Investment Analysis and Portfolio Management.* New York, Harcourt Brace Jovanovich, 1981.

Moak, Lennox L. and Killian, Kathryn W.: *Operating Budget Manual.* Chicago, Municipal Finance Officers Association of the United States and Canada, 1974.

Mogulof, Melvin: Future funding of social services. *Social Work,* 19:607–613, 1974.

Montana, Patrick J.: *Marketing in Nonprofit Organizations.* New York, AMACOM, 1978.

Moyer, R. Charles, McGuigan, James R., and Kretlow, William J.: *Contemporary Financial Management.* St. Paul, West, 1981.

Munro, Donald M.: *Basic Basic.* London, Edward Arnold, 1981.

National Health Council, National Assembly of National Voluntary Health and Social Welfare Organizations, Inc., United Way of America: *Standards of Accounting and Financial Reporting for Voluntary Health and Welfare Organizations.* New York, 1975.

National Institute of Mental Health: *Accounting and Budgeting Systems for Mental Health Organizations.* Mental Health Service System Reports, Series FN No. 6, by J.E. Sorensen, G.B. Hanbery, and A.R. Kucic. Washington, D.C., U.S. Govt. Printing Office, 1983.

_____: *Integrated Management Information Systems for Community Mental Health Centers* by Smith, Todd S. and Sorenson, James E. (Eds.). Rockville, 1974.

New York Times, March 13, 1988, p. 16, Section 3.

Osborne, Adam with Cook, Steven: *Business System Buyer's Guide.* Berkeley, Osborne/ McGraw-Hill, 1981.

O'Toole, Patricia: Picking the right financial planner. *Money, 13*(3): 131–138, March 1984.

Park, Jae C.: Budget systems: make the right choice. *Financial Executive, LII* (3):26–35, 1984.

Patti, Rino J.: *Social Welfare Administration.* Englewood Cliffs, Prentice-Hall, 1983.

Pendleton, Niel: *Fund Raising.* Englewood Cliffs, Prentice-Hall, 1981.

Pescow, Jerome K.: How to utilize computers in small and medium-sized accounting firms, pp. 1273–1309 in J.K. Pescow (Ed.). *Accountant's Encyclopedia, Volume 2, Revised.* Englewood Cliffs, Prentice-Hall, 1981.

Pietzner, Cornelius M.: Holding a community event. *Nonprofit World,* 3(6):11,30, 1985.

Powell, Ray M.: *Accounting Procedures for Institutions.* Notre Dame, University of Notre Dame Press, 1978.

_____: *Budgetary Control Procedures for Institutions.* Notre Dame, University of Notre Dame Press, 1980.

_____: *Management Procedures for Institutions.* Notre Dame, University of Notre Dame Press, 1979.

Pyhrr, Peter A.: *Zero-Base Budgeting.* New York, John Wiley, 1973.

Public Service Materials Center: *The Corporate Fund Raising Directory.* Hartsdale, 1987.

Rabin, Jack and Lynch, Thomas D. (Eds.): *Handbook on Public Budgeting and Financial Management.* New York, Marcel Dekker, 1983.

Racek, Timothy J.: Nonprofit accounting and financial reporting. pp. 6-3 to 6-46 in Tracy D. Connors (Ed.), *The Nonprofit Organization Handbook.* New York, AMACOM, 1982.

Ramanathan, Kavasseri V.: *Management Control in Nonprofit Organizations.* New York, John Wiley, 1982.

Ramanathan, Kavasseri V.: *Readings in Management Control in Non-Profit Organizations.* New York, John Wiley, 1982.

Reilly, Frank K.: *Investment Analysis and Portfolio Management.* Hinsdale, Dryden Press, 1979.

Rosales, Emmanuel: Learning to compute: "no train, no gain"? *Nonprofit World,* 5(2):10, 12, 1987.

Ross, Joel E.: *Modern Management and Information Systems.* Reston, Reston Publishing, 1976.

Rubright, Robert and MacDonald, Dan: *Marketing Health and Human Services.* Rockville, Aspen Systems, 1981.

Rust, Brian: Five steps to progressive fundraising. *Nonprofit World Report,* 3(1): 11,29–39, 1985.

Sarri, Rosemary: Administration in social welfare. *Social Work Yearbook, 16th Edition, Vol.1.* New York, National Association of Social Workers, 1971.

Schattke, Rudolf W. and Jensen, Howard G.: *Managerial Accounting: Concepts and Uses (2nd Edition).* Boston, Allyn and Bacon, Inc., 1981.

Schoech, Dick: A microcomputer-based human service information system. pp. 329–344 in Simon Slavin (Ed.), *Managing Finances, Personnel, and Information in Human Services.* New York, Haworth Press, 1985.

Schoech, Dick: Reflections of a proposal reviewer. *Research Review,* 11(9): 2–3, May 1984.

Schoech, Dick, Schadke, Lawrence L., and Mayers, Raymond Sanchez: Strategies for information system development. *Administration in Social Work,* 5(3/4):11–26, 1981.

Schultze, Charles L.: What program budgeting is, pp. 23–32 in Murray L. Gruber (Ed.). *Management Systems in the Human Services.* Philadelphia, Temple University Press, 1981.

Schwartz, Edward E. (Ed.): *Planning Programming Budgeting Systems and Social Welfare.* Chicago, The School of Social Service Administration, The University of Chicago, 1970.

Scrivner, Gary N.: Checklist for charitable nonprofit organizations. *Journal of Accountancy,* July, 1981.

Setting accounting standards in the public sector. *The Journal of Accountancy,* 147(3):83–87, 1979.

Shapiro, Benson P.: Marketing for nonprofit organizations. *Harvard Business Review,* 51:123–132, 1973.

Simonse, Arnold B.: Nonprofit accounting: the search for a solution. *Nonprofit World Report,* 3(1):23,24,30, 1985.

Skidmore, Rex: *Social Work Administration.* Englewood Cliffs, Prentice-Hall, 1983.

Silver, Alvin M. Data processing systems, pp. 765–824 in J.K. Peskow (Ed.). *Accountant's Encyclopedia, Volume 1, Revised.* Englewood Cliffs, Prentice-Hall, 1981.

Solomon, Ezra and Pringle, John J.: *An Introduction to Financial Management.* Santa Monica, Goodyear, 1980.

Solomon, Lanny M., Vargo, Richard J., and Schroeder, Richard G.: *Accounting Principles.* New York, Harper & Row, 1983.

Stevenson, R.A. and Jennings, E.H.: *Fundamentals of Investments (3rd Edition).* St. Paul, West, 1984.

Stretch, John J.: Seven key managerial functions of sound fiscal budgeting. *Administration in Social Work,* 3:441–452, 1979.

Swan, Wallace K.: Theoretical debates applicable to budgeting, pp. 3–59 in Rabin, Jack and Lynch, Thomas D. (Eds.): *Handbook on Public Budgeting and Financial Management.* New York, Marcel Dekker, 1983.

Sweeny, Allen and Wisner, John N., Jr.: *Budgeting Fundamentals for Nonfinancial Executives.* New York, AMACOM, 1975.

The Taft Group: *Taft Corporate Giving Directory.* Washington, D.C., 1987.

Tamari, M.: *Financial Ratios: Analysis and Prediction.* London, Paul Elek, 1978.

Taylor, James B.: *Using Microcomputers in Social Agencies.* Beverly Hills, Sage, 1981.

The Foundations Grants Index (*14th Edition*). New York, The Foundation Center, 1985.

Thomas, William E.: *Readings in Cost Accounting and Control (6th ed.).* Cincinatti, Southwestern Publishing, 1983.

Trost, Arty and Rauner, Judy: *Gaining Momentum for Board Action.* San Diego, Marlborough, 1983.

United Way of America: *Accounting and Financial Reporting: A Guide for United Ways and Not-For Profit Human Service Organizations.* Alexandria, 1974.

_____: *Budgeting: A Guide for United Ways and Not-For-Profit Human Service Organizations.* Alexandria, 1975.

Vanderleest, Henry W.: Needed: a clear understanding of the marketing process. *Nonprofit World,* 3(6):20–22, 1985.

Vargo, Richard J. (Ed.): *Readings in Governmental and Nonprofit Accounting.* Belmont, Wadsworth, 1977.

Vargo, Richard J. and Dierks, Paul A.: *Readings and Cases in Governmental and Nonprofit Accounting.* Houston, Dame Publications, 1982.

Vinter, Robert D.: Analysis of treatment organizations. pp. 35–50 in Yeheskel Hasenfeld and Richard A. English (Eds.). *Human Service Organizations.* Ann Arbor: The University of Michigan Press, 1974.

Vinter, Robert D. and Kish, Rhea K.: *Budgeting for Not-For-Profit Organizations.* New York, Free Press, 1984.

Walker, Michael C.: Determining the appropriate discount rate for private, not-for-profit organizations. *Management Accounting,* 60:54–56, 1979.

Weis, William L. and Tinius, David E.: Does anyone understand nonprofit reports? *Management Accounting,* 61:25–29, 1980.

Whalen, William J.: The basis of accounting, pp. 269–277 in Tracy D. Connors and Christopher T. Callaghan (Eds.). *Financial Management for Nonprofit Organizations.* New York, AMACOM, 1982.

Wildavsky, Aaron: A budget for all seasons? Why the traditional budget lasts, pp. 4–12 in Richard J. Vargo and Paul A. Dierks (Eds.). *Readings and Cases in Governmental and Nonprofit Accounting.* Houston, Dame Publications, 1982.

Williams, Larry and Teutsch, Clifford: Suite Charity. *Dallas Times Herald,* October 16, 1983.

Young, David M.: "Nonprofits" need surplus too. *Harvard Business Review,* 60:124–131, 1982.

Zaltman, Gerald (Ed.): *Management Principles for Nonprofit Agencies and Organizations.* New York, AMACOM, 1979.

Appendix A-1

REGIONAL COLLECTIONS OF
THE FOUNDATION CENTER

The following reference collections are operated by the Foundation Center. They offer a number of services and have extensive information on foundations and grants.

The Foundation Center
79 Fifth Avenue
New York, New York 10003
212-620-4230

The Foundation Center
1001 Connecticut Avenue, N.W.
Washington, D.C. 20036
202-331-1400

The Foundation Center
Kent H. Smith Library
1442 Hanna Building
1422 Euclid Avenue
Cleveland, Ohio 44115
216-861-1933

The Foundation Center
312 Sutter Street
San Francisco, California 94108
415-397-0902

Appendix A-2

GUIDE TO GRANT SOURCES

Annual Register of Grant Support
Marquis Professional Publications
Chicago, IL

Catalog of Federal Domestic Assistance
Superintendent of Documents
U.S. Government Printing Office
Washington, D.C. 20402

The Grantsmanship Center
650 S. Spring Street, Suite 507
P.O. Box 6210
Los Angeles, CA 90014

Federal Grants and Contracts Weekly
Capitol Publications, Inc.
2430 Pennsylvania Avenue, N.W.,
Washington, D.C. 20037

The Foundation Center
888 Seventh Avenue
New York, New York 10019

Foundation News: The Magazine of
Philanthropy
Council on Foundations, Inc.
1828 L Street, N.W.
Washington, D.C. 20036
202-466-6512

Public Service Materials Center
111 N. Central Avenue
Hartsdale, NY 10530

The Chronicle of Philanthropy
1255 Twenty-Third Street, N.W.
Washington, D.C. 20037

The Nonprofit Times
P.O. Box 468
Bladensburg, MD 20710-0468

Appendix A-3

EXCERPTS FROM SECTION 501 OF
THE TAX CODE*

s 501. Exemption from tax on corporations, certain trusts, etc.

(a) Exemption from taxation

An organization described in subsection (c) or (d) or section 401(a) shall be exempt from taxation under this subtitle unless such exemption is denied under section 502 or 503.

(c) List of exempt organizations

The following organizations are referred to in subsection (a):

(3) Corporations, and any community chest, fund, or foundation, organized and operated exclusively for religious, charitable, scientific, testing for public safety, literary, or educational purposes, or to foster national or international amateur sports competition (but only if no part of its activities involve the provision of athletic facilities or equipment), or for the prevention of cruelty to children or animals, no part of the net earnings of which inures to the benefit of any private shareholder or individual, no substantial part of the activities of which is carrying on propaganda, or otherwise attempting, to influence legislation (except as otherwise provided in subsection (h)), and which does not participate in, or intervene in (including the publishing or distributing of statements), any political campaign on behalf of any candidate for public office.

---

*United States Code, 1982 Edition, Vol. 10, Title 26, Internal Revenue Code, s s 1–2000, Washington, U.S. Government Printing Office, 1983.

Appendix A-4

FUND ACCOUNTING SOFTWARE VENDORS

American Fundware, Inc.
P.O. Box 773028
Steamboat Springs, CO 80477
800-551-4458; 303-879-5770

Blackbaud MicroSystems
160 East Main Street
Huntington, NY 11743
516-385-1420

CMHC Systems, Inc.
555 Metro Place North, Suite 200
Dublin, OH 43017
614-764-0143

Corbin Willits Systems
35754 Mission Blvd.
Freemont, CA 94536
415-790-5600

Data Pro, Inc.
787 10th Street
Plainwell, MI 49080
616-685-9214

Easter Seal Society
Easter Seal Systems
2023 West Ogden Avenue
Chicago, IL 60612
312-243-8400

Echo Consulting Services, Inc.
Box 1199
Conway, NH 03818
603-447-5453

Executive Data Systems
1845 The Exchange, #140
Atlanta, GA 30339
800-272-3374; 404-955-3374

Great Lakes Behavioral
Research Institute
214 Boulevard of the Allies
Pittsburgh, PA 15222
412-261-5577

Hewitt-Anderson Co.
P.O. Box 42858
Tucson, AZ 85733
602-326-5664

IMS (Innovative Management
  Systems, Inc.)
Koger Executive Center
8401 Northwest 53rd Terrace
Miami, FL 33166
305-593-2911

Institutional Data Systems, Inc.
2 Hamilton Avenue
New Rochelle, N.Y. 108012
800-322-IDSI

International Micro Systems, Inc.
6445 Metcalf
Shawnee Mission, KS 66202
800-255-6223; 917-677-1137

Micro Information Products
505 East Huntland Dr., #304
Austin, TX 78752
800-647-3863; 512-454-500

Technology Consulting Corp.
4811 South 76th Street
Milwaukee, WI 53220
414-282-9700

National Computer Systems, Inc.
P.O. Box 9365
Minneapolis, MN 55440
800-328-6172; 612-830-7652

United Way of Penobscot Valley
161 Center Street
P.O. Box H
Bangor, Maine 04401
207-941-2800

INDEX

A

Abels and Murphy, 25
Accountability, 6, 12
Accounting
   accrual basis, 190
   cash basis, 190
   cycle, 217–225, fig. 218
   defined, 187
   equation, 196, 201, 216–217
   functional basis, 196
   fund (*see* Fund accounting)
   funder, 214
   modified accrual, 190–191
   nonprofit (*see* Nonprofit accounting)
   principles, 191–194
Accounting entity concept, 191, 198
Account payable, 197, 199
Account receivable, 200
Adjusting entries, 223–224
Allocation, defined, 7
American Institute of Certified Public
      Accountants (AICPA), 189
Amling, 162, 163
Anthony and Herzlinger, 10
Annual Register of Grant Support,
      111–112
Assets, defined, 197
"Audit guide," by AICPA, 189, 191, 195, 196,
      214, 215, 252
Audit,
   benefits of, 262
   opinions, 262–263
   procedures, 260
   purpose of, 260

B

Balance Sheet, 201, 259–260, table, 258

Bodnar, 13, 14, 17
Bonds, 161–163
   corporate, 162
   government, 162–163
Bowers and Bowers, 307
Budget,
   as control mechanism, 28
   as political activity, 28
   balanced, 62
   Capital, 55
   cash flow (*see* Cash flow budget)
   defined, 25
   expense, 56–58, 144
   functional (*see* Functional budget)
   functions of, 26–28
   line-item (*see* Line-item budget)
   Master, 36, 55–62
   presenting, 77
   program (*see* Program budget)
   public support and revenue, 58–60
   salary expense, 58
   summary, 145–146
   variance (*see* Variance budget)
Budgeting,
   and planning, 47–62
   bottom-up, 49
   defined, 25
   incremental (*see* Incremental
      budgeting)
   PPBS (*see* Planning, Programming,
      Budgeting System)
   Process, 25–26, fig. 27, fig. 51,
   Program-Planning and (*see* Program-
      Planning and Budgeting Cycle)
   top-down, 49
   Zero-base (*see* Zero-base budgeting)
Burch, et al, 173, 299, 306

C

Capital, 197
Cash flow budget,
    defined, 60
    preparation of, 60, fig. 61
Catalog of Domestic Assistance, 109–110, fig.
    110
Certificates of deposit, 164
Chart of accounts, 137, fig. 138
Christy and Clendenin, 173
Closing entries, 224–225
Coalition for nonprofit accounting, 237
Common stock, 164–165
Computer(s),
    acquisition process, 294–307
    advantages and disadvantages of, 289–294
    hardware, 294, 299–300
    software, 294 (*see also* Fund accounting
        software)
    systems, 289
    vendors, 305
Conservatism, Principle of, 193
Consistency, Concept, 191
Consumer Reports, 176, table 173
Consultants (*see* Investment counselors)
Contracts, 81
Contributions, defined, 82
Control,
    defined, 7
    management, 133, fig. 134
    of cash, 146–147
    of costs, 136–146
    of personnel, 147–148
    of time, 139–140, fig. 141
    physical, 149
    system requirements, 135–136
    transaction, 148
Corporate Fund Raising Directory, 112–113
Cost Principle, 192
Costing
    average cost per employee, 142–143
    per person, 142
    unit, 142
Costs,
    allocating, 138–140
    figuring, 140–143
Current restricted fund, 215
Current unrestricted fund, 159, 215

Custodian fund, 216

D

D'Ambrosio, 163
Debits and credits, 219, fig. 221
Decision packages, 30, fig. 31
DeJacimo et al, 290, 305, 307
Depreciation, 259
DiGuilio, 84
Disclosure Principle, 192
Donor mandated restrictions, 159
Doherty, 181

E

Echo Consulting Services, 304
Emergency Management Institute
        Professional Development Series, 105
Endowment
    defined, 159
    fund, 216
Evaluating, defined, 7
Expense,
    budget, 56–58
    defined, 56, 200
    fixed, 57
    semivariable or mixed, 57
    variable, 56
Exempt organization,
    501 (c) (3) organization defined, 335

F

Federal Emergency Management Agency,
    70, 121
Federal Register, 110
Fees, 10, 81
Fiduciary responsibility, 196
Financial Accounting Standards Board
        (FASB), 8, 189–190, 206, 208–211, 248,
        250, 251, 252
Financial information systems, functions of,
    288
Financial management,
    defined, 6
    elements of, 6–7
    process, 20–22, fig. 21
Financial Statements,

Financial Statements (*continued*)
   analysis of, 263–264, 267–273
   budgeted, 61
   purpose of, 196, 246–248
   qualitative aspects, 250–252
   relationship to accounts, fig. 224
   required, 223, 252 (*see also* specific
      statements)
   users of, 248–250
Financial strength, 263, 264–270
Financial subsystem, 18–20
Financial World, 181
Fiscal compliance, 263–264
Fixed assets, 196
Fort Worth Star-Telegram, 5
Foundation Directory, 111
Freyd, 85, 86, 91
Functional budget, 35, Tab. 37
Fund(s)
   defined, 214
   categories of, 215–216
   current restricted (*see* Current restricted
      fund)
   current unrestricted (*see* Current
      unrestricted fund)
   custodian (*see* Custodian fund)
   donor restricted, 215
   endowment restricted, 216
   land, building, equipment (*see* Land,
      building, and equipment fund)
Fund accounting,
   defined, 195
   equation, 216–217
   software, 300–301, table 302, 303–304
Fund balance, 217
Fundraising,
   approaches, 90–93, table 91
   defined, 79, fig. 80
   programs, 85–87, table 86
Funding sources,
   evaluating and selecting, 113–115
   types, 213

G

Gaertner, 58, 59
Generally accepted accounting principles
   (GAAP),
Genkins, 84

Gitman and Joehnk, 164, 169
Going Concern Concept, 192
Grant(s), 82, 103
   corporate, 112–113
   foundation, 111–112
   governmental, 109–110
Grant proposal preparation, 121–129
Grantwriting,
   defined, 104
   process, 104–116, fig. 105
Gross, 141, 262
Gross and Warshauer, 10, 147, 191, 195, 260

H

Haakenson, 95
Hasenfeld, 14
Henderson and Peirson, 187
Hicks and Leninger, 301
Huang, 163, 168, 169, 170, 171

I

Importation, defined, 6
Incremental budgeting, 29
Investment counselors, 174–177
Investment planning, 167–174
Investment(s),
   defined, 161
   fixed-income, 161
   mix, 159
   planning, 167–174
   risk, 168–170
   safety, 171
   strategy, 170
   variable-income, 161

J

Journal, general, 219–221, fig. 220

K

Kamerman, 9
Katz and Kahn, 14
Khoury, 162, 166
Kotler, 83
Koontz, O'Donnell & Weirich, 133, 136
Kugajevsky, 30

L

Land, building and equipment fund, 159, 215
Lauffer, 105
Ledger, general, 220–221, fig. 222
Leduc and Callaghan, 147
Letzukus, 29, 32
Liabilities, 197
Line-item budget, 34, table 36
Lindholm et al, 105
Listro, 190
Loan and annuity fund, 216
Lohman, 136
Lynn and Freeman, 214

M

Market audit (*see* Marketing process)
Marketing,
    components, 84–85
    defined, 83
    exchange concept of, 83
    mix, 84–85
    process, 87–94
Matching Principle, 193
Materiality, Principle of, 193
Meigs and Meigs, 193, 217
Milani, 144
Miringoff, 25
Moak and Killian, 68
Monetary Principle, 193
Mutual funds, 165–166

N

National Institute of Mental Health (NIMH), 223
Nation's Business, 206
Net income/net loss, 198
Net profit, 200
Nonprofit human service agencies,
    characteristics, 10–13
    constraints on, 12
    defined, 8
    similarities with for-profits, 8–19
Nonprofit accounting,
    characteristics of, 195–196
    equation, 216–217

Notes payable, 197

O

Objectivity, Principle of, 194
Operating efficiency, 270–272
Osborne and Cook, 305
O'Toole, 174
Owner's equity, 197

P

Park, 43
Pendleton, 89
Pescow, 301, 305
Planning,
    and budgeting, 25, 47–62
    defined, 6
Planning Programming Budgeting System (PPBS), 32–33
Plant fund (*see* Land, building and equipment fund)
Posting, 219–220
Preferred stock, 163–164
Program budget, 34, table 36
Programming, 54, fig. 55
Program-Planning Budgeting Cycle (PPB), 47–62
Proposals (*see* Grantwriting)
Powell, 58, 160
Public support, 58, 144, 226
Public support and revenue budget, 58–60, 144
Pyhrr, 30

R

Racek, 188, 189, 245
Ramanathan, 62, 263
Realization, Principle of, 194
Recording, defined, 7
Reilly, 168
Reporting, defined, 7
Requests for Proposals (RFP's), 110–111, 116–117
Restricted funds (*see* Current restricted fund)
Revenues, 58, 144, 199, 226

Revenue budget (*see* Public support and revenue budget)
Richardson, 150
Rosales, 316
Ross, 288, 307
Rubright and MacDonald, 87, 90
Rust, 98

S

Salary expense budget, 58
Sarri, 10
Schiffman, 242
Schoech, 128
Schoech et al, 290, 294, 295
Schultze, 32
Scrivner, 280
Service volume, 56
Silver, 290
Simonse, 310
Solomon, Vargo, and Schroeder, 197
Sorenson, 147
Standards of Accounting and Financial Reporting for Voluntary Health and Welfare Organizations, 139, 188, 195, 214, 215, 252, 253
Statement of Functional Expenses, 256, table 257, 259
Statement of Support, Revenues and Expenses and Changes in Fund Balances, 252–253, table 254–255, 256
Stevenson and Jennings, 164, 171
Stewardship, 6, 12, 196, 263–264
Subsystems, 17–20, fig. 18
Swan, 35
Systems theory, 13–17, fig. 15

T

T-account, 221
Taft Corporate Giving Directory, 112
Targeting (*see* Marketing process)
Texas Department of Mental Health and Mental Retardation, 155
Time Period, Principle of, 194, 217
Trial balance, 222–223, 225

U

United Way of America, 137, 195, 219, 221, 224, 256, 259, 260
accounting coding system (UWAACS), 138
budget system (PPB), 33, 47–62
chart of accounts (*see* Chart of Accounts)
Unrestricted funds (*see* Current unrestricted funds)

V

Vanderleeest, 85
Variance budget, 143–145
Vinter, 14

W

Whalen, 207, 214
Wildavsky, 29
Williams and Teutsch, 274
Worksheet, 222–223, fig. 232–233

Z

Zero-based budgeting (ZBB), 29–32